EVENTS THAT WORKED FOR US

Best Practices for Ministry With Children and Families

Edited by JUDY COMSTOCK

International Network of

children's
MINISTRY

Events That Worked For Us

Best Practices for Ministry With Children and Families

ISBN 9781426714856

Table of Contents

A Note From Judy Comstock

This is the second book in the Abingdon Press series on "Best Practices for Ministry with Children and Families." The theme of this one is all about Events. You will find the book practical and relevant. It contains step-by-step plans to help you present your next big event with excellence. The idea of addressing a broad range of topics allowed us to bring together just about every kind of event provided by Children's and Family Ministry leaders. The chapters focus on specific age levels, seasonal events, events for certain groups of children, families, volunteers, mission events, and even fundraisers. You will reach for this book again and again.

I have enjoyed representing International Network of Children's Ministry as the ideas for this project came together. Kudos to the Abingdon Press team, especially Daphna Flegal. She patiently allowed changes and offered to help me select the Scriptures for each chapter. When I sought Daphna's input, she responded with helpful suggestions. We had fun seeing this book on Events become a reality.

Perhaps no other area of the church has more stories than our ministry niche. At the time of the event, we may have wanted to scream, but the joy of the Lord shined through and we smiled . . . eventually. Sharing some of these stories is a unique feature. Laugh along with us and recall some of your own ministry stories.

A major thank you is reserved for the contributing writers. What an amazing group of leaders! These practitioners offer proven ideas and plans. They were willing to share their experiences with you without compensation. All of the royalties from this book will be put into the CPC Scholarship Fund. This fund helps provide training and encouragement for children's and family ministry leaders who might otherwise not be able to attend Children's Pastors' Conference (CPC).

My prayer is that this book will be a blessing to your ministry on the multiple times you use it to plan your next successful event.

Judy Comstock

Reproducibles and the CD-ROM

You will find reproducible resource pages throughout *Events That Worked For Us*. These pages are printed with the articles and also available on the CD-ROM. You have permission to photocopy the pages or download them from the CD-ROM.

4 EVENTS THAT WORKED FOR US

Camps

The LORD is my shepherd, I shall not want. He makes me lie down in green pastures; he leads me beside still waters.

(Psalm 23:1-2)

Summer Skills Camps

by Eric Hamp

I wanted to be able to get into every aspect of the lives of the children I minister to, so I began looking at what seemed to be important to them. One thing that I observed is that if a parent has a minivan, the parent is hauling kids somewhere for practice during the week, whether it is for sports or music lessons. This led to offering skills camps. Not every student is an athlete, but all students have something that they love to do or would like to try and do if they could learn. It has become a safe environment for them to try something new that they may have been too shy to try. We began replacing our VBS for the older elementary children with a skills camp. I modeled this after a place I had ministered and their camp stood for: Shaping Kids With Innovative LifeLong Skills.

I want to share with you the *who, what, when, where, why,* and *how* to conducting a successful skills camp in your community.

Who is Skills Camp?
• Campers
I believe the best age group to work with is elementary children in grades 1 through 6. These children are at beginning levels of skill and can be mentored by coaches who may not be professionals. They are still easily excited about the chance to learn something new and the completion level is not as serious now.

Your target audience could be only the children in your church, or this could be a great hook for outreach into the community. People may not come to a church service you are having, but they will sign the kids up for a summer skills camp. Then after your camp is over, follow-up with your guests and invite them to your regular church services or other events you may be having.

• Coaches:
If you are fortunate enough to have professional athletes or gifted people in certain skills, by all means ask for their help. There may be people in your congregation or community that are not professionals but have a knowledge and passion for a skill; they are your greatest resource. Be sure to appreciate all of your volunteers at the end of the event and during the event with small tokens throughout the day.

What is Skills Camp?
This is simply another avenue to reach, teach, and keep boys and girls for Christ. We have a continually evolving menu for skills camp, but basically it consists of the following:

1. Basketball
2. Football
3. Soccer
4. Baseball/Softball
5. Golf
6. Karate
7. Photography
8. Cooking
9. Scrapbooking
10. Cheerleading

Other examples would include: dance, piano, writing, drawing, painting, technology (computer animation or video game development). The possibilities are endless.

Here is a sample description of a class:

The Cheerleading Camp is being extended to novice as well as experienced cheerleaders while promising to be fun, energetic, and spirited. During this three-day camp, young girls will learn the basics of cheering while experienced cheerleaders will be challenged to improve every aspect of their skill levels. They will learn different cheers and chants, jumps, how to keep the crowd involved, and how to be creative when combining basic steps with their cheers. Limited to 25 participants.

• Spiritual Emphasis/Chapel

We have a seamless thread of spiritual emphasis running throughout the entire camp, from the logo and designs to each coach weaving the gospel message into the skill each is teaching. There are numerous "teachable moments" to learn about sharing and forgiveness on the sports field and God's creation in the arts. Don't forget this is first and foremost a time to minister to the children of your community.

> We have a seamless thread of spiritual emphasis running throughout the entire camp, from the logo and designs to each coach weaving the gospel message into the skill each is teaching.

We like to keep the main thing, the main thing during skills camp. Our chapel services are a top priority. This is the time to connect the children (who may be only coming for the skill) to God. We have a high-energy, power-packed service which includes songs, games, a themed message, and showcases of the skills being taught. We have done the chapel service both in the morning, before the skills, and before lunch after the first skill. We found it works better doing it right away in the morning while everyone is gathered in the auditorium. A typical chapel service looks like this:

5 min. — Opening Song & Prayer
5 min. — Ice Breaker Game
10 min. — Action Songs
10 min. — Offering Lesson and Contest (We use this as a fundraiser for a local or international project. Boys vs Girls with an unwanted, but fun, penalty for the leader of the second place team.)
5 min. — Worship Song
15 min. — Message
5 min. — Closing Activity

We try to keep this to an hour to allow the rest of the day to flow smoothly. Chapel is always a great time to present Christ to some of these boys and girls for maybe even the first time. On the last day of Chapel, we allow the cheerleaders or dance team an opportunity to perform and practice for the evening service.

When is Skills Camp?

You can do this from three days to a full week. I have found with the elementary age group, three days works best for us. You will find a Monday through Wednesday schedule below.

Times can vary depending on personal taste. We give each student the option to choose two different skills, and we offer a morning and afternoon session. This way they may learn more than one skill. This also gives the coaches an opportunity to modify the instruction for different age levels. We have one session for 1st through 3rd graders and the other session for 4th through 6th grades.

We then have a Family night on Wednesday, where we invite the entire family back in the evening from 5:30 PM – 7:00 PM. We have inflatable games and bounce houses, food for sale or free, and a time of fellowship outside. Then we move into the auditorium from 7:00 PM – 8:30 PM for a family service with games, songs, a message, and give away prizes for every age. This is a great time to showcase the skills the children have been learning all week.

Skill's Camp Times

9:00 AM – 10:30 AM	Session 1
10:35 AM – 12:00 PM	Chapel in Sanctuary
12:05 PM – 12:30 PM	Lunch in Gym
12:35 PM – 2:00 PM	Session 2
2:00 PM – 2:10 PM	Dismissal in Sanctuary

Where is Skills Camp?

If you have a facility with tons of rooms, you are in luck, if not you will need to get creative. We use every space in the building, and then we contact a local school about a mile away and we transport children there for the field events, knowing they will be in a secure area. You may look for a recreational center or YMCA in your area, or the local high school could aid in making your event a success.

Why Skills Camp?

Consider breaking out of the box. Skills camp is a great way to meet kids where they are: at play. You can touch them on so many levels. There are the kids who are very confident in the skill, and you can teach them leadership. There are the kids who are just so-so in the skill, and that is where you can teach empowerment. Then there are the kids who do not know anything about the skill, and this is a perfect place to teach them about opportunities and having no fear. Collectively they learn how to encourage each other through experiencing this skill.

Another teaching opportunity with the skills is applying God's Word. An example of this would be scrapbooking. Throughout the Scriptures God tells us to remember: remember my covenant, remember my commands, remember what I have done for you. Preserving our memories through scrapbooking helps us remember all the things God has provided for us and all he has carried us through. It becomes not only a book of remembrance but one of praise and thanksgiving.

Through the teaching of the skills, you can relate those skills to God's Word. It is a new innovative way to reach the kids of our community for Christ.

How to do Skills Camp:

Below are the essential steps in creating a successful Skills Camp.

1. **Plan.** Plan out the dates, locations, and positions. Make detailed job descriptions for each position (i.e., coaches, assistant coaches, lunch helpers, water runners for outdoor sports, setup, cleanup, and so forth). Also, set up a planning calendar of what to do on certain dates to make sure you are on task.

2. **Set the date.** Check your local schools' schedules to ensure your dates do not conflict. Check with the leadership at your church to make sure your facility/staff is available.

3. **Secure the location.** If your facility is not conducive to this type of event, check with your local parks or schools.

4. **Enlist coaches.** Begin asking around for church members who have experience and passion for the skill.

5. **Enlist volunteers.** Put out the call to your congregation, sharing with them the value of helping to host a skills camp at your church.

6. **Promote.** You can either promote it within your church only or put it out there to the community through local radio stations, bulletin boards, and so forth.

7. **Stick to your plan.** At this point double check your dates, locations, and volunteers to make sure you are on task so that your event is successful.

8. **Have fun.** Don't forget to have fun. It is all about the kids and reaching, teaching them for Christ while having fun!

9. **Follow-up.** Bless and thank your volunteers. Mail cards to the new families that attended your skills camp in hopes they may become involved in your church.

Eric comes to INCM with over twenty years experience in ministering to children. His experience includes conducting children services for the Oral Roberts International Bible Ministries Conference in Tulsa, Oklahoma, Victory Christian Center's Word Explosion in Tulsa, and a weekly inner-city ministry to 700–800 children. He is married to his best friend, April, and they are the proud parents of their infant daughter, Areyna. Eric and April serve as the Directors of Children's Ministries at Word of Life Christian Center in Denver, Colorado.

Through the teaching of the skills, you can relate those skills to God's Word.

Sizzling Science Camps

by Dienna Goscha

Imagine walking into your church to find rockets whizzing above your head or concoctions bubbling in a lab down the hall. Perhaps you might catch miniature CSI agents with magnifying glasses searching for fingerprints, or inquisitive campers testing water samples from your nearby lake. Consider the possibility of turning your church or nearby venue into an oozing, popping, and sizzling science camp as an outreach to your community.

Children love to experiment and invent. Science camps capitalize on their natural curiosity. When you have captured a child's attention, spiritual truths can be taught by using science experiments as object lessons.

Shooting off rockets in a Space Camp, for example, starts a discussion about hitting the "target" of correct conduct for Christ. Dissecting a shark in a Creation Camp embeds in a child's mind the day God created sea creatures. Investigating a crime scene in a CSI Camp firmly places the events of a Bible story into a child's memory. Cleaning up a simulated oil spill in an Environmental Camp will stimulate discussion on ways that families can take care of God's creation. The spiritual lessons that springboard from science experiments leave a lasting impression in a child's heart and mind.

Many churches have found that science camp was one of the biggest hits of the year. Children, years later, will still talk about not only the fun they had but also what they learned. The spiritual outcomes from a science camp make the effort put into the camp worth it. When planning a science camp of your own, a few initial steps should be taken to help ensure that your camp becomes a successful, rewarding experience.

Step 1: Determine your purpose

- Is it to hold the camp as a bridge between the church and the community? For this type of camp, the church may wish to contract with a local museum, community-education leader, or science teacher as a resource. This type of camp's purpose is more as a community service to the community and as a way to "advertise" the church. Care should be taken that whoever is contracted to do the camp is in harmony with your church's theological beliefs.

- Usually a science camp's purpose is to connect children with Jesus through science. If this is the purpose of the camp, church leaders should direct the camp. With this type of camp, consideration should be made whether the camp is for outreach to the community or more as a summer program for the children in your church. Also, this type of camp works well for districtwide events within a denomination or network of churches.

Step 2: Choose your format

- Deciding when and how long the camp will be held is essential. Will it be overnight or only held during the day? Overnight camps could be a weekend away, a week at a campground, or simply a night's stay at the church. For day camps, consider whether the camp will be an all-day event or a morning or evening event such as a VBS. If done during the school year, after school camp works great.

- An overnight camp will bring extra considerations with it as more activities will be needed along with the logistics of sleeping arrangements, overnight counselors, and transportation that will need to be addressed. However, the intense focus that an overnight camp brings makes it well worth considering. A day camp is easier to plan and to recruit helpers. However, some science activities might have to be curtailed due to time limitations.

- One new trend is to offer specialized camps during Christmas break, spring break, or on teacher workdays. For families who must find daycare during these school breaks, a science camp is a welcome and needed event. Kids also love to have something fun to do on these days off from school.

Step 3: Target your audience

- What ages will you include? Targeting a narrow age range such as grades 3 to 5 will allow you to hone in on specific age-appropriate skills, while targeting a wide age range such as preschoolers through 5th graders will allow all children within a family to participate.

- Consider running a family science camp. A monthly family science night that offers an abbreviated science camp would be a great hit with families. For those who live in colder climates, a Cabin Fever day during January is a welcome event for a family. A week-long camp during the evening hours similar to a VBS is also a great option for families.

Step 4: Choose your venue

- Where should the camp take place? Having the camp in your own church makes planning, setup, and cleaning easier. It also gives the community a view of your church. However, a neutral location can also be advantageous. Many people might not bring their kids into a church building

but would be willing to take them to a park or community center. Also, any outdoors setting lends itself well to many science experiments and activities.

- Some facilities outside the church to consider would be the local park, a campground, a community center, the library, a school (especially for an after-hours program), the YMCA, or a nature center.

> Consider the possibility of turning your church or nearby venue into an oozing, popping, and sizzling science camp as an outreach to your community.

Step 5: Choose the subject matter and curriculum

- Decide on the type of camp you will run. Will it have general science-type experiments, or will it be specialized? Examples of specialized science camps include Forensics Science (CSI), Creation, Environmental, Inventors, Space, Mythbusters, or Amusement Park Science. Look at curriculum to find the different kinds of camps offered, or have a science lover in your church write the curriculum for you.

- Make sure that the curriculum has a strong spiritual content if this is the purpose of your camp. The idea is not to teach the science but to use the science as a springboard to teach spiritual concepts.

What would the activities in a camp look like?

- Large group: Drama, Science Lab, Bible Story, Real Life Scientist Story, Object Lesson
- Small group rotations: Science Lab, Craft, Snack, Bible Memory Activity, Games, Small Group Discussions

Looking beyond these initial steps, what might a typical day in a science camp be like?

- First, the day may begin with different welcoming stations as the kids check in. These stations would have simple science trivia or activities that could be read or completed quickly as the kids wait for the camp to begin. Next, the kids would gather for a large group time. During this time there might be a drama introducing the biblical point for the day, a science experiment demonstrated for the group by a "mad scientist," the Bible story told in a creative way followed by a real life story of a scientist. The kids would then break into their small groups where they would travel between rotations of a science lab where they would do hands-on science activities, games, crafts, snacks, Bible memory activities, and small group discussions. Each of these rotations would support the Bible point for the day. Finally, the kids might gather back together in a large group for a dramatic end to the day with an eye-catching science experiment that would create a visual memory of the biblical point.

- Once the curriculum is determined, recruiting should take place. Some non-science people will need to be reassured that science skills are not needed to participate in this event. Do find those who love science to take on the roles that are more science oriented. Their natural enthusiasm will spill over onto the kids.

- Many science camps use simple kitchen supplies. Be sure to call on the church community to supply these items. Also, check for specialty items and order them well in advance. Science supply stores are easily found online through search engines.

- When planning, consider ending the event with a science night for families, including a special guest such as an FBI agent, someone from the recycling center, a weather person, or a specialty science

entertainer. Another possibility is setting up a fun science lab where kids can show their families different science experiments they did during the week.

- A science camp experience includes quality benefits such as long-term retention of the subject matter, special memories created from unusual and unique biblical lessons, and a heightened enthusiasm for the children's ministry of your church. Those of us who want to reach our culture for Jesus need to be willing to step outside the box. We must show children that God is not closed up in the walls of a church. A science camp is a great way to begin that process.

> A science camp experience includes quality benefits such as long-term retention of the subject matter, special memories created from unusual and unique biblical lessons, and a heightened enthusiasm for the children's ministry of your church.

Dienna Goscha, owner and principle writer of River's Edge Curriculum, has over twenty years of experience leading children's ministries. Her creativity and her background in math and science are a springboard for developing and writing innovative curriculum. She has written four different science camp curriculums and has had a blast implementing them. Currently, she is a pastor on staff at Real Life Community Church in Elk River, Minnesota.

Contact information:
www.riversec.com
dienna.goscha@gmail.com

Day Camp Schedule:
3 Hours

Opening: 45 minutes

- Worship Music *(10 minutes)*
- Sizzle and Fizzle Drama *(5 minutes)*
- Dr. Beaker Science Lab *(5 minutes)*
- Bible Story *(15 minutes)*
- Real Life Scientist Story *(5 minutes)*
- Life Application Object Lesson *(5 minutes)*

Rotate through stations: 25 minutes each

Divide the large group into five equal groups. Divide either by age or mix ages. Assign a small group leader for every group of ten children.

- Dr. Beaker's Laboratory — hands-on lab experiments
- Bible Memory Activities
- Game Lab
- Creation Crafts
- Sizzling Snacks/Small Group Discussion

Closing: 10 minutes

- Wow! Experiment — Choose an experiment from Dr. Beaker's Lab.

Overnight Camp: Schedule for the Week

Monday
2:00 PM – 4:00 PM Check In/Tours/Large
                    Group games
4:00 PM Small Group
4:20 PM Welcome Meeting — Chapel
5:00 PM Supper
5:45 PM Small Group
6:30 PM Chapel
8:00 PM Large Group Games
8:45 PM Small Group in Room
9:00 PM Bedtime

Tuesday
8:00 AM Breakfast
8:30 AM Quiet Time/Journal
8:45 AM Small Group
9:15 AM Games — Front Lawn
9:45 AM Bathroom/Water Break
10:00 AM Chapel
11:30 AM Games — Front Lawn
12:00 PM Lunch
12:40 PM Mail Call
12:45 PM Gym/Crafts
1:45 PM Slime Time
2:15 PM Swim/Snack Shack
3:15 PM Clean Up
3:30 PM Environmental Project
4:30 PM Game — Front Lawn
5:00 PM Supper
5:45 PM Free Choice — Front of Dorm
6:30 PM Chapel
8:00 PM Bonfire
8:45 PM Small Group in Room
9:00 PM Bedtime

Wednesday
8:00 AM Breakfast
8:30 AM Quiet Time/Journal
8:45 AM Small Group
9:15 AM Hike
10:15 AM Bathroom/Water Break
10:30 AM Chapel
12:00 PM Lunch

Wednesday (con't)
12:40 PM Mail Call
12:45 PM Gym/Crafts
1:45 PM Slime Time
2:15 PM Swim/Snack Shack
3:15 PM Clean Up
3:30 PM Environmental Project
4:30 PM Game — Front Lawn
5:00 PM Supper
5:45 PM Free Choice — Front of Dorm
6:30 PM Chapel
8:00 PM Games
8:45 PM Small Group in Room
9:00 PM Bedtime

Thursday
8:00 AM Breakfast
8:30 AM Quiet Time/Journal
8:45 AM Small Group
9:15 AM Environmental Project
10:00 AM Chapel
11:30 AM Games — Front Lawn
12:00 PM Lunch
12:40 PM Mail Call
12:45 PM Gym/Crafts
1:45 PM Slime Time
2:15 PM Swim/Snack Shack
3:15 PM Clean Up
3:30 PM Environmental Project
4:30 PM Game — Front Lawn
5:00 PM Supper
5:45 PM Small Group
6:30 PM Chapel
8:00 PM Bonfire
8:45 PM Small Group in Room
9:00 PM Bedtime

Friday
8:00 AM Breakfast
8:30 AM Quiet Time/Journal
8:45 AM Pack/Clean Up
9:30 AM Chapel
10:30 AM Small Groups/Check Out

Fitness Camp

by Michelle Romain

Health and fitness are vital concerns for families more than ever. Giving kids keys to health early in life is priceless.

The World Health Organization stated, "Many of the most significant modern diseases take many years to develop. Heart disease doesn't happen overnight, it is the end result of a lifetime of bad habits . . . and this process begins in childhood."

Obesity among children has almost tripled in the last 20 years, and medical experts are calling obesity an epidemic disease. In addition to the increase in overweight children, illnesses, such as Type 2 diabetes, are developing in kids today at much younger ages than they did 20 years ago.

Even if kids aren't overweight, they are still bombarded with unhealthy choices made to look healthy by the media. For example, many kids think fruit-flavored drinks and cereals, fruit roll-ups, and fruit pastries are healthy because of the way commercials portray them. Lack of physical activity from sedentary lifestyles is also causing many of the health problems kids have.

There are several public programs in schools and clubs teaching kids to take care of their bodies. Parents are sending their kids to these because they want fitness help, and kids are joining in and having a great time. How much better is it for churches to offer fitness programming because

they can add the one aspect that public programs cannot — disciplining on why God created us and how he intended for us to take care of our bodies. Therefore, a successful, well-rounded Fitness Camp includes physical fitness and nutritional training based on God's Word.

Our bodies are spiritually designed to need God and physically designed to need nutrition and exercise. When churches focus on shaping up people's hearts as well as their bodies, they develop people who serve God with their hearts, souls, minds, and bodies (Mark 12:30).

When people understand why they were created and how their bodies were designed, they begin to develop life-long healthy habits including eating and exercising correctly, avoiding harmful substances, and living a life with self-control.

Planning:
There are many details that must go into planning a camp program. *Shapin' Up Fitness Camp* comes complete with exercise DVDs, Bible and health lessons, PowerPoint® presentations, daily handouts for parents, extra-curricular activities, snack ideas, and more. *Shapin' Up Fitness Camp* also includes registration forms, promotional handouts and videos, certificates, graphics; and planning, safety, and budgeting guides.

> **H**ow much better is it for churches to offer fitness programming because they can add the one aspect that public programs can not — disciplining on why God created us and how he intended for us to take care of our bodies.

The beginning step in planning your camp is scheduling. When scheduling, decide the dates and location for your camp. Plan for five days in a row, one day a week, half day or full day. Select your location based on your format — decide if you will teach in a large group setting where all campers are in one room or use a rotation basis such as different rooms for different activities (fitness, Bible, health, snack, games, and so forth).

Then establish your budget. Decide if your camp will be free of charge or if you need to charge a nominal fee. Cost is based on items such as T-shirts, giveaway items (e.g. resistance bands or pedometers), snacks, lunch, field trips, and so forth.

Thirdly, determine your registration process — determine the maximum number of campers you can have and how you will implement a registration process — paper forms, website, etc. On the registration forms, ask for pertinent medical information and have a statement of permission in regards to medical treatment, field trips, and so forth.

Recruit volunteers based on the number of campers and teachers you will need. Establish training events for volunteers at this time, as well.

Finally, construct a promotional campaign using mailers, flyers, promotional videos, website, and so forth. Since health and fitness is such a relevant topic in all communities, often public organizations, such as schools and child-care facilities, will allow you to advertise through them.

Fitness Camp Schedule

- Opening Activities: As adults, we would love to sit kids down and tell them everything on our hearts — all about what we've learned from our life experiences. However, we know that kids don't learn that way. Kids need fun and activity mingled into their learning experience. So start your Fitness Camp with quick opening games and ice-breaker activities. This motivates kids to be involved, excited, and listening.

- Fitness Training: The next area of your camp should encourage physical fitness in a way that is appealing to kids. Kids tend to view exercise as a dreaded word. Tell them they're going to run laps in PE class and their eyes roll up. Focusing on sports is not appealing to some kids because they are not comfortable or interested in sports. The US Government recommends at least one hour of physical activity per day for kids. So showing kids how to make physical activity, or exercise, fun and easily doable is key.

Physical fitness ideas for your camp could include high energy games or inviting a local fitness instructor to lead the kids in a kid friendly aerobic-type session. *Shapin' Up Fitness Camp* includes six fitness DVDs that you can play for the kids to exercise along with. In the videos, kids are encouraged to be in proper form and march in place if they're too tired to do the exercise. Always lead kids through a warm up, physical activity, and a cool down.

> The most important aspect of a Fitness Camp is the Bible training.

- Bible Training: The most important aspect of a Fitness Camp is the Bible training. Review a key verse or Scripture passage daily and offer an opportunity for kids to speak with a counselor about salvation. Typically, a Fitness Camp will bring several visitors to a church, often from unchurched homes.

Kids don't think about food as being right or wrong. They often don't realize the importance of treating their body like a sacred temple. A health program should start with the fact that our bodies were made by and belong to God. Therefore, we need to take care of our bodies the way God intended. He gave each of us special gifts and talents to use for him. Challenge kids to understand that God created them with unique abilities for a special purpose and that through self-control they can live a healthy lifestyle. The Bible Challenges should coincide and prove the nutrition training in the Health Challenges.

• Health Training: The health training should teach kids about the nutrition their bodies need and how their bodies use it. Health training always focuses on nutrition and fitness — never body size or shape or diets.

Research the Internet or your local health department for interesting props, experiments, fun facts, demonstrations, and more to use in your teaching. Each day send home handouts for parents to use at home to reinforce what the kids learned that day.

Optional Activities:

Extend your camp to a full day camp experience by adding optional activities. Examples include serving kids lunch and taking them on an active field trip such as swimming, hiking, skating, and so forth. Afterwards, serve a healthy snack allowing the kids some hands-on opportunities to make it themselves. Or, keep the kids on campus and offer a cooking class, game time, class on developing health ideas, and so forth.

Reinforce your campers' experiences with fitness equipment they can use at home. Send them home at the end of the week with exercise bands, pedometers, flying discs, jump ropes, and so forth. Show them fun ways to use these and the benefits they can receive from using them.

Relevant Need

A Fitness Camp is unique from what most churches are offering for special events. A successful Fitness Camp prepares kids for a healthy lifestyle by demonstrating physical activity is fun, teaching kids how to make good nutrition choices, educating parents to model healthy lifestyles, and focusing on pleasing God rather than our peers.

Churches where a Fitness Camp for kids and/or parents is provided are offering an excellent way to reach out to the community and meet a critical need in society today.

_____

Michelle Romain has over 20 years experience in Children's Ministry as a minister, speaker, and writer. She is the author of Shapin' Up Fitness Camp *and Director for ACMA. Michelle lives in Lexington, Kentucky, with her husband, Denny, and has three incredible children.*

Fitness Camp Registration

_____

Student Name

M   F   _____   _____

Circle One   Birth Date   Last Grade Completed

_____

Street Address

_____

City State Zip

_____

Allergies / Medical Concerns

_____

Parents'/Guardians' Names

_____   _____   _____

Home Phone   Cell Phone   Work Phone

_____   _____

Emergency Contact   Phone

I give permission for my child to attend and participate in the activities for Fitness Camp.

_____   _____

Parent/Guardian Signature   Date

Fine Arts Camp

by Annie Waterman

> **W**orship the LORD in the splendor of his holiness; tremble before him, all the earth. (Psalm 96:9, NIV)
>
> **A**scribe to the LORD the glory due his name; worship the LORD in the splendor of his holiness. (Psalm 29:2, NIV)
>
> **C**ome, let us bow down in worship, let us kneel before the LORD our Maker. (Psalm 95:6, NIV)

The Psalms are prolific in descriptions of worship — what it is, how to do it, and why.

But what are our children learning about worship? Do children today ascribe worship to the twenty minute music set (in "big church" or in their Sunday School class) that is typically found at the beginning of corporate worship times? Do they realize that worship is an expression/outpouring of our very being — that worship is essential to our relationship with Christ?

It is true that in the Scriptures there are many references to music in the context of worship, but this is not the sole way to enter into worship. And music, while a great tool for worship, is not the only artistic expression of worship that exists.

Those who work with kids are very aware that abstract concepts are grasped more readily when broken down and when an experience is well — experienced! The elementary- to early adolescence-aged kids are in what Piaget calls "Concrete Operational Stage." This age group demonstrates intelligence through both logic and manipulation of symbols as they relate to concrete objects. Egocentrism begins to diminish during this stage of development.[1] In the case of worship, we, the teachers, have an opportunity to free our kids from the confines of a limited definition through hands-on interactions. Fine Arts Camp serves as a tool to teach our kids how to free their limited concept of worship and to experience new ways to view their relationship with their Maker.

Fine Arts Camp allows kids to see how they are using their creative gifts and talents to express love for Christ — to, in essence, give back to their maker. The specific goal of Fine Arts Camp is to give kids an opportunity to see how their interaction with the arts is an expression of worship. This concept is outlined for the kids at the beginning and end of each camp day, as well as in the classes themselves. The beauty of the camp setting is that it allows kids to try new things — experience a new art form and above all use it in worship.

The Nuts and Bolts

After five years of managing a camp for approximately seventy-five kids, our team has discovered that the following format works best:

- Monday through Friday for one week during the summer.
- Hire professionals (or at the very least people with a passion and evidence of artistic ability).
- Charge enough money per child to cover the cost of the paid professionals, extended care, food for volunteers, and supplies for the classes.

Offer a preschool program (9:00 AM to 12:00 PM) for kids three years old through entering kindergarten. Limit the number of enrollees by determining the number of staff needed and the ability of the teacher. Offer three or four thirty-minute sessions for the kids (dance/movement, clay, music and/or crafts). Set the fee in such a way as to cover the cost of hiring the staff and teachers as well as supplies. A sample preschool schedule is printed below.

Preschool

Time	Event	Staff	Where
9:00 AM – 9:20 AM	Big Group Time	2 paid Childcare Workers	Sanctuary
9:25 AM – 9:55 AM	Dance/Movement	2 paid Childcare Workers 2 Dance Instructors	Fellowship Hall
10:00 AM – 10:30 AM	Music	2 paid Childcare Workers, Music Instructor, 1 Volunteer	Sanctuary
10:35 AM – 10:45 AM	Snack/Bathroom	2 paid Childcare Workers	Foyers
10:50 AM – 11:20 AM	Clay	2 paid Childcare Workers, Clay Instructor, 1 Volunteer	Large classroom with sinks, small tables and chairs
11:25 AM – 11:45 AM	Craft	2 paid Childcare Workers, Volunteer	Large classroom with small tables and chairs
11:45 AM – 12:00 PM	Lunch	2 paid Childcare Workers, Volunteer	Large classroom with small tables and chairs
12:00 PM	Pick up	2 paid Childcare Workers	Large classroom with small tables and chairs

Offer a program for kids entering first through second grade that are together in a special group (we called ours Next Level) that has a set schedule for the day. Like the preschool program, this group attends the same three classes per day (dance/movement, percussion, and junk art are popular classes for this age group). The fee charged covers the costs of the supplies, teachers, and staff. This program runs from 9:00 AM to 12:00 PM. Our program offered "extended care" for an additional fee. Extended care is childcare only but allows working parents to have their children participate. The additional cost of extended care is to cover the paid childcare workers. Any child who stays for extended care also brings a lunch each day. A sample schedule is on page 21.

First through Second Grade

Time	Event	Staff	Where
9:00 AM – 9:20 AM	Big Group Time	Part of larger group	Sanctuary
9:25 AM – 10:10 AM	Junk Art	Junk Art Instructor Volunteer	Large classroom
10:15 AM – 11:00 AM	Dance/Movement	2 Dance Instructors , Volunteer	Foyer
11:05 AM – 11:50 AM	Percussion	Music Instructor, Volunteer	Sanctuary
11:50 AM – 12:00 PM	Closing	Staff	Sanctuary

Fine Arts Camp participants who are entering third through seventh grade are given the choices of classes to take within each of the 3 sessions (2 sessions before lunch, 1 session after lunch). The classes offered depend upon the number of sign ups, the available teachers, and the ability to separate out by age group. Once payment is received, families receive an e-mail with the specific class choices. The classes are assigned on a first come, first serve basis (in regards to forms being returned). A sample schedule is printed below.

Third through Seventh Grade

Time	Event	Staff	Where
9:00 AM – 9:20 AM	Big Group Time	Part of larger group	Sanctuary
9:25 AM – 10:35 AM	Session 1	Instructor and Volunteer per class	Specific space for each class
10:40 AM – 11:50 AM	Session 2	Instructor and Volunteer per class	Specific space for each class
11:55 AM – 12:20 PM	Lunch	Staff to oversee lunch	Large space for eating and games
12:25 PM – 1:35 PM	Session 2	Instructor and Volunteer per class	Specific space for each class
1:40 PM – 2:00 PM	Closing Time	Part of larger group	Sanctuary

Sessions offered might look something like this:

Session I: Guitar, Piano, Dance, Watercolor, Praise and Worship, Puppets

Session 2: Clay, Junk Art, Watercolor, Piano, Guitar, Voice, Drama, Puppets

Session 3: Dance, Drawing, Recorder, Junk Art, Voice, Clay, Drama

When the same class is listed more than once, we can break the children into different age groups in order to have an optimal learning environment with a specific age group. For example: Dance in Session I might be for kids entering third through fourth grade and in Session 3 the Dance Class would be for kids entering fifth through seventh grade. Make sure when scheduling to include a wide variety of choices for each age group (i.e. not all musical instruments only for a specific age group in one session).

Offer extended care for families who need their child to be in an all-day program. Charge extra for children who stay until 4:30 PM in order to cover the cost of the childcare workers.

> Whenever possible it's also great to have the kids participate in the worship services. In our experience, utilizing the kids in both kid's church and BIG church helps to enforce the idea of worship over performance.

Recital

On the last day of camp if the lunch time and third session are slightly altered, time wise, then there is time for a recital that highlights the things learned by the kids the week of camp. Recital can include all performance-based groups as well as an art show of the classes that produced works (i.e. clay, watercolor, drawing, junk art, creative crafts). Parents and families should be invited so that kids have an opportunity to share what they've learned. Whenever possible it's also great to have the kids participate in the worship services. In our experience, utilizing the kids in both kid's church and BIG church helps to enforce the idea of worship over performance.

Opening and Closing Sessions

Have your staff use the beginning and end of the day as a way to connect the concept of worship to the classes the kids take. We have used musical worship to begin the day, as well as reading Scriptures related to worship. At the closing time, kids can talk about how they learned about worship through their classes that day. A worship wall is available for kids to express their thoughts directly to God. This has been an effective tool used during closing sessions as well.

Extended Care

As mentioned, offering extended care provides the families needing all-day care an opportunity to participate. Hire paid childcare workers to run the extended care. During this time provide snack, a movie, simple craft and/or a time to run around and play an active game. Parents and kids will appreciate the time of less structured activity.

Cost

Each church will need to determine the costs for their supplies, instructors, and staff time. Think about budgeting for volunteer lunches (each day of camp), volunteer appreciation gifts, technical support for the recital, and instructor pay.

See the CD-ROM for additional forms and information as done by our camp.

1. Citation: Huitt, W., & Hummel, J. (2003). Piaget's theory of cognitive development. Educational Psychology Interactive. Valdosta, GA: Valdosta State University. Retrieved [date] from http://www.edpsycinteractive.org/topics/cogsys/piaget.html

Annie Waterman is the Children's Ministries Director at the Aurora Campus of Colorado Community Church.

Fine Arts Camp Notes

All Ages 9:00 AM – 9:20 AM — opening time in Sanctuary

Preschool $60
    9:25 AM – 9:55 AM Dance/Movement
    10:00 AM – 10:30 AM Clay
    10:35 AM – 10:45 AM Snack — bathroom — run around
    10:50 AM – 11:20 AM Music
    11:25 AM – 11:40 AM Craft Project
    11:40 AM – 12:00 PM Lunch

Next Step (kids entering first through second grade) $60
Aftercare 12:00 PM – 4:30 PM $40 (additional)
    9:25 AM – 10:10 AM Percussion
    10:15 AM – 11:00 AM Dance/Movement
    11:05 AM – 11:50 AM Junk Art
    11:50 AM – 12:00 PM Wrap it up

Third through Seventh Graders $75
Aftercare 2:00 PM – 4:30 PM $25 (additional)
    9:25 AM – 10:35 AM Session 1
    10:40 AM – 11:50 AM Session 2
    11:55 AM – 12:20 PM Lunch
    12:25 PM – 1:35 PM Session 3
    1:40 PM – 2:00 PM Closing Session

Session 1 (grades)
(2–4) Junk Art
(2–4) Piano
(2–7) P & W
(5–7) Guitar
(5–7) Watercolor

Session 2 (grades)
(2–4) Clay
(2–4) Guitar
(2–4) Watercolor
(2–4) Drama
(5–7) Junk Art
(5–7) Piano
(5–7) Voice
(5–7) Dance

Session 3 (grades)
(2–4) Dance
(2–4) Percussion
(2–4) Voice
(5–7) Clay
(5–7) Drawing
(5–7) Drama

Instructors
Preschool Instructors $60 for the week (per sessions taught)
Next Level Instructors $80 for the week (per sessions taught)
3rd – 7th Grade Instructors $110 for the week (per sessions taught)

COSTS

Instructor Pay	$2,270 (includes all instructors + paid childcare worker for Preschool program)
Extended Care	$ 475 (2 workers at $9/hour for 5 hours a day)
Gift Certs	$ 100
Lunches	$ 450
Supplies	$ 700
Total	$3,995

Permission granted to copy for local church use. \ This page is on the CD-Rom.

Class Choices
PLEASE NOTE THE AGES FOR EACH CLASS in the Session
(grade most recently completed)
Fine Arts Camp July 13-17th

Name:_____**Grade in Fall:**_____

Please indicate your **first and second choice for each session**

Session 1

____ **Group Guitar (5th – 7th)** — Learn some basics of guitar. For beginner students who want an introduction to this great instrument. ****Need to have an acoustic guitar to use during this week.****

____ **Recorder (3rd – 4th)** — Kids will have a blast learning some basic music theory while learning the recorder. The recorder is a great way to introduce kids to music for the first time!

____ **Praise & Worship (3rd – 7th)** — Kids will learn cool new praise songs, complete with hand motions, and even improve their singing voices. At the end of each day, they will get to be up front and lead the large group in worship.

____ **Watercolor (5th – 7th)** — Kids will learn some basics of drawing and painting with watercolor. Like what you see in our Children's School of Fine Arts Gallery? Get ready to be amazed at what YOU can do!

Session 2

____ **Clay (5th – 7th)** — Kids will have fun learning different types of sculpting. A new and exciting project each day.

____ **Group Piano (3rd – 7th)** — Come learn some basics of piano. For beginner students who want an introduction to this great instrument!

____ **Watercolor (3rd – 4th)** — Kids will learn some basics of drawing and painting with watercolor. Like what you see in our Children's School of Fine Arts Gallery? Get ready to be amazed at what YOU can do!

____ **Group Guitar (3rd – 4th**) — Learn some basics of guitar. For beginner students who want an introduction to this great instrument. ****Need to have an acoustic guitar to use during this week.****

____ **Dance (5th – 7th)** — Kids will have fun learning different styles of dance. Get ready for a high energy class and a fun performance on the final day.

____ **Drama (3rd – 4th)** — Kids will have fun putting together and imaginative performance. They will learn the art of drama and put on a performance for the final day.

Session 3

____ **Drama (4th – 7th)** — Kids will have fun putting together an imaginative performance. They will learn the art of drama, and put on a performance for the final day.

____ **Clay (3rd – 4th)** — Kids will have fun learning different types of sculpting. A new and exciting project each day.

____ **Drawing (3rd – 7th)** — Come learn some drawing techniques from the same instructor who has been teaching watercolor. You will be excited to see what you can do!

____ **Group Voice Class (3rd – 7th)** — Have you wanted to learn to sing better? Do you like music but wish you could sing more? Sign up to learn some basics and have some fun!

____ **Dance (3rd – 6th)** — Kids will have fun learning different styles of dance. Get ready for a high energy class and a fun performance on the final day

FOR OFFICE USE ONLY: Date Form Received:_____

Tutoring Camp Ministry

by Gwen Bowles

The generous gift to our church of a farm equipped as a retreat center started the ideas flowing. On the farm there is a swimming pool, a retreat center with a kitchen, and two large rooms for group activities. There are restrooms and showers, a workshop, a barn with table games, a fishing pond, trails though woodlands, and large open areas for games. A dream of combining the farm and the talents of our church members to provide a mentoring experience for at-risk children began to evolve into plans for a free day camp.

Tutoring camp has been held for the last three years at Spring Hill. We have expanded the camp to two weeks so that twice the number of children can be reached. Half of the children who attend are the ones we tutor and mentor twice a month during the school year.

Our church has partnered with a local school, and we work through their social worker to meet the needs of some of their students. The social worker identifies the children who will benefit from the extra attention that Tutor Camp includes.

We provide registration brochures in English and Spanish. They are distributed by the school social workers. On the weekend before camp opens, each home of a camper is visited by some of the Tutor Camp personnel. Parents are reminded of the pick-up times. The camp staff member answers questions and strives to start developing a relationship with the parents and child.

Our camp personnel are all volunteers. Some of the adults serve as the camp director, assistant director, nurse, and pool attendant and are present at all times. Other adults help with woodworking, crafts, serving meals, and helping during academic practice time. These volunteers are able to come and go during the day. A volunteer lifeguard is available throughout the camp.

College and high school students serve as counselors for the groups. Our ratio is at least two counselors per eight to ten children. As campers grow out of the program, they may return as junior counselors.

Each day an adult volunteer from our church or the community comes as our special guest for the day and shares a hobby or interest. Their shared talents have included activities such as cooking, fishing, golf, disc golf, geocache, scouting activities, magic, music, and visits from local Christian athletes.

The first year transportation was provided by church members. Since then we have partnered with the school system. The school district provides the bus and the driver. Our church pays for the cost of the gas. This relationship with the school system has brought some limits to direct evangelism during camp, but we have been able to provide character education and have connected with many families in our community who we might not have been able to know.

Our follow-up allows us to be more direct. Some of these families have attended events and worship services at our church. For most families our encounters that occur as a result of the Tutor Camp provides the opportunity for these families to "know we are Christians by our love."

> The key is to realize that these children may or may not ever attend our church but they will forever know that they are loved.

The first two years, breakfasts were provided by Panera Bread and lunches by groups within the church. We were blessed after that to be awarded a grant from the US Department of Agriculture. One of the stipulations required by the grant was to wait three hours after breakfast before we served lunch. This grant may not be repeated, so we will most likely ask church members to again prepare the food.

Due to the size of our camp swimming pool, we must limit the swimming sessions to ten children. We usually have three groups of ten children attend each week of camp. We assign the children to groups by sex and age.

The camp schedule we have used is on the following page.

The final day of camp each week is met with tears by both campers and volunteers, coupled with requests to come back. It is not unusual to hear statements like, "This was better than Christmas." It is humbling to see how much it means to a child-at-risk to participate in the ordinary activities.

Repeat campers start asking in September about the following summer. The campers have experienced God's love through his people and now want to have that kind of love in their lives.

The key is to realize that these children may or may not ever attend our church, but they will forever know that they are loved.

_____

Gwen Bowles is a Christ-follower currently serving at Spring Hill Baptist Church. She is wife to her best friend, Russell, and the proud mother of two daughters, Lynn and Jennifer. Gwen is the doting grandmother to seven! She is a retired teacher, having worked for thirty years teaching children with special needs.

Tutoring Camp Schedule

10:00 AM – 10:20 AM — Breakfast and Read Aloud
Selected picture books are used to facilitate discussions about specific character development.

10:20 AM – 10:50 AM — Woodworking
Projects have been toolboxes, birdhouses, craft stick, bowls, and boxes.

10:50 AM – 11:30 AM — Academic Practice
Individualized packets of worksheets correspond to the Standards of Learning Objectives of the grade just completed by the child. Children choose to work alone, with a counselor, or in small groups. Incentives are used to motivate the children to remain on task. Each completed assignment earns a check. The checks result in candy at the end of the week.

11:30 AM – 11:50 AM — Wacky Games
The games serve the purpose of providing relaxation time after the tutoring session. Game time also results in laughter, and groups compete for winner's bragging rights. (All of our volunteers participate with the groups.) Games include:
- Spitting Skittles — like watermelon seed spitting.
- Straw Fishing Relay — kids use straws to suck up construction paper fish and transport to buckets.
- Shaving Cream Contest — kids use shaving cream and plastic spoons to shave a counselor. The first group whose counselor has a clean face is the winner.
- Toilet Paper Wrap-up — "wrapped up in love" — the first group to unroll entire roll of toilet paper around all members of the group is the winner. The group decides shape they will assume — circle, straight line, and so forth.

11:45 AM – 12:00 PM — Prepare for Groups

12:00 PM – 1:00 PM — First Rotation

Group 1	Group 2	Group 3
Swimming	Special Guest	Recreation/Crafts

1:00 PM – 1:30 PM — Lunch

1:30 PM – 2:30 PM — Second Rotation

Group 1	Group 2	Group 3
Recreation/Crafts	Swimming	Special Guest

2:30 PM – 3:20 PM — Third Rotation

Group 1	Group 2	Group 3
Special Guest	Recreation/Crafts	Swimming

3:20 PM – 3:30 PM — Prepare for home

The Inside Scoop

Our children's sleep-over camp was held in a small, lovely facility with a private lake, a distance from our church but not far from where I grew up. My brother still lived in the area, and, with brown hair and beard, struck a similarity to popular images of Jesus. So one afternoon I took the children to the lakeshore and waited until my brother, dressed as Jesus, emerged from the woods and walked across a scenic bridge. They were awestruck as "He" came to them, and listened attentively while "Jesus" told them a story of his life and love for them.

After sweet interaction, "Jesus" got up to leave. As "Jesus" crossed back over the bridge, the children silently watched until Michael broke the silence, calling out, "Jesus! Come back some day! Maybe we can go bowling together!"

Cindy Ziemba, Director of Children's Ministry
Ward Evangelical Presbyterian Church
Northville, Michigan

First United Methodist Church of Midland, Michigan, is located on Main Street, next to banks, shops, and offices. It is a beautiful, modern structure designed by a famous architect. Although the church building takes up an entire city block, there is very little grass available for outside activities.

It was summertime and we were using the marketplace format for VBS. Because we did not have outside space, the marketplace was inside. We had decorated the youth center with merchant booths complete with awnings and other Bible-times decorations. We had built a well in the middle of the space where the children gathered to hear the Bible story. All the volunteers and all the children dressed in Bible-times costumes.

On one of the days a friend of one of our volunteers brought a lamb for the children to pet. We could not house the lamb inside, so we set up an old wooden playpen outside on a very small patch of grass. Then we placed the lamb in the playpen.

Unfortunately the lamb was small enough to get through the slates of the playpen. The downtown workers enjoyed the sight of three women dressed in Bible-times costumes chasing one small lamb down Main Street. Thankfully, we did catch the lamb.

It was a different way to advertise our marketplace.

Daphna Flegal
Lead Editor, The United Methodist Publishing House

Christmas

And she gave birth to her firstborn son and wrapped him in bands of cloth, and laid him in a manger, because there was no place for them in the inn.

(Luke 2:7)

Little Town of Bethlehem Advent Fair

by Joel Bullock

For churches looking for a way to share the story of the birth of Jesus, this Advent Fair prepares families for the journey to Bethlehem during the Advent season. Whole families and congregation members are invited to this hands-on event. The goal of the event is to have families spend time together and give them opportunities to talk about the story of how Jesus was born. So not everything will be one hundred percent historically accurate, but everything will be one hundred percent about Jesus. The event is designed to help families participate and enjoy being together.

Congregation members should receive by mail a summons for a census to be taken. The summons will list the details of the event and emphasize that people of all ages are encouraged to attend and that families with children should attend together. The summons also suggests that people wear Bible-times costumes. (A simple costume can be made by cutting a hole for the head in the middle of a piece of fabric and then wearing the fabric like a poncho, or by wearing a bathrobe with a towel tied over the head.)

On the night of the event, have signs posted outside the church directing families to the event. The signs should direct them toward a hallway with sand on the ground. As the families enter they walk through the desert on the way to Bethlehem.

At Bethlehem, families are greeted by the census taker. There they are welcomed and given a map of the town and a money bag with coins. Families must use a quill to write their names on a scroll to sign in to the census. Then they proceed to the tax collector's table where the tax collector decides what the fair tax is for each family. If some try to get by without paying the tax, the Roman guards will find them.

Next, families can go from merchant to merchant, making crafts and experiencing the sights and sounds of Bethlehem. Families can visit the fabric merchant and borrow clothes to dress in for the night. Children can make toys, lanterns, and leather goods. Families can smell and grind spices, have their pictures taken, and visit the stable where animals live.

Perhaps the most meaningful part of this event is for families to participate in a mission project at the "Room at the Inn" merchant. Parents loved the idea that they were doing something meaningful for others with their children.

At the end of the night, two travelers, Mary and Joseph, arrive looking for a place to stay. The couple mingles with families and may even pose for a few pictures with families. But the baby is not here yet. Finally, someone calls everyone together and reads the story of the birth of Jesus from a children's Bible.

After the event, follow up by sending a note or a Christmas card to families who attended the event, along with their family's picture.

General Setup

Possible Investments

- Fake Fire Lamps — to be used for campfires or on top of pillars for a dramatic city gate. This can be purchased online for discount prices. They can be used repeatedly in children's ministry, especially whenever you act out Bible stories.

- Blankets — Mexican blankets work well and can be found online for about five to seven dollars. These blankets are great to have anytime for children's ministry. You can reuse these for events like picnics or VBS. We use the blankets at every merchant for kids to sit on and work on crafts.
- Household palm trees (live or fake) — Our church invested in six live palm trees at a very low cost. But we keep them around the church throughout the year and use them to create scenes for Holy Week and Easter.
- Workers lights with clamps — these small silver lights are great for creating inexpensive spotlight effects. You can put any color or size bulb in the lamp and create a new effect. For this event, overhead lights alone don't set the mood well. You can reuse these for special effect lighting for musicals, church programs, or VBS, or just as a work light for projects around the church.

Borrow or Buy

- Canopy tents — ask church members to loan canopies for the event. 10 feet x 10 feet is the best size, but they also come 8 feet x 8 feet or 12 feet x 12 feet. The diversity in size will create atmosphere. These can be a good investment, but unless there is a great sale, borrow them.
- Variety of fabric in earth tones
- Earthenware pots
- Natural-colored woven baskets
- Natural-colored rope (not synthetic) — used to hang material or baskets

Make

- Signs for each town merchant
- Backdrop of town at night — This reusable backdrop can be made from 2-inch foam core board. Plan to use it for the backdrop for pictures. Cut a skyline with mostly square roofs and a few rounded roofs (there should not be any steeples). You can either paint or

cut out holes for windows. Paint the skyline in a dark brown, blue, or black. Alternately, you could use a wall and cut out the city from bulletin board paper.

Details

The real key to this experience is allowing the volunteers to decorate their own businesses. The more the volunteers are encouraged to bring in decorations and dress and act like merchants, the more successful the event will be.

Walk Through the Desert

If there is a long hallway, you can create your own desert road to Bethlehem. Cover the floor with a heavy duty plastic or tarp. Secure it to the floor with tape so it does not slide. Spread sand on top of the tarp so families must walk through the desert on the way to Bethlehem.

Census Taker

This is the first station families visit. Set up an 8-foot table covered with a natural-colored cloth. Lay out a long piece of butcher paper that is at least six feet long. Quills suitable for writing may be purchased online. Make your own ink mixture by adding a little water to black washable paint. The census taker welcomes each family and gives each child a pouch of gold coins for the experience. Fabric pouches and gold plastic coins may also be purchased online.

Tax Collector

Drape a table and chair with red or purple cloth for the tax collector. Placing a gold metal box or wooden carved box on the table gives the tax collector a place to store his money. Another option would be to make a box from a shoebox with gold wrapping paper taped neatly around it. Add a few jeweled stickers, and it is a box fit for a tax collector.

Fabric Merchant

Look in your church closets for Bible-times costumes to display and share with attendees.

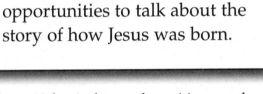

The goal of the event is to have families spend time together and give them opportunities to talk about the story of how Jesus was born.

Another option is to purchase a roll of muslin or lightweight natural-colored material. Measure a length of material that is twice the height of a person. Cut a hole in the folded edge for a head to fit through. Small lengths of material can be cut about two inches wide for belts or head wraps.

Room at the Inn

Churches can coordinate in advance to make a project for a local homeless shelter. One project that both parents and children enjoyed making was jars of dry soup ingredients to give as gifts to low income families or used to make soup at the shelter. Everyone made as many jars as they wanted. The kids loved scooping the ingredients up and putting them in the jars.

Spice Trader

To set the mood for the spice trader, place a variety of spices in small bowls. Some of the typical spices are whole cinnamon, star anise, and cardamom. The best location to purchase spices is at an Indian or Middle Eastern grocery store. Often they sell the whole spices in large quantities for a modest price. These stores also may have a well-priced pistol and mortar to crush the spices.

There are many ways to make perfumes that are oil-based. Search online to find resources for making oil-based perfume. Small vials can also be purchased online for children to make their own perfumed oil.

Leather & Woodworking

Since families will be pounding hammers and leather, this merchant is quite loud. If possible, have this area outdoors or in another room.

Contact the local Boy Scout troop for leather working tools. You might even invite them to come and lead that area. We actually bought leather bracelets that were precut with holes so kids could just string bright colored thread and cord through the holes. Leather goods like bracelets or key chains can be found online from discount suppliers. You can also check at a local craft supply store.

Ask members of your congregation to bring in woodworking tools for kids to look at and learn about. We also supplied a board with hammer and nails for kids to try. They could also paint a wooden cross necklace or color a precut wooden ornament.

Candy Merchant

These are simple recipes that usually include honey, dates, figs, and cinnamon. When you heat these together, it makes a delicious topping for ice cream. You can also go online and search for Middle Eastern recipes for desserts. The important thing to remember is that there should not be any nuts in the recipes. Children with nut allergies are very sensitive to foods and can have life-threatening reactions.

Photos

Use the backdrop created for the set for this merchant. Add a campfire by placing sticks around a fake fire lamp. Baskets stacked up are an easy way to make pictures come alive. We even had some pretend animals like a chicken that children loved to hold in the picture.

It is important for the photographer to keep a list of the order of photos, names, and addresses of each family, and a basic description of how to identify each family (woman in red hat, child holding chicken).

Stable

4-H groups often have children who are raising animals for projects. Contact a local group and see if anyone would be willing to bring their animal in for the event.

Joel and Kristin have served as pastors in Ohio, Indiana, and California. Their greatest joy is empowering others to serve in ministry by mentoring them to discover their gifts and use them in the kingdom. Additional information about their ministry can be found at www.bereleased.com.

The Best Ever Christmas Pageant

by Joel Bullock

We wanted to make the Christmas Eve service very family friendly and participatory for children. We planned to use a storybook instead of a meditation or sermon, and we were committed to letting everyone know that there will be extra noise and movement — perhaps even some wandering children.

Usually we have big children's choirs involved in our Christmas Eve service, and the children have a part to act out and speak. The children had been learning the songs they would sing and the hymns for the service. But, we also realized that there were many children who came to the service who were either not involved in choirs or were visiting.

So, we decided to have a Christmas pageant that would allow the children to re-enact the events leading up to the birth of Jesus. The leaders chose to have a script that was narrated by adults and youth. The script would communicate the story for anyone who does not know the Scriptures. This also allowed for children to be involved in the movement and actions of the story without the added pressure of remembering and saying lines.

Weeks before, we began gathering children for each part. We designated a youth or young adult to lead the wise men procession from the back, we had the shepherds hunch down by the fire in the center of the platform, and we had angels stand on risers. Mary and Joseph were young adults who came forward as one of the children's choirs, dressed with animal headdresses, sang a song about the animals at the manger.

Then the night of the event arrived. As people came into the sanctuary, our church staff asked the children who were coming to attend the service if they wanted to help act out the story.

We told them all they had to do was follow the youth leader — and they would get to wear a costume. It worked beautifully. In fact, after Mary and Joseph placed the baby Jesus in the manger, all of the children were invited to come forward to see the baby as the congregation sang carols. As the children returned to their seats with their families, the congregation closed the service by singing "Silent Night." During the song, we passed the light of a candle to adults and older children. We had glow sticks for younger children.

After this wonderful service, a mother of sixth-grade twins came to me and said, "My son was just saying on the way to church that he wished that he could be part of the service. He doesn't really sing in the choirs and really isn't comfortable talking in front of people like his brother, so he knew that there was not anything for him to do. But, when you asked him to be a shepherd and that he did not have to say or sing anything, he was so excited!"

Another girl, when asked if she would help, enthusiastically asked if there was anything else she could do. And a few even persuaded their families to stay for the next service so they could be a part of it again.

The set we constructed on the chancel stayed up for the rest of the Christmas Eve services. It was the first time that our church had decorated with more than candles for this special evening service.

Joel and Kristin have served as pastors in Ohio, Indiana, and California. Their greatest joy is empowering others to serve in ministry by mentoring them to discover their gifts and use them in the kingdom. Additional information about their ministry can be found at www.bereleased.com.

An Advent Event: The Family Tree of Jesus Christ

by Pamela Riedy

It seems that by the age of five, most children know the basics of the Christmas story. By the age of ten, they can recite most of the story. By adulthood, a fresh approach can engender a spiritual journey that is often lost in the rush to accomplish all of those holiday chores before December 25. That is the challenge of the Christian Educator in December: how to create a program that enriches the entire congregation and triggers that spiritual journey.

Many churches have advent festivals; they are often craft-oriented, like making advent wreaths, and focus on young families. The Family Tree of Jesus event is an opportunity to add far more depth, encouraging the whole congregation to attend. Imagine an all-church potluck the Sunday after Thanksgiving. The fellowship hall is ready to buzz with activity in a variety of stations. This whole church family is going to learn about the family tree of Jesus.

The Gospel of Matthew traces the lineage of Jesus back to Abraham. The Gospel of Luke traces it all the way back to Adam. Known as the Jesse Tree, these Scriptures become the foundation for understanding the Old Testament roots of our New Testament faith. They hearken back to the prophets who proclaimed that the Messiah, the Anointed One, the Christ, the Savior would come out of the root of Jesse, the father of King David. The purpose of this Advent event is to build anticipation that salvation is delivered in a baby born from the house of David; his name was Jesus.

Using the free unit of eleven lessons from the Cornerstones curriculum, find people in the congregation with particular talents who will enhance the activities. These can be run as a Workshop Rotation Model; select a favorite four and spend 15 minutes in each workshop. Or they can be activity centers in the fellowship hall.

Start the event with the Bedouin Encampment lesson. Hear a storyteller dressed as Jesse relate the genealogy of Jesus. Perhaps a person who has done research on family trees could make a chart. Use the table on the following page to select four other activities. Add Advent wreath-making if that is a tradition in your church.

If your church has a computer lab, consider using the "Bible @ Your Fingertips" lesson to explore a Bible dictionary, Bible Atlas, and genealogies. The software *Life of Christ* (from www.sundaysoftware.com) is a great piece of software with animation, resources, and quizzes.

After everyone has experienced the four activities, bring them back together to sing a few of the carols that anticipate the birth of Jesus.

An interesting addition to this event is a crèche display. Ask people to bring a crèche set of their own and witness the variety that appears. Send everyone home with the suggestion that they put their crèche in a room where the nativity figures are scattered throughout; each day the figures can be moved closer and closer to the manger scene until Christmas Day when all of the "witnesses" are crowded around to see the birth of the Messiah. It is amazing how this simple daily exercise becomes a Christmas meditation.

Use this Advent Festival to guide your congregation through this holiday season along a path that creates awe, wonder, and witness of the incarnation.

Pamela Riedy is the co-founder of Cornerstones Publishing, the premier curriculum for the Workshop Rotation Model. A talent-based curriculum, the workshop lessons invite teachers to use their talents to pass the faith onto the next generation. Cornerstones Publishing, Inc. www.cstones.com; pam@cstones.com; 866-851-7102

Check Four	Talent	Workshop	Activity
	Acting Director	Bible Improv	Act out stories from the lives of the people on the Jesse Tree, discovering how these people create Jesus' family tree. Consider people in their own lives who share character traits similar to the people on the Jesse Tree.
	Graphic Artist Crafter	Created by the Spirit	Chose a person on the Jesse Tree and create a symbol for that person. These symbols will become a decoration on a tree you create.
	Baker	Eat Your Way through the Bible	The creation of a traditional French Christmas dessert — Buche de Noel — will help the class remember the story of Jesse and how the Messiah came from this humble beginning.
	Church Historian	Faith Today	Create a Church History Tree with the ancestors of Jesus in the roots and Christian denominations as the leaves. Briefly explore your own denomination and local church history.
	Storyteller Cook	Mary & Martha's B&B	Hear from Rahab, the great-great grandmother of David who greeted the Hebrews as they entered Canaan after their Wilderness experience. Make a root vegetable salad to symbolize the root of Jesse.
	Set Designer PE Teacher	Moved by the Spirit	Create family groupings and a timeline for some of the names in the Jesse Tree. Play a game of checkers on a human scale, with callers who tell their classmates (names from the Jesse Tree) where to move on the board.
	Puppeteer Native American	Puppetry	Enact a puppet show to illustrate the book *Knots on a Counting Rope*. This story is a Native American tale of the value of passing the family stories on to the next generation.
	Photographer Scavenger for props	Video Live!	Learn about the term Messiah and the Jesse Tree. Create a family picture album portraying sixteen members of the Jesse Tree.
	Environmentalist Gardener	Where in the World	Look at roots in the rain forest to see how important they are and how they can be a symbolic connection to the Jesse Tree. Either take cuttings from plants or prepare bulbs to be forced and shared with members of the congregation.

The Inside Scoop

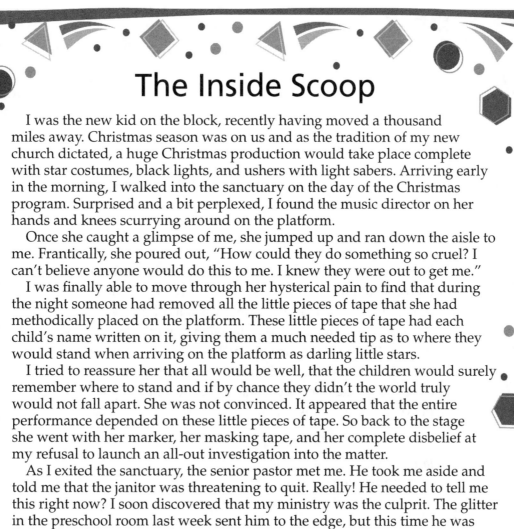

I was the new kid on the block, recently having moved a thousand miles away. Christmas season was on us and as the tradition of my new church dictated, a huge Christmas production would take place complete with star costumes, black lights, and ushers with light sabers. Arriving early in the morning, I walked into the sanctuary on the day of the Christmas program. Surprised and a bit perplexed, I found the music director on her hands and knees scurrying around on the platform.

Once she caught a glimpse of me, she jumped up and ran down the aisle to me. Frantically, she poured out, "How could they do something so cruel? I can't believe anyone would do this to me. I knew they were out to get me."

I was finally able to move through her hysterical pain to find that during the night someone had removed all the little pieces of tape that she had methodically placed on the platform. These little pieces of tape had each child's name written on it, giving them a much needed tip as to where they would stand when arriving on the platform as darling little stars.

I tried to reassure her that all would be well, that the children would surely remember where to stand and if by chance they didn't the world truly would not fall apart. She was not convinced. It appeared that the entire performance depended on these little pieces of tape. So back to the stage she went with her marker, her masking tape, and her complete disbelief at my refusal to launch an all-out investigation into the matter.

As I exited the sanctuary, the senior pastor met me. He took me aside and told me that the janitor was threatening to quit. Really! He needed to tell me this right now? I soon discovered that my ministry was the culprit. The glitter in the preschool room last week sent him to the edge, but this time he was teetering on the edge. He had spent hours late into the night on his arthritic knees trying to scrape tiny pieces of masking tape off the stage before the big performance this morning. He knew that someone would be angry if these little pieces of tape were on the platform, ruining the performance. Who in the world would put little pieces of tape on the platform and leave it for him to clean? He was outraged that this type of work had been left for him. Could people in this church not clean up after themselves?

It didn't take long to put two and two together. I went to reassure the music director that no one was out to sabotage her musical but rather a well meaning, yet misguided, janitor was just trying to do his job. I left the janitor to the senior pastor. After all, how much should one new kid on the block have to endure?

Dienna Goscha, owner
River's Edge Curriculum
www.riversec.com
dienna.goscha@gmail.com

At our annual Christmas pageant, Mary and Joseph go out-of-sight into the stable to secretly receive the baby Jesus. But on this night the secret was not hidden well enough. A preschool girl saw the woman who was playing Mary receive the baby and cried out, "Jesus is here! Baby Jesus is here." Spontaneously everyone came close to see Jesus, and someone started to sing, "Joy to the World, the Lord is come!"

Joel Bullock
www.bereleased.com.

Early Childhood

$$C$$ome, my children, listen as I teach you
to respect the LORD.

(Psalm 34:11, CEV)

Family/Baby Dedication

by Kal Otis

Let's face it! One of the most significant milestones in any family is the birth of a baby. This gift of life awakens feelings of love, awe, responsibility, wonder, protectiveness, fear, and uncertainty. It is the deepest desire of every parent to do their best as they enter parenthood. How many times have you heard parents long for a custom-designed "instructional manual" to help them raise their children?

The Bible has these "instructions," and the church is best positioned to not only help parents abstract those nuggets, but also to create a biblical support system as they partner with parents for the first eighteen years of a child's life.

Our staff realized that we needed a strategic plan to achieve this, and we found our answer in revamping how we did Baby Dedication. I want to warn you that if you choose to do this, it will not be an overnight process. It will take tremendous teamwork from both staff and volunteers, but the end result is powerful for the sake of both parents and the Kingdom!

Start by making a list of goals.
- What do you want to achieve?
- Why change what you are doing now?
- How can you use this event to teach parents to be actively involved in their child's life for the next eighteen years?
- How can you inspire and empower them to be Godly parents?
- How can you help them set spiritual goals for themselves and their children for the next eighteen years?

- How can you help them achieve them?
- How will you inform them (and keep in front of them) what the Children, Student, and Family Ministry's mission, goals, and objectives are as these goals relate to the spiritual upbringing of their children?
- Do the parents understand that the church wants to partner and support them and what that means?

From the above list of questions, you might have concluded that it is vital that all levels of staff be involved in this process. This integrated approach ensures that the staff aligns what they have to offer for the sake of children, teens, and parents to achieve the same end result.

Parenting is an exhausting and overwhelming job, and the routine of life robs all of us of what our focus needs to be. Our ultimate goal was to ensure that both parents and their children had the opportunity to have a personal relationship with their Savior Jesus Christ and learn how to grow and maintain it.

This meant we needed to find a platform to encourage parents to make daily decisions that pointed them and their children in that direction. It was also evident that parents would need a network to keep them accountable, focused, and encouraged.

As you might have already deduced, we needed to impart a lot of information to the parents. The best solution was to create a few classes that the parents would attend before the actual

> How many times have you heard parents long for a custom-designed "instructional manual" to help them raise their children?

Family/Baby Dedication Celebration. Let me talk you through what our entire process looks like:

Step 1: Registration
A parent or parent-to-be registers to dedicate their baby or child. We like to call it "Family Dedication." When you read this article in its entirety, you will see why. You will have to decide how many times you will offer a Family Dedication Celebration Service in a given year. The size of your church, the number of babies or children, volunteer availability, and space are some factors to consider. You will want to gather information during this time to create certificates as well as get their availability to attend orientation classes. Provide a list of classes and dates for the whole year, as well as their preference of dedication date. Provide all the dates for the year.

Step 2: Orientation Classes
Once registration is completed, both parents have to attend a series of classes in a linear manner. In order to advance to the next class, they must complete the homework. These classes are taught by a combination of staff members and child-rearing experts. This is a great opportunity to engage midwives, nurses, doctors, counselors, or any other experts from your church to give parents tips and Godly advice.

We do three, two-hour classes. The class content includes all the questions posed at the beginning of this article. The homework questions are designed for the parents to discuss and answer them together. The parents will be sharing part of their homework with their closest family and friends on the day of the dedication.

Some of the homework questions include:
- What spiritual and character traits do you want to see in your child by the time he or she turns 18 years old?
- How will you pattern your lifestyle to achieve these goals?
- Write letters to your child that he or she will read when they turn twelve, sixteen, and eighteen.

Your part does not end once the event ends but is rather the first step towards providing on-going ministry to families. Holding parents accountable as well as encouraging and equipping them can help your church set a path of meaningful ministry that meets the needs of the people at a perfect time in their life.

- How will you invest in your own relationship with each other and with God?

They are encouraged to become members of the church, small group, attend classes, and volunteer. Other than themselves, whom will they invite (we ask them to pick at least four to six people) to be part of their child's spiritual life for the next eighteen years? What part will each of those people play?

Provide opportunities in this class for parents to get to know each other. This is a place to establish network for parents that are in the same phase in life. We all need constant support and practical help, and this group can provide it for each other.

Step 3: Family Dedication Celebration Service
Dedicating a child should be a memorable experience, and for this reason we wanted to create an intimate time and setting for those dedicating their children. Dedications used to be part of our regular services on a Sunday morning, but now they are part of a specially designed service on a Sunday evening. Your budget and volunteer base will decide how involved this process will be.

The front of the room is set with round tables that seat ten while the back of the room has rows of chairs. Each family dedicating their child is assigned a table. Families are asked to invite friends and family, including those who may not know the Lord. As part of their homework, parents select four to six people to be a significant part of their child's life. Only those are invited to sit at their table. The rest of the invitees are asked to sit in the rows of chairs. We thematically decorate the room and tables. We provide snacks as well as childcare.

The staff plans the order of service and works hard at making this a personal time. Some of our elements include welcome, skit, music, videos, personal slide show, Scripture reading, message, and prayer of dedication. During the service we provide seven to ten minutes for parents to share some of their homework with those hand selected people at their table. It is a great time to reveal their dreams for their child for the next eighteen years. They also ask those around the table to be a part of their child's life as well as communicate the role they want each one to play.

I do acknowledge that this is a lot of work, but I cannot emphasize enough that the results will bless you, your staff, your church, and your relationships. This event is crafted to be a beautiful beginning of a lifelong partnership between the church and a family to raise God-loving and -fearing families that will change our world for Christ.

Your part does not end once the event ends but is rather the first step towards providing on-going ministry to families. Holding parents accountable as well as encouraging and equipping them can help your church set a path of meaningful ministry that meets the needs of the people at a perfect time in their life.

The celebration of Family Dedication milestone can lead to recognizing and celebrating other significant milestones that nurture spiritual growth in families. This event has caused our staff to evaluate what we have been doing in other areas of ministry and to recognize missed ministry opportunities. The end result is that we have started to embark on some new journeys by creating events that allows us to partner with parents in a very effective manner.

Some of these milestones include Bible Dedication, a celebration of when a child enters first grade and is developing skills to read. This is a great time to teach parents and kids to pray, how to read the Bible, and memorize Scriptures.

We are also working on Purity Commitment, a celebration of God's design for every boy and girl as they enter teenage years; and Freedom Riders, a celebration of the gift of freedom that a teen gets when he or she gets their driver's license and the responsibility it carries. All these provide opportunities for us to partner with parents when they need us the most.

Kal Otis has over 24 years of team building experience in both secular and ministry settings. In her current position as a Family pastor, she leads high performance teams that are both multigenerational and multifunctional. She has been instrumental in leading the charge of envisioning and implementing an integrated approach to Family Ministry at her church. She is passionate about equipping others to "think outside the box." A published author, she has been involved in evaluating church systems and assisting leadership to creatively align and synchronize all areas of ministry towards a common vision.

Room Around the Manger

by Darlene Abbott

We wanted to do something different with preschoolers for Christmas. We wanted to do more than just dress them up in funny costumes and stick them on the stage to sing. We wanted to find a way to involve parents in more ways than running the video camera. We wanted them to see that we were teaching children much more than just to sing a song. Plus we were afraid the kids' paper costumes would be louder in the microphones than their voices. Enter Kathie Hill Music Preschool Praisentations (www.kathiehillmusic.com). We used the *Christmas Journey Praisentation, Volume 1*, in the Room to Room format. It was our very first Room to Room experience, and it was a huge success.

Progressive Dinner meets Preschool Music . . .

Have you ever been to a progressive dinner? This is where you have the appetizer at one house, the salad at another, the main course at yet another house, and the dessert at final location. People used to do this to show off their Christmas decorations.

Well, the Room to Room Christmas Journey is much the same way. A group starts in an Orientation Room where everyone is given instructions for the Christmas Journey. Next they are taken to the second room, which is the Shepherd's Room. The third room is the Wise Men's Room, and the fourth, the Manger Room. Through a very short script and three songs, the group experiences the part of the story of the room they are in. For instance, in the Shepherd's Room the group interacts and experiences only the shepherd's part of the Christmas story.

Let me pause here and say that this is very interactive in each room. The teachers that were in our preschool choir were dressed in biblical costumes as the shepherds, wise men, and of course, Mary and Joseph. The children sat in a

singing circle with one parent. By doing so, guests and parents could see their preschooler do much more than just sing. Between the three rooms, they saw that their children had learned to keep a steady beat, how their hand/eye coordination had been improved by playing instruments, how they could move to the beat with scarves, how they could duplicate rhythms, and how they had gained knowledge of music symbols and simple note patterns. Of course the children sang too. And believe me, parents and grandparents got pictures and video of it all.

Now, back to the journey . . .

Each room is where the magic happens. The rooms and costumes are what bring this experience to life for the children. In our case, we went so far as to hide the Shepherd's Room CD player inside a tree so that it didn't take away from what was supposed to be an outside setting. In the Wise Men's Room the CD player was placed in a traveling trunk. And in the Manger Room, it was placed behind some hay. Instruments were hidden in baskets or disguised in some other way. All of these details helped to bring this program to life for the children.

We couldn't disguise the parents, but we did remind them that they were a part of the action. In fact we encouraged the parents sitting in the singing circle to participate instead of just watching the children. It is sometimes difficult to explain this experience to new parents because they never seem quite sure what to expect. But once they see it, they want to see it again. One year, when a member of our cast became a father, he was adamant that we plan ahead so that he could share this experience with his daughter once she was old enough.

Each group of parents and children is guided from room to room by a "Star Guide." The groups travel in the same order: Orientation Room, Shepherd's Room, Wise Men's Room, and the Manger Room. Each room takes about ten to twelve minutes, but the presentation as a whole only takes about forty minutes to complete. A group consists of six or seven families that sign up for the same time slot. The time slots are ten minutes apart.

We started at 5:00 PM. Groups signed up every ten minutes: 5:10, 5:20, 5:30, and so on, up until 7:30 PM. We asked several teenagers from the youth group to be the Star Guides, and they too dressed in biblical costumes. Everyone gathered at a check-in table for their time. Once a group was present, they were led by a Star Guide to begin their journey. Unless we were running two sets of rooms, five or six Star Guides was enough to keep the groups moving smoothly.

We also decided to put some decorated areas around the check-in table as photo opportunities. These were areas that parents could take family photos or just photos of their children while they were waiting on their group to begin.

For the Christmas Journey, we also put up a tree where we hung the paper ornaments the children decorated. These ornaments had their name and age on them as well as what they would give Baby Jesus for Christmas.

More than a Musical . . .

The teacher's book for *Christmas Journey Praisentation* had a wealth of great instructions for how to pull this program together, as well as lesson plans to teach these songs to the children ahead of time. This book helped our teachers approach each song with a variety of activities to help the children get the full experience.

The best part about the songs is that even a child who hasn't been in choir could still follow along

> W e serve each week so that children can have real-life, stick-to-your-memory, make-the-Bible-come-alive experiences that help them know the one true and living God.

with almost every activity that we did in the Room to Room Christmas Journey. We decided to invite our Chinese congregation. Some of them have never had a child in preschool choir. They had so much fun that we realized that this would be a great outreach to our community.

Each of the programs also comes with a script that allows for performance of the songs on a stage with just the preschoolers. The programs also include an option for inviting the parents into the choir rooms as the choir teachers lead them through some of the more favorite songs and games. However, we have enjoyed the new Room to Room format so much that we recently completed our sixth such experience this past Christmas. Kathie Hill Music now has several different Christmas programs for us to choose from, so we didn't have to do the same one year after year.

There's Room Around the Manger . . .

This past Christmas we chose the Room to Room format for Room Around the Manger (*Praisentations, Volume 4*). This program is the Christmas story from the perspective of the inn keeper. He did not have room for Mary and Joseph, but Jesus always has room for us. The rooms on this journey are the Orientation Room, the Market Room (where we all prepare for our journey to Bethlehem), the Inn (where we see how there was no room for Mary and Joseph and we also help count all the people), and finally the Manger Room (where we eventually catch up with Mary, Joseph, and Baby Jesus).

After several of these programs, we discovered that saving the workers' children for the last groups helped the workers themselves get to experience the journey with their own children. When we finished in the Market Room and Inn Keeper's Rooms, the workers from those two rooms came with us to the Manger Room.

Room Around the Manger

It is so sweet to see the children and all of their parents as biblical characters worshipping baby Jesus. After worshiping, "Mary" picked up the manger and moved it into the middle of the singing circle as she had with every other group that day. The children, just like every other group of children, hurried around the manger without being prompted. But this time, there was one little blonde girl who did not move quickly enough to get close to the manger. Her lip instantly turned outward in disappointment.

"Mary" quickly made room and, with her arm, ushered the little girl right in front of her while saying, "Oh sweetheart, Jesus has room for everyone around the manger." The little girl's frown flipped quickly into a smile stretching from ear to ear. At that point "Mary" started to sing . . .

> There's a place for you
> A place for me
> There's room around the manger . . .

© 2009 Kathie Hill Music, used by permission

So we sat there, as many of the other groups did that day, realizing that we were all family — God's family. We were reminded why we do what we do, why we continue to tell children about Jesus. We serve each week so that children can have real-life, stick-to-your-memory, make-the-Bible-come-alive experiences that help them know the one true and living God. We serve God and we look for things like this experience to help us remember as well as communicate to our preschool families that God truly has room for anyone who will accept him and his love.

_____

Darlene Abbott serves as Preschool and Children's Choir Coordinator at Brentwood Baptist Church in Nashville, Tennessee. She has written preschool music and curriculum and has served as a teacher for instructional videos. She is a graduate of the University of North Alabama in Florence, Alabama. Between projects Darlene travels as a clinician and speaker. She resides in Nashville with her husband, Brandon, and their three children.

Trike Nite

by Jennifer Huddleston

Overview

Trike Night is an event for families with preschoolers where kids get to ride on their bikes around the parking lot to visit different stations. The purpose of this two-hour event is for families to make connections with each other in an informal setting. It is a great entry level event to bring in non-churched friends and neighbors too. We have hosted this event at our church for the past two years in July. The first year the event was held entirely outside in our parking lot. The second year we moved a lot of the activities inside due to extreme heat in our area that week. Both ways worked well.

Our big concern in preparing for this event was safety. When we promoted the event, we requested that kids bring their own 3-wheel and 4-wheel bikes. We wanted to avoid having a lot of older kids who could ride very fast on 2-wheel bikes that would pose a safety issue for young preschoolers. Our target audience was preschoolers, but we knew that some families had older kids too, so we planned with that in mind.

Stations

Welcome Station — This was their first stop. We asked everyone to make a nametag and wear the nametag so that everyone could get to know each other better. We gave them a map of the event stations so they didn't miss anything. We also handed out tickets for free snow cones. The welcome station was also stocked with a first aid kit, and we had a doctor on call at the event in case of any injuries.

The second year we included some simple Bible thoughts on the back of the map that parents could share with their kids at the various stations. Our goal is to help parents begin to see everyday opportunities as places to share the Bible with their preschoolers.

Tracks — The first year we set up three separate track areas using orange cones and lots of pennant flagging. The "Toddler Track" was for our littlest kids whose bikes did not have pedals. The "Green Track" was the biggest area and was for all our 3-wheel and 4-wheel pedal bikes. The "Red Track" was for bigger kids who were on 2-wheel bikes. Again, our goal was to keep the faster riders separate from the slower ones for safety reasons.

The second year we did away with the three track idea and made one really big track which worked even better for us. The riders were spread out enough so that we didn't have any safety problems. We used duct tape arrows on the parking lot to show kids which direction to ride, and we insisted that everyone go the same direction. We had volunteers stationed around the tracks to help kids as needed.

Snack 'N Go — This is where we served snow cones, lemonade, and water. We set up tables and chairs for families to take a break and enjoy a treat. We had some older kids serve as waiters and waitresses. All our snacks were free.

Car Wash — Using PVC pipe, we built a frame that the kids could ride their bikes through. We used zip ties to hook a soaker hose to the top so they got misted as they drove through the car wash. We also provided buckets and sponges for them to wash their bikes by hand. The car wash was about 5 feet tall, 4 feet wide, and 6 feet long. It was a huge hit!

Driver's Test — We set up an area using orange cones that kids drove their bikes through in order to "pass" their driving tests. When they finished this they made pretend driver's licenses. We found that the preschoolers didn't really understand this very well and we omitted this station the second year.

Decorate Your Bike — We provided six-inch long crepe paper streamers, a variety of die cut shapes, and masking tape for the kids to decorate their bikes with. The first year we also let them make foam license plates and had alphabet rubber stamps for them to stamp their names on the license plates. They used yarn to tie the license plates to their bikes. We encourage the kids to finish the car wash station before they visit the decorate station since the decorations didn't hold up well when they got wet.

> O ur goal is to help parents begin to see everyday opportunities as places to share the Bible with their preschoolers.

Drive-in Story — We had a storyteller come and read books to the kids while they sat on their bikes or on blankets in the grass near the parking lot. We opted to not do this the second year as we found it was hard for the kids to hear the story and focus with all the other stations going on around them.

Grocery Store — We set up bookshelves to resemble aisles in a grocery store. We stocked the shelves with pretend food and provided toy grocery carts and let the kids have fun pretending to shop. We also had a checkout area with cash registers and grocery bags.

Doctor's Office — We provided dolls, doll beds, vinyl rest mats, and lots of doctoring supplies along with doctor and nurse dress-up clothes. We also set up a waiting area and receptionist station. The kids had a blast caring for their friends and parents.

Auto Shop — Here we put out lots of toy tools for the kids to pretend to fix their bikes. We also had some large battery operated jeeps that they could "fix." We removed the batteries from these jeeps so that they didn't get driven away. We also had some "pit crew" dress-up shirts for them to wear while they worked. We purchased various bike bells and horns and mounted them on a wooden dowel and let the kids make lots of noise testing all the horns and bells.

Art Gallery — Note: All of our activities were done without paper because we didn't want families to have to carry stuff around all night. It is also very windy here and things tend to blow away. We decorated the sidewalks with chalk and painted them with water. We also froze water in lots of small containers and let the kids create "Ice Sculptures" by spraying the ice with colored water using small spray bottles.

Promotion

We began promoting our event through our weekly worship bulletin and church e-mail newsletters about six weeks out. Three weeks out we mailed a postcard to the homes of all preschool families in our database. Two weeks out we sent home a flyer with all preschoolers who attended during our weekend services. The final Sunday before the event we put "Take me to Trike Night" stickers on all the kids as they were leaving their Sunday classes. We also hung checkered flag pennants around our check-in area for a few weeks to help build excitement and remind parents about the event.

Setup

The year we did this event outdoors we did all the setup the day of the event. We made signs for each station. We kept decorations simple with just balloons and pennants. One advantage to having it indoors the second year is that we could start setting up earlier in the week and therefore didn't have such a rush at the end. We used a sound system outside so we could make announcements and also play kid's worship music at this popular event.

Jennifer Huddleston has served as the Director of Preschool Ministries at Westside Family Church since January 2002. Her education is in Elementary Education with Early Childhood Emphasis. Jennifer is married to Brian Huddleston and has four children.

© 2010 Abingdon Press

PRESCHOOL TRIKE NIGHT
All Campuses, July 23, 6–8PM
Lenexa Campus Parking Lot

Grab your trikes and helmets and get ready to hit the road! Preschoolers are invited to bring their 3 or 4 wheel bikes and cruise to the parking lot of the Lenexa campus for an evening of family fun. Parents will have the opportunity to share some great Bible thoughts with their kids as they ride some laps on our track, do some shopping at our grocery store, help care for patients at the doctor's office, shine up their bike at the car wash, create a masterpiece at the art gallery, and much, much more.

For more INFO or to VOLUNTEER *(there are still many opportunitities for you to help make this a fun and safe night for all!)* **please contact Jennifer Huddleston at jhuddleston@westsidefamilychurch.com or 913 890 4202. Please register your family by July 18th.**

PRESCHOOL TRIKE NIGHT
All Campuses, July 23, 6–8PM
Lenexa Campus Parking Lot

Grab your trikes and helmets and get ready to hit the road! Preschoolers are invited to bring their 3 or 4 wheel bikes and cruise to the parking lot of the Lenexa campus for an evening of family fun. Parents will have the opportunity to share some great Bible thoughts with their kids as they ride some laps on our track, do some shopping at our grocery store, help care for patients at the doctor's office, shine up their bike at the car wash, create a masterpiece at the art gallery, and much, much more.

For more INFO or to VOLUNTEER *(there are still many opportunitities for you to help make this a fun and safe night for all!)* **please contact Jennifer Huddleston at jhuddleston@westsidefamilychurch.com or 913 890 4202. Please register your family by July 18th.**

This page is on the CD-Rom.

Westside Family Church
8500 woodsonia dr
lenexa ks 66227

913 422 8257
westsidefamilychurch.com

PRESCHOOL TRIKE NIGHT
All Campuses, July 23, 6–8PM
Lenexa Campus Parking Lot

Grab your trikes and helmets and get ready to hit the road! Preschoolers are invited to bring their 3 or 4 wheel bikes and cruise to the parking lot of the Lenexa campus for an evening of family fun. Parents will have the opportunity to share some great Bible thoughts with their kids as they ride some laps on our track, do some shopping at our grocery store, help care for patients at the doctor's office, shine up their bike at the car wash, create a masterpiece at the art gallery, and much, much more.

For more information contact Jennifer Huddleston at jhuddleston@westsidefamilychurch.com or 913 890 4202. Register your family by July 18th.

This page is on the CD-Rom.

© 2010 Abingdon Press

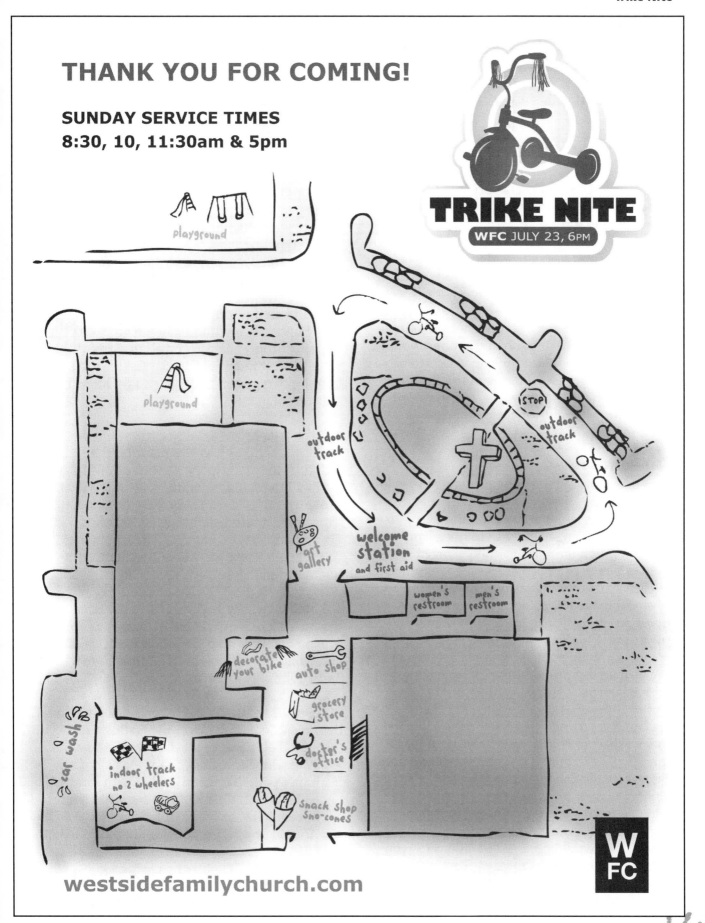

THANK YOU FOR COMING!

SUNDAY SERVICE TIMES
8:30, 10, 11:30am & 5pm

TRIKE NITE
WFC JULY 23, 6PM

playground

playground

outdoor track

outdoor track

STOP

art gallery

welcome station and first aid

women's restroom

men's restroom

decorate your bike

auto shop

grocery store

doctor's office

car wash

indoor track no 2 wheelers

snack shop sno-cones

WFC

westsidefamilychurch.com

This page is on the CD-Rom.

A Very Merry Morning

by Jennifer Huddleston

Donkeys, sheep, and goats, OH MY! Come and experience the nativity story through the eyes of a preschooler during "A Very Merry Morning." This family friendly event will take you through a variety of stations designed to share the Christmas story with your preschoolers. Activities include practicing your woodworking skills in Joseph's carpentry shop, dressing up in nativity costumes for a family photo, making ornaments, decorating cookies, and many more! You can also take a step outside to experience a live petting zoo! Christmas is a busy time of year, but what better way to spend the morning than with your family focusing on the true meaning of Christmas.

Overview

This event is designed to help equip parents to share the biblical story of Christmas with their preschool age children. We offer this event on a Saturday morning in early December. Families travel through the various stations together, guided by the parents. We provided volunteers in each station for the purpose of re-setting and re-stocking materials and answering any questions parents may have. The parents do all the teaching and interacting. We did not just want to provide an event to entertain families. We wanted to train parents and provide them with resources.

As families arrived at each station, we handed them a sheet that listed the instructions for all the activities in that room as well as some simple Bible conversation ideas about how to relate this activity to the Christmas story. Originally we had about ten stations planned, but as our registrations began pouring in, we quickly realized we would need more stations to keep things from being too crowded. This event could be done very successfully with less stations and a smaller crowd.

Promotion

We began promoting our event through our weekly worship bulletin and church e-mail newsletters about six weeks out. Three weeks out we mailed a postcard to the homes of all preschool families in our database. Two weeks out we sent home a flyer with all preschoolers who attended during our weekend services. The final Sunday before the event we put "Very Merry Morning" stickers on all the kids as they were leaving their Sunday classes. We did ask families to register in advance so we knew how many to plan for.

Stations

Welcome station — As parents enter the building, they stop at the welcome table to get a list of all the stations and the locations. We also provided tables for coats so they didn't have to carry them around all morning. We asked everyone to make a nametag so that parents could get to know each other by name as they interacted in the various stations.

Ornament Factory — Kids picked a wooden ornament that they wanted to decorate. The ornaments were shaped like stars, angels, trees, and balls. We offered watercolor paint, markers, and glitter glue to use in decorating.

The Sensory Stop — This room is designed to help preschoolers discover the Nativity story through their sense of touch. Activities include:
- Walk along the sandy road — a Contact paper path that we sprinkled with sand. Kids take off their shoes to see what it might have felt like as Mary and Joseph traveled.
- Animal Touch Board — Mount pieces of fabric to represent different animal skins onto a posterboard. Let kids feel it and guess what it is, then lift it up and see the animal pictured underneath to see if they are correct.

- Sand table — Bury characters from a Nativity set in the sand. Let kids find them and set them up in a stable, then retell the story with their parents.
- Felt board — create different scenes using the Nativity felt set.
- Manger of hay — Decorate a large flat cardboard box to look like a manger and fill it with hay. Kids can lay down in the box and see what it might have felt like for baby Jesus to lay in a manger. You can also have blankets that parents can wrap their kids just like Mary wrapped up baby Jesus.

This event is designed to help equip parents to share the biblical story of Christmas with their preschool age children.

Tool Time — As kids play and explore in the tool time room, they can think about the differences between the things Joseph used in his workshop and the things we use today. Activities include:

- Play with toy tools and wooden blocks.
- Find tool items in sawdust — fill a plastic tub with saw dust. Hide tools and large nuts and bolt for kids to find.
- Sand pieces of wood — make sure the wood is smooth to prevent splinters.
- Paint wood pieces with water.
- Dress up like a carpenter.

Tell the Good News — Mary heard the good news from an angel. You can help tell the good news about Jesus! Activities include:

- Toy phones and cell phones to call each other and tell them Jesus is born.
- Computers — Mount pictures simulating computer monitors on the wall above a table. Set old computer keyboards on the tables. Kids can have a pretend computer to e-mail people about the good news that Jesus is born.

- Post Office — set up an area with Christmas stationery and cards for kids to decorate and write on. They can put on stickers for stamps and "mail" them in the mailboxes. Provide mail bags and dress-up outfits for kids to be mail carriers and deliver their letters.
- Megaphones: Tell a friend what the angel said to Mary.

Games Galore — A variety of party games designed to reinforce the Christmas story:

- Hopscotch — Create a hopscotch mat that shows pictures of the Christmas story. As the kids hop along, they can retell the story. Another hopscotch mat can have the letters J-E-S-U-S for the kids to hop on.
- Pin the Tail on the Donkey.
- Bean Bag Toss — cover three hula hoops with garland to make them festive. Lay the hoops in a triangular shape on the floor. Inside each hoop tape a Bible verse card. Kids can throw the beanbag into a hoop and parents read the verse to the kids.
- Magnetic Nativity Sets — Dress up the characters in the Nativity story using magnetic sets.
- Tic Tac Toe — Make two different colored sets of angels to use as markers. Put masking tape on the carpet to create a tic tac toe board. Talk about the angels that visited Mary, Joseph, and the shepherds to tell the good news about baby Jesus.

Bethlehem Baby Care — Kids can help care for the baby dolls just like Mary cared for baby Jesus. Provide a variety of baby care items including doll beds, doll blankets, rocking chairs, strollers, bottles, and clothes. Also provide a small manger and some strips of cloth for wrapping the babies.

- Mary wrapped baby Jesus in strips of cloth. Help dress the baby dolls.
- Jesus slept in a manger filled with hay. What kind of bed do you have? Help put the baby to bed.
- Mary rocked and sang songs to baby Jesus. Sing songs to the dolls as you care for them.
- Talk about ways mommies and daddies care for their babies.

The Shadow Shop — Set up a large, bright flashlight to shine on a blank wall. Provide lots of room for moving around. We cut out simple Nativity shapes and put them on large sticks for the kids to hold in front of the light to cast shadows on the wall. There are many ways to play in the Shadow Shop:

- Dance and sing to the music with the ribbon streamers while watching your shadow on the wall. The angels sang to God, too!
- You can use the stick puppets to create Nativity shapes on the wall by holding the stick puppets in front of the light. Talk about the shadows you see, or ask your child to guess which character of object's shadow they see on the wall.
- You can create poses or mini fingerplays using your hands or bodies to reflect Nativity animals or characters on the wall. Have fun experimenting with your shadow!

Merry Music — Provide fun Christmas music for the kids to sing and dance with. You can also include instruments for them to play and small parachutes to play with.

Starry Night Portrait Studio — Set up a Nativity backdrop of a night sky with some plants and a manger. Provide a variety of sizes and styles of biblical dress-up clothes and props for families to dress up in. We had a photographer take pictures of each family and post the pictures on a secure website where families could download the photo for free at home. Some families preferred not to dress up for their pictures, and that was certainly okay too. We had red, green, and white foam frames on tables for kids to decorate with stars and pom-pons while they were waiting for their turn for pictures.

Journey to Bethlehem — We used pipe and drape to create a path around a large room. Kids rode on tricycles and scooters around the path. At the end of the path they discovered a large display showing Mary and Joseph and Jesus in a stable. We decorated this room with lots of white lights and made the lighting slightly dim.

Bethlehem Bowling — We put jingle bells inside water bottles and wrapped them with pictures of Mary, Joseph, Jesus, shepherds, angels, and animals. Kids rolled soft balls to try to knock down the "pins." We used foam pool noodles as bumpers to separate the bowling lanes.

Cookie Design Shop — Provide plain sugar cookies with icing and sprinkles and let kids enjoy decorating.

Follow the Stars Story Path — This station was set up in our worship center. It took the most work to set up but was a huge success with families! As families enter this room, each child receives a blank stable picture. We set up five small decorated scenes portraying parts of the Christmas story (Mary's house, Joseph's house, Traveling to Bethlehem, the Manger, Shepherds' Night sky). As they travel to the five stops, they will add stickers of all the characters they hear about. Each stop is labeled with a large star taped to the floor. The scenes were created using cardboard and bulletin board paper and a few props. When families arrive at each star stop, they unclip the story picture, read the story found on the back of the picture to their child, give a character sticker from the basket to add to your Manger Scene, then continue on to the next stop.

Petting Zoo — A local petting zoo company came and brought sheep, goats, donkeys, and a cow for the kids to feed and pet. This was set up outside. Although it was freezing cold, the kids loved visiting the animals.

Jennifer Huddleston has served as the Director of Preschool Ministries at Westside Family Church since January 2002. Her education is in Elementary Education with Early Childhood Emphasis. Jennifer is married to Brian Huddleston and has four children.

A VERY MERRY MORNING

WHO: **FAMILIES OF KIDS IN THE REEF**

WHERE: **THE REEF, LENEXA CAMPUS**

WHEN: **SAT, DEC 5TH 9–11AM**

ALL CAMPUSES INVITED!

Donkeys, sheep, and goats, OH MY! Come and experience the nativity story through the eyes of a preschooler. This family friendly event will take you through a variety of stations designed to share the Christmas Story with your preschoolers. Activities include practicing your woodworking skills in Joseph's carpentry shop, dressing up in nativity costumes for a family photo, making ornaments, decorating cookies and many more! You can also take a step outside to experience a live petting zoo! **REGISTER ONLINE.**

PLUS:

We are also collecting new and gently used books to benefit patients at Children's Mercy Hospital. Please bring your books on the weekend of December 5 & 6. Children's Mercy is a non-denominational hospital so they ask that everyone respect that by not including books with religious content. We will be able to place a "Donated By" label in each book which includes our church name and web address.

This page is on the CD-Rom.

Westside Family Church
8500 woodsonia dr
lenexa ks 66227

913 422 8257
westsidefamilychurch.com

DATED MATERIAL

_____

Donkeys, sheep, and goats, OH MY! Come and experience the nativity story through the eyes of a preschooler. Go online for info and to **REGISTER.**

WHO: **FAMILIES OF KIDS IN THE REEF**
WHERE: **THE REEF, LENEXA CAMPUS**
WHEN: **SAT, DEC 5TH 9–11AM**

PLUS:
We are also collecting new and gently used books to benefit patients at Children's Mercy Hospital. Please bring your books on the weekend of December 5 & 6. We will be able to place a "Donated By" label in each book which includes our church name and web address.

NONPROFIT ORG
U S POSTAGE
PAID
SHAWNEE MISSION KS
PERMIT NO 963

ADDRESS SERVICE REQUESTED

This page is on the CD-Rom.

Follow the Star
A Christmas Event for Preschoolers & Their Families

by Karen Apple

Preschoolers may sit quietly as a master storyteller presents the Christmas story, but I want more than starry-eyed listeners. I long to see totally, engaged learners. Creating a multi-sensory event for preschoolers and their families can be challenging if you want more than a bouncy castle or a barrel full of plastic fish. We found a solution with "Follow the Star." It includes drama stations, a birthday party, and live animals, including a dog dressed in sheep's clothing.

It's easy and fun to create a multi-sensory Christmas learning adventure that will keep families talking about the wonder of God's great love. They will visit six stations. At the first three, they will listen for five to eight minutes. The manger scene and birthday party will take longer.

Stations

- inside the Temple with Simeon and Anna
- on a hillside with a shepherd and his sheep (a dog dressed in sheep's clothing)
- outside the inn where the grumpy innkeeper speaks from the doorway
- inside the stable with Mary, Joseph, baby Jesus, the shepherd, and a sheep (the dog dressed in sheep's clothing)
- present-day birthday party for Jesus
- room or outdoor area with real sheep and goats

Creating an environment is as simple as king-size sheets painted with sample or left-over wall paint, props, scents, low-key lighting or spot lights, and costumes. Preschoolers need large scale simple graphics and décor at eye level. Make it a night adventure to ensure excitement and long-lasting memories.

A guide in Bible-time costume welcomes each group of twenty to thirty parents and children at the entrance. Schedule the departure of each "caravan" in fifteen-minute intervals. Each caravan has a guide and a star. The guide begins the journey at the entrance. "Long ago, in a far away land, wise men saw a bright new star. They followed it hoping to find the promised newborn king. Tonight YOU are going on a trip through time as you follow the star." The star lights up.

(The star is a black box with a large star cut out. It is attached to a black flashlight held high by a teenager dressed in black.)

The guide continues, "Each time the star appears, follow it just like the wise men did that first Christmas long ago. At each place the star stops, you stop, sit down, and listen until the star lights again to lead you on." Suddenly the star moves along for all to follow while the guide leads the way.

At each location, the guide instructs his caravan to quickly and quietly sit. A character then briefly tells his part of the story from first-hand

> **I**t's easy and fun to create a multi-sensory Christmas learning adventure that will keep families talking about the wonder of God's great love.

experience. The focus of each story is "God loves you. God sent his Son, Jesus, for you. Jesus wants to be your forever friend."

Enhance each story station by stimulating the senses. Fill the Temple with the scent of incense and the glow of candles and lanterns. Encourage each child to pet the shepherd's sheep (dog in sheep's clothing), to knock on the door of the inn, then sing "Away in a Manger" at the Nativity scene. Joseph can explain why God sent his Son from heaven's glory into the world. "For God so loved the world that he gave his one and only Son, that whoever believes in him shall not perish but have eternal life" (John 3:16, NIV).

Conclude the tour with one birthday cake for each caravan and a visit to a room or outdoor area with live sheep and goats to pet. The sweet taste of cake and soft touch of wool will cement memories.

If you have several caravans exploring at the same time, set up two or three birthday party locations. Families can visit with friends at the party and proceed on their own to the petting area.

After one event our Joseph said, "I looked out at the kids and it seemed like they were painted on the inside of my glasses. Perhaps I shouldn't have linked Jesus' birth to eschatology!" He was kidding, but simplicity is critical. AND Joseph probably should not wear glasses.

My husband, Steve, was especially moved after one of these events, "When I petted that new born lamb, I realized for the first time how small and helpless the "Lamb of God" chose to be."

His comment reminded me how the simplest experiences can touch the hearts and lives of volunteers, parents, and children for eternity.

Notes

A dog in sheep's clothing — Our dog, Josh, was a gentle, loving, cocker/terrier. I cut a pillowcase to cover his head, back, and sides. I glued cotton balls all over and attached two elastic bands to keep it snug around his chest and tummy. The children adored the "sheep," and he loved the attention.

Gifts to the world — Samaritan's Purse provides a way for individuals or groups to choose how they want their donations to be distributed. Their catalog includes goats and lambs. If you charge for the event, you can donate the money to Samaritan's Purse and tell each "caravan" about this wonderful opportunity to help children and families around the world. If you don't charge for the event, an offering is another option for families to contribute to this cause. After all the money was collected, our preschoolers were excited to hear how many animals we "gave away." This is especially effective if the children pet lambs and goats. www.samaritanspurse.org

Large church — Schedule this event for more than one night. Small to medium caravans and moving people along are two keys to success!

Karen Apple has been a children's pastor for over 25 years. She currently writes and speaks to equip, encourage, and motivate children's ministry leaders to be all they are designed to be. Karen adores apples, especially her husband Steve.

The Inside Scoop

I was visiting Carrie, one of the volunteers on my children's council. I always enjoyed a visit to her home. She and her husband had become good friends, and I particularly enjoyed interacting with her two children.

On this particular visit I was still in her home when her son, Bobby, came home from kindergarten. When Carrie asked Bobby how his day had gone, Bobby immediately started complaining about a classmate named Kevin.

"Sounds like you and Kevin are having some problems," said Carrie. "Have you prayed about it?" she asked.

"Yes," answered Bobby. "But Kevin hasn't been sick yet."

Daphna Flegal
Lead Editor, The United Methodist Publishing House

In the midst of all your planning for an event, don't forget the human factor. Working with children requires patience, commitment, and most of all love. One Sunday at the end of class a little girl told me that she had really had fun in Sunday school that day. I asked her what she liked the best. After thinking, she looked at me and said, "I think I liked you the best." What she loved the most was time, attention, and the love she felt from an adult.

Kerry Blackwood
Editor, The United Methodist Publishing House
Sunday school teacher for three- and four-year-olds

Easter

God has raised this Jesus to life, and we are all witnesses of the fact.

(Acts 2:32, NIV)

The Hunt Is On!

by Kurt Goble

An Easter Egg Hunt seems like a simple thing. You hide the eggs. They find the eggs. That's it, right?

It's one of those events where the details tend to sneak up on us at the last minute. We are just about to get things underway when we realize that there are lots of questions staring us in the face.

- Where are the children going to put their eggs?
- What about smaller kids who aren't going to find as many eggs?
- What about older students who are going to find too many?
- Did we get enough eggs?
- Did we get too many?
- What if the actual "hunt" only takes 5 minutes? What do we do after that?

There is, of course, no single way to do an Easter Egg Hunt. The look and feel of your event will vary according to factors like your intended purpose, location, number of participants, and personal leadership style. You will want to design an event that works in your church setting.

Below are ideas, tips, and critical questions you can use to customize your own event.

Ideas

Not all of these ideas will work together. Note the ones you like.

• Pre-hunt

Have your students build and decorate their own baskets or egg holders. You can use chenille wire and strawberry baskets. Add ribbons and Easter basket "grass" to decorate them. If you let each student fill his or her basket, it will limit the

child to six to nine eggs, depending on the size of the eggs. Or you could use empty egg cartons to limit each child to 12 eggs. You could gather these for months in advance, or ask each child to bring one to the hunt (be prepared with extras). Have stickers, markers, and various craft items ready so that children can decorate their "customized egg carrier."

• Fillers

Don't just give out candy. Remember that small novelty toys can be purchased in bulk very inexpensively. But be careful to avoid toys for younger children that can pose a choking hazard.

• Special Prizes

If this is a community outreach event, you may want to promote that you will be giving away a special prize. You may even be able to get a business owner in the community to donate a prize. Put a ticket in one egg announcing that the child has won. Or you may want to have lots of eggs with raffle tickets. Then, you can hold a raffle at the end to give away special prizes.

• Color-Coded Rounds

Use the different colored eggs to coordinate controlled "rounds." For example, you may have a certain kind of candy hidden in the pink eggs. During round one, let students gather pink eggs only. Move through the different colors one at a time. This will allow you to do different activities within your Easter Egg Hunt.

• Competitive Puzzle Hunt

This one will work best with upper-elementary aged kids. Purchase two puzzles (100 pieces or less) of the empty tomb or Calvary. Hide the pieces from one puzzle in yellow eggs, and pieces from the other puzzle in green eggs. Divide the students into two teams. One team can only gather yellow, and the other can only gather green. The team who can locate all of their eggs and construct their puzzle the fastest wins.

• Color-Coded Control

Suppose you have some eggs with candy, some with toys, and some with raffle tickets. You want to make sure that each student gets some of each item. Put the candy in the pink and blue eggs. Put novelty toys in the green and yellow eggs. Put tickets in the purple eggs. Then you can tell your students that they are allowed to find two of each color egg.

• Egg Trade

At the end of your hunt, have an "egg trade." Allow the children to circulate, exchanging eggs with each other. You could also make this a more social time by providing refreshments as the students trade their eggs.

• Program

Have a short and entertaining program at the end of your hunt. This can be a great opportunity to introduce people to your church and share the Gospel message in a non-threatening way.

Tips

• Get a lot of eggs.

There is no such thing as too many. Although lots of leftovers may invite a bit of criticism, being shorthanded is much worse. Imagine having a first-time family visit your event to find that you ran out of eggs. This would leave a lasting negative impression. Stock way up on supplies, and if you have too many, that's okay!

• Use individually wrapped candy.

Although this will be more expensive, and limit your options, it is much more sanitary than

having volunteers scoop handfuls of jellybeans into plastic eggs.

• Don't use real eggs.

There are far too many quality control and safe food-handling issues to make the use of real eggs worthwhile. There are also better things to do with your time and money than hard boiling 1,000 eggs.

Customize your own Easter Egg Event! Have fun with it! Trust your own unique understanding of your own unique ministry setting to innovate a program that is tailored to meet the needs of your kids.

• Help!

Tell your kids that when they are finished finding their eggs, they need to help others who have not done so. This will keep older kids busy while assisting the younger ones

• Fruity is better.

Stay away from chocolate candy and opt for the fruity stuff. Chocolate is more expensive, triggers more allergies, and has a shorter shelf life. It can also melt if your hunt happens to be on a warm day. Aside from that, most children prefer the fruity stuff.

• Controlled Environment.

Unless you get a permit that gives you exclusive use, public parks are generally not a great idea. A controlled environment such as a church campus is much better. When working with children, you don't want to operate in a place that you cannot ask people to leave, if necessary.

Critical Questions

• Why are we doing this?

Is it an outreach? If so, how are we going to promote it to the community? Do we require children from within the church to bring a friend? How can we connect with families during the event? What are we going to do to motivate people to come back to our church?

Or is it a teaching experience that takes place within our church service? What are we going to teach through this? How do we get that point across?

Or is this for fellowship? How do we make it social? What do we do to encourage interaction and help our kids connect to one another?

• Where are we doing this?

What are the inherent strengths and weaknesses of our environment? Is it safe and secure? Do we need to rent portable fencing to secure all or part of our church campus?

• Who is this for?

What age groups are we serving? Are we allowing parents to drop off, or must they stay with their children? Is this a family event? If so, how can we best serve the parents? Are we focusing on church members or on people who are not connected?

• What is my budget?

Think about your budget in terms of both money and time. Decide from the get-go if this event is going to be simple or extravagant because things that start simple and turn extravagant tend to be tough on the budget.

• How are we going to pull this off?

During holidays our volunteer availability tends to be diminished. Get commitments well in advance. Get help stuffing and hiding the eggs and setting things up.

A Sample Example

Suppose we wanted to put on an Easter Egg Hunt as an outreach event. We've decided to hold our event the evening of Good Friday. Here is what it might look like:

We have not promoted the event within our community. Instead we have been encouraging our church families to invite their friends with children to our Easter Egg Hunt, where there will be crafts and prizes; including a bicycle and a Nintendo DSi.

Part of our campus lies against a busy street, so we've rented a portable fence to close it off.

Upon arrival, we have parents sit with their kids to assemble and decorate their baskets for collecting eggs. We are anticipating a high turnout, so we opened our doors fifteen minutes early.

As soon as a child's basket is complete, the child is told that he or she may go into the "Easter Garden" and collect two eggs of each color. We have color coded the eggs to assure that each child will get eight eggs with candy, four with novelty toys, and two with raffle tickets.

We have an area set up with refreshments so that people can socialize while waiting for the raffle that will take place as soon as everyone has had a chance to gather their eggs.

We gather everyone into our Worship Center for the raffle. We've decided that our goal is to get families back for our church services, so before raffling off the prizes a staff member gets up on the stage and shares:

"Welcome to our Church. We are so glad that you have joined us today to celebrate Easter by throwing this party for our kids. If you have never been here before, we want to thank you for joining us, and we hope you will be back for our Easter Services this Sunday, where we celebrate the foundation of what our faith is all about."

It's Your Turn

Customize your own Easter Egg Event! Have fun with it! Trust your own unique understanding of your own unique ministry setting to innovate a program that is tailored to meet the needs of your kids.

Kurt Goble has made more mistakes than anyone in the history of Children's Ministry. But he loves sharing what he's learned from all those mistakes. For fourteen years Kurt has served as children's pastor at First Christian Church of Huntington Beach, where he shares God's Word with kids through innovative programs. He is a graduate of Bethel College and a curriculum writer. He and Heidi are happily married with two kids.

Angel Breakfast

by Tina Houser

Many churches do an angel breakfast as a special Christmas event, and after seeing the promotion for several of these, I wasn't content to do what everyone else seemed to be doing. The angel plays a significant part in the story at the other end of Jesus' time on earth. Why not have a Resurrection Angel Breakfast?

The Resurrection Angel Breakfast that we put together was intended to be a dress-up special morning for grandparents and grandchildren to share, but could actually be any group you prefer.

The morning started with everyone ooohing and aaahing when they came through the doors. That was because the lights were low. The tables were covered with white linen tablecloths and a centerpiece of a string of 100 twinkle lights hidden under a thin white cloth. A gold spray-painted matte board glittered castle set in the middle of each twinkling cloud.

Each place setting had a small clear plastic box of silver-wrapped chocolate candies tied with a white ribbon as the take-home favors. Gold plastic dinnerware for each table setting was wrapped in a napkin and held together with a gold handmade wire angel napkin ring. We asked that the people not take the napkin rings.

Posts made from 4" x 4"s that were eight-feet tall were wrapped in more twinkling lights. Lightweight white material was stapled to the top of each post and draped to the floor. A bouquet of pearlized white balloons made a crown for each post.

The menu for the breakfast was posted on white card stock table tents that had been garnished with gold glitter. Items on the menu were Sinless Sausage, Crown of Jewels (fruit salad), Gabriel's Eggs-ellent Eggs, Heavenly Hash Browns, Golden Streets Toast Sticks (French toast), and Jubilee Juice. The kids were delighted with the quirky menu but loved even more that their table servers were dressed as angels. Each server wore a white satin thigh-length poncho with gold lame' belt, and donned a gold halo made by hot gluing a length of gold Christmas tinsel into a ring.

The highlight of the morning was the appearance of the Resurrection Angel himself. Ours was a neighboring children's pastor, Joel Bullock. I purchased a white tuxedo from a discount men's wear store and hemmed it with packing tape so nothing was cut off (for whoever might be the next Resurrection Angel). We spray painted a tie gold, made him a tinsel halo like the angel servers, and just happened to have a set of white feather theatrical wings. He came in with a heavenly megaphone and did a monologue about what he saw when Jesus' left the tomb. Joel memorized the script I provided for him, word for word, which was not my intention. (The script follows.) I just meant for him to tell it. He was amazing!

Grandparents had the opportunity to do a few things with their grandkids. We played a game of A-N-G-E-L Bingo with minimarshmallows as the markers. The prize was a beautiful angel food cake.

In a separate room, they could enjoy making a handkerchief angel craft together. All the supplies for making an angel had been pre-packaged in a zip close plastic storage bag, which also included the directions. Instead of using handkerchiefs, we found it was less expensive to cut the same size piece of white cloth from material we found on the cheapie table at a discount store. The directions for making the Resurrection Angel are on the following page.

1. Cut out the wings from posterboard. The pattern has already been drawn for you.

2. Put three cotton balls in the center of the white square of material (or a handkerchief).

3. Pull the material around the cotton balls to make a head. Secure it by wrapping a gold chenille stick around the neck. Twist twice and leave the ends out (fairly equal in length).

4. Using a paper punch, make two holes where the dots are on the wings.

5. Outline the wings with a tiny stream of glue. Take the wings to the glitter station. Sprinkle glitter on the stream of glue and then shake it off over the pan.

6. Put a ring of glue around the head to make a halo. Take the angel to the glitter station and sprinkle with glitter. Shake it off over the pan.

7. Attach the wings by pushing the ends of the chenille stick through the two holes. Twist the chenille sticks tightly twice against the wings.

8. You now have your very own Resurrection Angel to remember this special day.

Families were pulled away one at a time to have their photo taken with the Resurrection Angel under one of the beautifully lit posts. These pictures were developed and sent to the grandparents, along with a letter from the children's pastor. What a glorious keepsake from such a beautiful morning!

_____

For more ideas for Passion Week, see Tina's newest book Easter-rific: Teaching Kids about Passion Week. *Normally though, Tina is the publications director for KidzMatter where she oversees K! Magazine and writes The Kitchen Kids' church curriculum. "Children are the living messages we send to a time we will never see."*

Tina Houser is the Publishing Director for Kidz Matter www.kidzmatter.com <http://www.kidzmatter.com> and K! Magazine www.thekmagazine.com <http://www.thekmagazine.com>

Script for the Resurrection Angel

by Tina Houser

(*Walks out humming, not noticing the audience; he stops abruptly as he recognizes their presence.*)

Oh, hello. Maybe you can help me. I was invited to share breakfast with a group of people at First Church of God. My GPS has been a little off lately since they sent that new satellite up. The old way sure seemed to work a lot better. By the smell of things, I must be getting close. (*Kids will probably speak out.*)

Oh, this is it? Well, hello again. Pastor Tina invited me to come so I could meet some of her very special little friends. Everyone who is a special friend of Pastor Tina say, "Hallelujah!"

Oh, how I love to hear hallelujahs. How I love to sing hallelujahs. (*Sing a line.*) How I love to surprise people and hear them yelp, "Hallelujah!"

Oh, by the way, I'm the Resurrection Angel. I was going to bring one of my fellow angels along with me, but he got another assignment, so I'm flyin' solo today.

God has lots of special assignments for us. Sometimes we don't even realize what a big assignment we have. That's kind of what happened to my friend. God gave him an assignment about two thousand years ago, in your time measurement.

We were missing God's Son, Jesus, really badly in heaven. But, Jesus had an assignment of his own. God had sent Jesus to this earth to show people how to live, how to treat each other, how to love each other. It wasn't easy, but God sent Jesus anyway. The hardest part of it was knowing that Jesus came here to take the punishment for everyone's sins. Jesus was going to have to experience death to do that.

That's where my friend comes in. Jesus knew that it was going to be difficult, so he went to the Garden of Gethsemane to pray. Jesus always talked everything over with his father. As he bowed his head, God gave the immediate order that my friend needed to go and be by Jesus' side to give him strength for the days that were coming. It was a good thing, too, because the guys that Jesus had asked to pray with him kept falling asleep. My angel friend brought strength straight from heaven to Jesus.

Now, I had an assignment of my own. I really didn't know what it was, but God had me working out at Jehovah's Gym. He said the assignment was going to call for me to be in shape. (*Flex your angelic muscles.*) So, I was doing my repetitions and working with my coach.

There were some Jewish leaders down on earth that really didn't like Jesus, and they got mad every time they heard him talk about his heavenly father. One night, they sent soldiers to arrest Jesus. They beat him with whips and sticks. They spit on him and took his clothes. Then, they put nails through his hands and feet to hang him on a cross. We all watched from heaven, waiting for God to do something. But, God was quiet.

It was really strange. God watched his Son do the most difficult thing that has ever been done. God was in agony as he listened to the people make fun of Jesus.

And, then it was like a loud speaker in heaven and we heard Jesus' words echo when he called out to his father, "Forgive them, Father, they don't know what they're doing." As we looked on the ball that is earth, it went dark. Jesus was dead.

All of heaven froze. We couldn't blink. What would happen now? God's Son was dead? We watched as Joseph of Arimathea took Jesus' body off the cross and placed it in his own tomb. Would we ever see Jesus again?

Then, I heard God cry out for me. He meant business! I flew as fast as my wings would take me and bowed in front of God. He asked how my training was coming. I thought it was a strange question at such a sad time, but I told God I was as strong as a tow truck. "Good," he said, "because you're going to need it." Then, he whispered in my ear as I nodded my head. He turned to the rest of heaven and said, "You don't want to miss this. Get ready for a celebration." The angelic choir looked confused because they had just watched Jesus die. What was God celebrating?

Off I went to the tomb where they had buried Jesus. It had taken several soldiers to push a big stone in front of the opening, but they wanted to make sure no one stole Jesus' body. Then, God blasted on his miracle megaphone and said, "Move . . . that . . . rock!" (*Extreme Makeover Home Edition style*)

I rolled up my sleeves, stretched a bit, and then gave a heave-ho and rolled that rock out of the way. I looked up and said, "Take him away, God!" The angelic choir didn't even bother to warm up; they just burst into some mighty high-powered hallelujahs!

But, my job wasn't done yet. I sat down inside the tomb to wait. (*Whistling to pass the time*) Sure enough, just like God told me, these women showed up to put spices on Jesus' dead body.

Boy, were they surprised to see me. Of course, I did the old faithful "Fear Not" thing. I was the one who got to tell the first people that Jesus was not dead. He wasn't there. He was alive, again, just as he had told them he would be.

Then, I said, "Shoo. Get out of here. Go tell his followers. They'll want to see this empty tomb for themselves." I sure didn't have to tell them twice.

From there on out, Jesus took care of it himself. We continued to watch Jesus surprise his followers over the next forty days, showing up when they least suspected it and proving that he was alive. Then he headed back to heaven. We're all busy now, getting heaven ready for all Jesus' believers to spend eternity.

Well, my assignment here is done. Got to get back to heaven . . . and I hope you'll be coming there some day too. I'll see you then.

"Why Am I Doing an Easter Egg Hunt on Good Friday?"

Creating Lenten Opportunities for Spiritual Growth

by Pamela Mers Riedy

An Easter Egg Hunt on Good Friday? How does that lead our church families to a stronger relationship to God and Jesus Christ? A community service group, like Kiwanis, can sponsor an Easter Egg Hunt; it's secular.

Churches are in the business of spiritual nurture; everything that happens in a church is an avenue to deepen our daily conversation with God. Churches can offer a faith journey experience that is wrapped around an Easter Egg Hunt.

Lent is that time in the church calendar between Ash Wednesday and Easter when we can travel down the road with Jesus through his ministry. Ultimately, because we have walked through the dark valleys of Holy Week, we want to be singing alleluias on Easter morning. Christian Educators can provide opportunities for congregations to have encounters with Holy Week. These become tangible lasting memories that are the building blocks of faith.

Ponder hosting an intergenerational series during Lent. It offers parishioners of all ages the opportunity to explore aspects of Holy Week through interactive Bible study. The presence of children does not preclude a meaningful experience for adults.

For example, imagine studying Leonardo da Vinci's *Last Supper*. A facilitator tells the history of da Vinci's painting, the event it portrays, and an analysis of the body language for each profile. With simple biblical costumes and a table staged with props, thirteen people at a time get into position, strike their various poses, and get their pictures taken. The first group then offers instructions on their poses to the next set of

thirteen and "snap," another photo is taken. This goes on in sets of thirteen until everyone who wants to be in a picture has been photographed.

These photos can be e-mailed to the participants who will likely send them to friends and family, post them on Facebook, and treasure the experience for years to come. Every time they bump into da Vinci's masterpiece, they will remember the moment when Jesus said, "The one who dipped his hand into the bowl with me will betray me." They will remember the experience of the Last Supper. They will remember being with Jesus just before he walked to Calvary. And they will rejoice at Easter sunrise that Jesus lives!

This recreation of da Vinci's Last Supper can be a one-time event, perhaps after worship on Palm Sunday or in a child-friendly Maundy Thursday service. It can also be just one of several experiences that are offered on Wednesday nights during Lent.

If you feed them, they will come: serve a simple soup and bread for dinner. The intention is to provide an interactive, intergenerational experience with Holy Week where everyone attending is spiritually fed.

The chart on the following page serves as a road map for envisioning a Lenten program that fits the local congregation. Use the ideas as a jumping off point to be developed in-house, or order well-developed lessons from Cornerstones Publishing.

Each lesson is cited by the (Yearly Theme of the curriculum: Bible Story/Unit: Workshop Lesson).

	Concept	Cornerstone Source
Ash Wednesday	Launch a Lenten series with a pancake breakfast on the Sunday before Ash Wednesday, decorated for Mardi Gras. Make the connection between Mardi Gras, pancake breakfasts, Fat Tuesday, and Ash Wednesday.	Quest for Identity: Samaritan Woman at the Well: Created by the Spirit
Lenten Series, One-time Event, Maundy Thursday Experience, Search for New Life (aka The Easter Egg Hunt)	Create a silhouette slide show about Holy Week and show it on Good Friday.	Test of Faith: Garden of Gethsemane: Video Live
	Ponder the emotional ups and downs of Holy Week by creating roller coasters.	*Roller Coaster of Holy Week* Creative Uses CD
	Create an art gallery from religious art collections in the church or library. Make a hanging acetate "window" of witnesses standing at the foot of the cross, painted by the participants.	Messiah: Jesus Washes the Disciples' Feet: Created by the Holy Spirit
	Eat your way through Handel's Messiah by creating images in response to the music using snack foods. It's deeper than it appears and gives a solid overview of Jesus' ministry, crucifixion, and resurrection.	Messiah: Handel's Messiah: Eat Your Way through the Bible
	Celebrate Easter the Bermuda way by launching kites on Easter morning as a symbol of the Resurrection. Make them on Palm Sunday after church and let them fly on Easter morning. (So much better than balloons.)	Quest for Identity: Easter around the World: Created by the Spirit
	Explore the body language in da Vinci's *Last Supper* and recreate it using parishioners and digital cameras.	Witness to God's Presence: Last Supper: Moved by the Spirit
	Learn about what Jesus said during the time he washed the feet of the disciples. Then create a miniature golf course based on John 13-17.	Messiah: Jesus Washes the Disciples' Feet: Moved by the Spirit
	Host an intergenerational Taste of the Seder and use this as a platform for introducing children to communion.	Host an intergenerational Taste of the Seder and use this as a platform for introducing children to communion.
	Connect a foot-washing ceremony with a sock drive for the homeless.Connect a foot-washing ceremony with a sock drive for the homeless.	Messiah: Jesus Washes the Disciples' Feet: Faith Today
	Create pysanky-style eggs, a Lithuanian tradition of painting Easter eggs with symbols of the faith.	Covenant: Crucifixion and Resurrection: Bedouin Encampment
Good Friday	Offer a child-friendly Tennebrae Worship service before the Good Friday service. Watch the silhouette slide show made earlier.	Witness to God's Presence: Last Supper: Mary & Martha's B&B
	Launch those kites made in Lenten Series.	
Easter Sunday	Try a butterfly launch.	*Word of God: Church Year: Bedouin Encampment*

Now stop reading and ponder the possibilities for a few minutes. Look at the list. Check the ones that interest you. Do you have a vision? Is it a one-time event? A family series? A Maundy Thursday experience?

Are you still thinking about that Easter Egg Hunt? Make it an opportunity to become aware of the awesome mystery of Holy Week.

Consider hosting a Search for New Life event on Good Friday when most children are off of school and many adults can get away for a one-hour lunch.

In advance, ask the congregation to bring in tens of dozens of dyed or plastic eggs. The plastic eggs can be filled with a variety of tokens that symbolize Holy Week.

Many churches hide eggs in three separate spaces for preschoolers, lower elementary, and upper elementary. Have adults lined up who will supervise the children in each area.

9:00 AM – 10:00 AM
Experiential Bible Study, perhaps using several ideas from the list.

10:00 AM – 11:00 AM
Rehearsal in sanctuary of a play to be performed when parents and young siblings join them.

Very successful performances have enacted the stories *The Tale of the Three Trees*, by Angela Elwell Hunt and *The Little Rose of Sharon*, by Nan Gurley with just that one hour rehearsal.

11:00 AM – Noon
Lenten crafts.

The children have spent two hours learning about Holy Week and pondering what it means. This is an opportunity to do a "keeper," something that is kept through every move, downsize, and natural disaster only to show up another generation later. That's one tangible way to pass the faith onto the next generation.

Noon – 12:30 PM
Lunchtime: parents and young siblings arrive with brown bag lunches.

12:30 PM – 12:45 PM
Performance in sanctuary.

12:45 PM – 1:15 PM
Search for New Life (formerly known as the Easter Egg Hunt).

Under supervision and with careful but brief instructions, release the children to search for new life in the form of Easter eggs. When every last egg has been found, encourage the families to return to a central place to share what they found in their plastic eggs. (Seriously, do you miss the bunny suit?)

Lent is indeed an opportunity to plant the seeds of faith that grow into glorious alleluias on Easter morning.

All referenced lessons can be found at www.cstones.com by looking at the "Six Year Scope and Sequence." For the sixty Bible stories that Cornerstones publishes, there is a choice of eleven different workshop lessons, from storytelling to arts/crafts, movement to puppetry, drama to geography, and more. In each yearly theme, the March lessons are Holy Week and the April lessons are the Resurrection. That's 132 lessons that can be utilized in planning your program. Pam Riedy will be glad to talk about Lenten programming with you. Call her toll free at 866-851-7102.

Pamela Riedy is the co-founder of Cornerstones Publishing, the premier curriculum for the Workshop Rotation Model. A talent-based curriculum, the workshop lessons invite teachers to use their talents to pass the faith onto the next generation. Cornerstones Publishing, Inc. www.cstones.com; pam@cstones.com; 866-851-7102.

The Inside Scoop

We were preparing for the Passion Week before Easter and wanted the triumphal entry of Jesus into Jerusalem to be celebrated in a way that children would remember. So we rented a live donkey and ordered palm branches for the children to spread as the biblical account describes.

Everything was in place. The actor portraying Jesus was appropriately dressed including an authentic beard grown for the occasion. The children were waiting attentively, ready to place palm branches and coats that they were carrying along the pathway as Jesus rode by.

Suddenly something strangely unfamiliar to this well-known story occurred. As the donkey rounded the corner of the building, in full view of the children, he bucked Jesus off his back.

Our Jesus "spoke not a word." He grunted, dusted himself off, gingerly climbed back on the donkey, and began the processional through the line of children shouting hosannas and spreading the palm branches and coats as if nothing unusual had happened.

We accomplished our goal of providing an event the children would remember.

Johanna Townsend

The night before Easter an unchurched mother from the church neighborhood called me at home, anxious about whether her child could attend our special Easter morning breakfast for kids. I gladly gave her the information and told her that a surprise Easter angel will make a visit and share what it was like to witness the Resurrection of Jesus.

On Easter evening I received an e-mail from the mom and she said, "Addison attended that Angel Feast Breakfast and enjoyed it. He told me that a fairy with wings dressed in white and gold visited and he heard a story about Gosh. Hmmmm . . . I guess there's some work to be done. Anyway, he's excited about coming back soon."

Addison and his family have started coming to the church regularly, and Addison has found out more about the Angel who witnessed Jesus' Resurrection.

Joel Bullock
www.bereleased.com.

Fall Events

For everything there is a season, and a time for every matter under heaven.

(Ecclesiastes 3:1)

Throw a Glow Party

by Katie Williams

We recently replaced our traditional October 31st Carnival with a new outreach. It isn't an alternative to Halloween but rather uses Halloween and the events surrounding it to promote our new event.

We threw a huge Glow Party, kind of like a minirave for kids with a Christian twist. It was amazing in many ways, and while not all of the ideas I share below will work for everyone, hopefully you can glean a few that will apply to your next great event.

The Glow Party was designed to be entirely evangelistic. Everything we did in promoting and planning the event was for the purpose of getting kids to come to the event, hear the gospel, and respond if God had spoken to their heart.

Getting the Word Out

Since this was a new event for us, I knew we would need to promote it like crazy, not only to our un-churched neighbors, but also to our own church family.

We created 15,000 Glow Party Invites, similar to a bookmark in size and printed on both sides. A glow stick was attached to each invite. We thought this might also motivate people to take an invitation versus feeling like someone was pushing something on them. (See the CD-ROM for the invitation.)

Then we contacted our local school PTA's and asked if we could sponsor a booth at their fall carnival. We told them we would provide the game, the volunteers, and the prizes. Thirteen out of the eighteen schools we contacted took us up on the offer. We did take time to make sure that each principal was aware of exactly what

the prizes were, as well as the wording on the invitation. We've learned that if we don't use biblical references, like Bible Stories, Worship, and so forth, the schools will be more permissive. Some of the schools were selling glow sticks, so we swapped those prizes out for Fun Dip candy with the invitation attached. The ones that did not need more booths or games were staffed with our volunteers, and we provided some prizes. This approach required about 6,500 of the invitations.

You can only imagine the impact we had on the school community because we supported them with our people. For weeks after the event we heard positive reports through various contacts about how grateful and surprised they were at the support we provided. It was a huge win-win.

Since one person could not possibly pass out the remaining 8,500 invitations, we enlisted the help of the entire church. We invited all our children's ministry families, members of Sunday Schools, Bible Studies, and the general congregation to help us spread the word. We gave them a variety of ways to do this:

- They could pick up a bag of 50 invites and hand them out to friends or neighbors during the two weeks prior to Halloween.
- They could pick up a bag of 50 invites and hand them out on Halloween.
- They could take a bag of invites and a carnival game and host a minicarnival in their front yard on Halloween.

Many people came to us with their own ideas for passing out the invitations. One gal talked her principal into passing them out to the entire school. Another volunteer was able to get her city's park and recreation department to approve passing them out to the kids in the afterschool program. Another person connected us with all of the afterschool Bible clubs, and we were able to pass out 800 invitations that way.

The response was overwhelming. We could have easily given out 20,000–25,000 invitations if the budget had allowed it.

Planning the Party

We chose to host the party on the Saturday after Halloween, hoping to capitalize on the holiday momentum. We also wanted to intentionally provide an opportunity for the parents to experience our Saturday Night "Live @ 5 Service." We knew it was risky hosting an event the night after Halloween, but we took the chance anyway.

Since we hosted the event during a regular service time, we needed to provide a program for all ages. We created a miniprogram for the nursery, and age-appropriate programs for the preschool and elementary kids.

All of the areas were decorated with black lights strategically placed to accent the programming. In the nursery and preschool they were placed in corners of the rooms so half the room could be lit with regular lighting and half with the black light. This approach created an environment that made the room not too dark for the little ones. In the elementary area, we used the black lights to accent the stage.

We also decorated with blinking light balloons, glow spheres, and fun shimmer decorations.

Age-Appropriate Programming

We adjusted the program for each age level and added lots of fun glow elements to the activities that were planned.

Nursery Area
- We provided UV reactive bubbles for the kids to play with.
- We had fun, kid-friendly glow-in-the-dark tattoos to put on their hands.
- They had glow-in-the-dark beach balls to toss around and use for games.

Preschool Area
- Made their own glow "Gak."
- Created fun shapes with UV reactive Chenille Sticks.
- Each child received a glow necklace at the door.
- Could get their cheek painted with UV reactive face paint.
- Decorated their arms with glow-in-the-dark tattoos.
- Had UV reactive bubbles to play with.
- Played games with a glowing beach ball and glowing hoops.
- Heard the gospel message using glow sticks to represent the wordless book.

Elementary Area
- Chose three Glow items from the "Glow Shop" (necklaces, sticks on lanyards, or bracelets).
- Could get their cheek painted with UV reactive face paint.
- Created pieces of art with UV reactive Chenille Sticks.
- Participated in some awesome worship with "The Stick People."
- Heard a message from Exodus 34:29 when Moses came down from the mountain and his face was glowing.
- The message led into an invitation to accept Christ.
- Saw a story presentation using UV painted props that floated across the stage as the story was told through music.

"The Stick People" were comprised of the elementary-aged worship team dressed in black with glow sticks duct taped to the front of their legs, arms, and torso. They wore glow glasses to provide a face, and they were extremely engaging to watch move around in the dark.

The story presentation was used as a reflective wrap-up to the salvation message. Three-foot props matching the lyrics were decorated with UV paint, and then we glued them to a stick. Using the music as the foundation for the story, we created choreography for the worship team, and they floated the glowing props across the stage accordingly.

The Results

The response from the community was more than we hoped for. There were more than 800 kids in attendance that night. Many kids accepted Christ, but there was such a crowd that we weren't able to capture the contact information like we would have liked.

When the pastor gave the invitation, he told the kids to find a leader and squeeze the leader's thumb if they wanted to accept Christ as their Savior. There were so many parents who decided to stay that the kids wouldn't have known who were leaders and who were parents.

One little girl approached my husband who was standing with his hands folded. She grabbed his hands, pried them apart, and squeezed his thumb. That made his night.

During the following weekends, we recorded at least four families who begun attending our church as a direct result of the Glow Party. One grandmother started coming to our Saturday night service with her five grandkids. She brings her other four grandkids on Sunday morning.

Even several months later, I recently greeted another family who was just returning to our church and sited the Glow Party as the reason for coming back.

Between the impacts we had at the public schools, the life saving impact of those who accepted Christ, and the fact that many families chose to begin attending church, we chalked this party up as a huge success.

My Evaluation

We learned a lot throwing this first Glow Party. I would definitely make a few minor adjustments next time we host one. Here are few suggestions:

- The word party seemed to imply that people could arrive at any time since they didn't know it had carefully planned timing for each activity. Other word choices would be: celebration, gala, jubilee, and so forth.
- Hosting it during a regular service time proved challenging in getting parents to the "Adult" worship service. They wanted to stay, so I would rework this as a really great family event.

Here is what was great about this event and what I worked hard to incorporate at our most recent events:

- Our families and congregation were empowered to invite their neighbors with the creative invitations.
- We built friendships and made a lasting impact at the local schools.
- Our team worked hard, utilized their strengths, and did an amazing job pulling everything off.
- We shared the Gospel with everyone who came.
- Families returned and have gotten plugged in to Shadow Mountain Church, our church, as a direct result of this event.

Links to Make it Happen

I hope you are as excited as I was to throw such a fun-themed event. Here are links to the retailers and places that helped make it all happen.

Windy City Novelties, Inc.™ — All the glow sticks & balloon lights

BlackLight®.com — UV Reactive Paints, UV Bubbles, UV Chenille Sticks

Oriental Trading® — Glow-in-the-Dark Tattoos

Silly Farm — UV reactive face paints

Party City® — All the black lights

Michaels® — UV/Glow-in-the-Dark Craft glue used for the Gak

Katie Williams accepted Christ at the age of eighteen after many years of wondering where God was and how she could find him. She overcame her uncertainty of knowing where to look and the fear of not being accepted when a friend invited her to a youth group in high school. This life history has given her a deep desire to try new approaches for sharing Christ and creative ways to get people involved in the local church. She brought her graphic and marketing skills to Shadow Mountain Community Church in 2004 and has served as the Designer of Outreach and Special Events ever since. During that time she has hosted more than forty annual events and many more creative events for kids and families. She cherishes her time with her husband Robert, of fifteen years, and loves taking time to carefully invest and develop the individual strengths of each of her three children, Becca, Jarrett, and Brendan.

This page is on the CD-Rom.

EVENTS THAT WORKED FOR US

Planning A Fall Festival

by Dean Stone

Why Fall Festivals

Fall is my favorite time of the year! Living in Oklahoma, we experience temperatures during the summer that often reach 100 degrees plus. Nothing says, "Get outdoors and connect with nature" anymore than a fall festival. The crisp air, beautiful autumn colors, and fresh aromas of nature are hard to resist.

Fall festivals are wonderful opportunities for families to bond together. It's also a great opportunity for churches to reach out to their community. Without a doubt the first consideration in planning a fall festival is to understand your purpose for such a festival.

Fall festivals take on many different formats. In my ministry, we've conducted four different types of fall festivals over the past ten years. In most situations, venues will largely determine what activities you will be able to offer.

Types of Fall Festivals

1. The first event we have conducted was a three-night event held at a nearby ranch. The event was called the Fall Family Funfest. The main purpose of the event was to attract as many people from the community as possible and introduce them to the church and its children's ministry. The ranch had an indoor riding arena that we turned into a huge indoor carnival for kids. Outside we set up inflatable games, pony rides, and a petting zoo. Food booths offered participants a wide selection of carnival style food. Although the church was small, over 1,700 people attended the three-night event.

2. Another church I served conducted its fall festival by renting an entire family fun zone, complete with driving range, go-carts, batting cages, bumper boats, corporate center, and minigolf. This festival was the easiest event to direct. Secure the facility, sell the tickets, provide food and beverages, and presto . . . the venue makes the event. We set up outdoor concerts featuring local talent. The women's ministry hosted a chili cook-off attracting many adults that wouldn't have otherwise attended. Hot dogs were made available for the kids. The event was totally financed with ticket sales.

3. The church I am currently serving conducts a "Trunk or Treat" as a part of the regular midweek program prior to Halloween. Adults are urged to bring their cars and park in a certain lot and pass out candy to trick or treaters. We have also turned the gym into a carnival. You'll want to start early promoting the event to your adults and seeking their commitment to hand out candy from the trunks of their vehicles. Encourage them to creatively decorate their trunks. We've been blown away by the creativity. Be forewarned that some will take the opportunity to scare the life out of kids if you don't put some safeguards in place. You'll also want to purchase a boatload of additional candy. Candy has a way of disappearing really fast. Lighting and adequate supervision is also critical.

4. The Fall event I enjoy most is our Fall Family Retreat. This event occurs the last weekend in September and has become a fall family tradition. Nothing can be more family oriented than a family retreat! Parents are encouraged (but not required) to attend. Families can choose to stay inside a lodge, outside in tents, or bring their RVs. The event begins on Saturday morning and concludes with lunch on Sunday. Activities include

horseback riding, ropes course, fishing, canoeing, wide area games, hayrides, hot dog roasts, and much more. Chapel sessions with family themes are also planned.

10 Steps In Planning A Successful Fall Festival

1. Determine the purpose of your event.

2. Set reasonable goals that will guide your planning.

3. Start early! Since the Fall Festival is a major calendar event in your children's ministry, the date should be set a year in advance. Less important details of your event can be determined sixty to ninety days in advance.

4. Select a venue. Most community venues suitable for a Fall Festival will be booked a year in advance. Don't wait till the last minute.

5. Recruit coordinators. Recruit "Get-er'-done" kind of people. Plan a limited number of meetings to brainstorm and plan. These people must "own" this event. Make sure they are part of the creative purpose. Cultivate relationships with your coordinators and encourage them to be a part of your festival staff each year. Examples of potential areas of coordination include: Publicity, Food and Beverage, Ticket Sales, Setup, Cleanup, Transportation, Security, Greeting/Hospitality, and, of course, Programming.

6. Promote. As a general rule, events that require moderate or greater commitment on behalf of families should know about the event at least 6–8 weeks in advance. A requirement of little or no commitment allows you to shorten the publicity window to four weeks or less. In either situation, people should hear of the event four to five different times in as many different ways as possible. Consider the following promotional strategies: e-mail, Facebook, church website, Twitter, video displays, church bulletin, banners, posters, fliers, direct mail, church newsletter, lobby displays, testimonials

during worship, pulpit announcements, and personal blogs.

7. Establish a budget and determine funding. How much will be needed and in what areas? Will tickets be sold, budgets utilized, or private funding sought?

8. Verify insurance coverage. As with all venues away from the church, make certain that your church insurance policy has you covered! Insist that outside vendors are also adequately insured.

9. Rehearse your event! As with any major children's ministry event, it is highly recommended that all details be reviewed prior to your big event. As a pilot reviews each detail of his aircraft and flight plan prior to takeoff, the festival director should carefully review every little detail of the event.

10. Determine a "Plan B." What should you do if it rains and the event is outdoors? How cold is too cold to continue with the festival? Are there alternative indoor venues located nearby that could be utilized on short notice?

Don't forget to appreciate your festival leaders. Provide them with a small thank-you gift. Be sure to evaluate the festival and record suggestions for next year's event.

Pumpkin Devotions

Countless devotions and spiritual applications have been shared from the pumpkin. Below are two ideas:

Devotion #1
Shrink-wrap a small New Testament (a small Gideon's New Testament will work fine). If you can't find a store to shrink-wrap the New Testament, use fine plastic wrap. Carefully cut a small rectangular opening in the side of the pumpkin. Remove the plug and insert the New Testament inside the pumpkin. Replace the plug.

Bring out the pumpkin with the plug side away from the audience. Proceed to cut open the pumpkin, removing the seeds. Announce to your audience that you see a rather unusual seed at the bottom. Remove the New Testament from the top and share how the Bible is much like a seed. You could even tell the parable of the sower and the seed. God's Word is like a seed and wants to grow in the hearts of boys and girls.

Devotion #2

Tell the children you're going to carve a pumpkin. The first step is to take a knife and open the top. Next you have to remove the nasty slimy stuff inside. Then proceed to carve a smiley face. Finally, set a candle inside.

Becoming a Christian is much the same. God opens us up (often using tragic circumstances) and removes the nasty stuff inside called sin. Only then can we begin to know his joy. Finally God places the Holy Spirit inside that enables us to shine in a dark world.

To Scare or Not To Scare

To be honest, as a child, I loved haunted houses, trails of fears, and hayrides with surprises. Most kids love them too! As a children's pastor, I must admit that I've either conducted or taken kids to all of the above. After years of children's ministry experience, I have reached the conclusion that it is not in the best interest of children's ministry to combine fearful Halloween related activities with fall festivals. My decision is based on the following:

1. Children struggle enough with fear. Real life situations are scary enough. Why should we contribute to a child's fear?

2. Halloween is generally understood as Satan's holiday. While I'd never become legalistic or condescending in this matter, it is unwise for a church to sponsor activities that promote Halloween themes of death and destruction.

3. Without a doubt there will be people in your church that are highly conservative and opinionated on this topic. You'll offend them if you conduct an event with strong Halloween themes. It just isn't worth it!

Dean Stone currently serves as Lead Children's Pastor of CrossPointe Church in Norman, Oklahoma. He and his wife Lisa also own and operate Cornerstone Kids' Ranch near Ada, Oklahoma, a ranch designed to teach children to love God and care for his creation.

Dean formerly served as Executive Director of International Network of Children's Ministry, a denominationally independent organization based in Englewood, Colorado. During his leadership, "INCM" grew to become a leading organization in America for training and resourcing leaders who minister to children from all Christian denominations.

Dean is a graduate of Oklahoma State University with further studies at Hillsdale College in Moore, Oklahoma. Dean, and his wife Lisa, have one daughter, Janelle, age 19.

Fall festivals are wonderful opportunities for families to bond together. It's also a great opportunity for churches to reach out to their community.

Potential Fall Festival Activities

Hayride
Hot Dog/Smore Roast
Carnival
Pumpkin Patch
Pumpkin Carving
Pumpkin Decorating
Pony Rides
Petting Zoo
Square Dancing
Hay/Corn Maze
Trick or Treating
Cake Walk
Inflatable Games
Face Painting
Chili Cook-off

Root Beer Chug
Pie Eating Contest
Haunted House
Cookie Decorating
Butter Churning
Diamond Dig
Tattoos
Tricycle Race
Toe Sack Race
Tug O War
Pie Auction
Popcorn Ball Making
Through the Bible Walk
Pumpkin Seed Roasting
Costume Contest

Sample Fall Retreat Schedule

Saturday

9:00 AM	Depart from Church
10:15 AM	Arrive at Cornerstone Kid's Ranch
10:30 AM	Orientation (arena)
11:00 AM	Unpack, set up tents, visit restrooms, free time
12:00 PM	Chuck wagon lunch (lodge)
1:00 PM	Worship & Teaching (arena)
2:00 PM	Ranch Activities (refer to map for location of activities)
3:00 PM	Lazer Zone Family Fun Center (bus loads at arena)
6:00 PM	Dinner around the campfire, "Ride Through the Bible" Hayride, Sardines Game
7:30 PM	Worship & Teaching (arena)
8:30 PM	Fireworks & Snack (lodge)
9:15 PM	Late night movie (arena)
10:00 PM	Get ready for bed

Sunday

8:00 AM	Breakfast (back of lodge)
9:00 AM	Free time/Get ready for Worship
9:45 AM	Worship & Teaching (arena)
11:00 AM	Ranch Activities (refer to map for location of activities)
12:00 PM	Lunch (back of lodge)
1:00 PM	Pack up & clean up
1:15 PM	Depart (bus loads at arena)
2:30 PM	Arrive back at church

Fall Children's & Family Retreat
September 25-26

- Horseback Riding
- Lazer Tag
- Hayride
- Fireworks Show
- Barnyard Festival
- Ropes Course
- Frisbee Golf
- Fishing
- Petting Farm
- Bowling
- Mini Golf
- & More!

Children in grades one through six and their parents are invited to attend the Fall children's retreat at Cornerstone Kids' Ranch just out side of Ada. We will depart from the church at 9:00am on Saturday, September 25th and return at 2:30 pm on Sunday, Sept. 26th. Late September is the perfect time for a family out- ing. Children may attend with or without a parent. Younger and older siblings may attend provided a parent attends.

Dads and boys will sleep in tents surrounding a campsite. Moms and girls will stay in the ranch house (slumber party style with limited beds) or in tents in the backyard. If your family plans to attend and wishes to stay together, plan to bring a tent. A family camping site will also be avail- able complete with RV restroom and shower. RVs or camper trailers can also be accommo- dated with water and electric hookups.

The retreat features a hayride, wiener roast, "ride through the Bible hayride," old fashioned games, 3 Chapel programs, a trip to the Lazer Zone Family Fun Center (Unlimited lazer tag, bowling, & mini golf) and the best fireworks show this side of Disneyland. The retreat also features a barnyard festival that includes a visit to the petting farm, horse riding, inflatable games, frisbee golf, barrel train, barn swing, and more.

The cost is $20 per person and families must register by Wednesday evening, September 23rd. After this date the cost is $25 **PLEASE NO EXCEPTIONS**! Four meals will be included in your registration fee. We will be able to pro- vide free transportation for approximately 125 people on church buses and vans. To register, complete the form below, detach and return to the children's welcome center at the church.

What to Bring: Change of clothes, light jacket, toiletries, sleeping bag, pillow, towel/wash cloth (if you plan to shower), flashlight, insect repel- lent, Bible. If you will be camping as a family, bring a tent.

Retreat Schedule

Saturday
9:00	Depart from church
10:15	Arrive at Cornerstone Kid's Ranch.
10:30	Orientation (Arena)
11:00	Unpack, set up tents, visit restrooms
12:00	Chuckwagon lunch
1:00	Fun Ranch Activities
3:00	Lazer Zone Family Fun Center
6:00	Dinner around the campfire, "Ride Through the Bible" Hayride, Games
7:30	Barnyard Festival (Inflatables, Petting Farm)
8:30	Chapel
9:30	Fireworks & Snack
10:00	Get ready for Bed

Sunday
8:00	Breakfast
9:00	Fun Ranch Activities
10:30	Chapel
12:00	Lunch
12:45	Pack up & Clean up
1:00	Depart
2:30	Arrive at CrossPointe Church

REGISTRATION FORM

Please complete this registration form (one for each family), detach, enclose $20 ($25 after 9/22) per person and drop this by the children's welcome center. Checks should be made payable to CrossPointe Church. The parental consent and waiver form below must be completed and signed by a witness. Questions? Call Children's Pastor, Mr. Dean @ 405-250-3214. Please Note: Check the box besides Mom and Dad's name if they are registering too. If they are not registering, leave box blank.

☐ Mom's Name _____   ☐ Dad's Name _____

Home Address _____ City _____ ST ____ Zip ____

Home Phone _____ Work Phone _____ Mobile _____

Child's Name (list only those registering)	Birthday (M/D/Y)	Age
1.		
2.		
3.		

Allergies? Please describe _____

Emergency Contact _____ Phones _____

As in prior years, we will be offering horse riding in an indoor arena. Please indicate ☐ **yes** if you want you child to be included in this event or ☐ **no** if you do not. If neither is checked, your child **will not** be allowed to participate!

CROSSPOINTE CHURCH
PARENTAL CONSENT AND WAIVER

I hereby declare my consent for my child (children) named above or I, if I am an adult participant, to participate in the activities conducted by CrossPointe Church.

First Aid and Emergency Medical Treatment

I recognize that there may be occasions where the child (children) named above or I, if I am a participant, may be in need of first aid or emergency medical treatment as a result of an accident, illness, or other health condition or injury. I do hereby give permission for agents of CrossPointe Church and Cornerstone Kids' Ranch to seek and secure any needed medical attention or treatment for the child (children) named above or me, if I am a participant, including hospitalization, if in the agent's opinion such need arises. In doing so I agree to pay all fees and costs arising from this action to obtain medical treatment. I give permission for attending physician(s) and other medical personnel to administer any needed medical treatment, including surgery and, again, I agree to pay for the medical treatment.

I further agree to indemnify and hold CrossPointe Church and Cornerstone Kids' Ranch and its ministers, leaders, em- ployees, volunteers, or agents from any and all claims arising from my participation in its activities and programs, or as a result of injury or illness of my child (children) during such activities.

Signature of Parent or Legal Guardian _____ Date ____

Print Name of Parent or Legal Guardian _____

Witness Signature _____ Date ____

This page is on the CD-Rom.

PUMPKIN PATCH

Saturday, October 17, 24, & 31

11:00 am - 5:00 pm

*(Weekdays for schools available...
call 405.250.3214 for more info)*

Held at Cornerstone Kid's Ranch

Cornerstone is located approximately three miles Northwest of Ada. Take highway 99 (the new 4-lane) north from Richardson Loop. Exit left onto Egypt road just past the new CLEET facility. Watch for signs. For more information call 405.250.3214.

- **Hayrides**
- **Pick your own pumpkin**
- **Hay Maze**
- **Inflatable Games**
- **Barrel Train Rides**
- **Pony Rides**
- **Petting Farm**
- **Diamond Dig**
- **Tricycle Racetrack**
- **Concessions & More**

$6 Kids *(2-12 years)*
$7 Teens/Adults
Kids under 2, free

This page is on the CD-Rom.

Fall Kick-Off

by Philip Biles

Fall Carnival. Trunk Treats. County Fair. Free Family Fun Fall Fair Festival. No matter what you call it, every church can benefit from some sort of Fall K.I.C.K.-Off event coming out of the summer. Naming it is the easy part. Making sure it serves its purpose without being a Fall Failure is the difficult part, but it may not be as hard as it seems! Let's K.I.C.K. it off . . .

K — Keep God in focus.
Remember the biggest kick-off event ever? Creation! God kicked it all off extremely well, so we want to make sure he is involved in every part. Stop and pray right now. Pray for direction and excitement. Pray for ideas to begin flowing from heaven into your noggin. Praise him for bringing you to this article!

Before this event ever gets on the church calendar, discuss with your team and/or your pastor and make sure you know why this event will occur. The last thing anyone wants to do is pull together a big event that reaps little fruit and becomes just another spot on the already busy church calendar.

After a busy summer of traveling, camps, and watching Phineas and Ferb, parents are eager to get back into the school routine. Having an event in the fall can really help jump start your families into the excitement and joy of your children's ministry.

A fall kick-off event is a great place to highlight your ministry and be used for either an evangelistic outreach, fellowship builder, discipleship catalyst, or all the above. As an evangelistic outreach, you will be introducing the community to a church body, not just a building with stained glass windows.

Serving the Lord together as believers brings a sense of genuine Christ-like fellowship. Fellowship as in Acts 2:42-47 fellowship. Working as a body of Christ in the planning, implementing, and follow-up brings joy and excitement for doing the Lord's work. As Acts 2:47 states, your church will be "praising God and enjoying the favor of all the people. And the Lord added to their number daily those who were being saved." Fellowship and serving builds community. After serving together during this event, your families will be proud to invite their friends and neighbors to church — ready to share more than just a free hot dog and pony ride!

I — Invite the world.
Remember, we want to think beyond our church walls. What one word brings people to any store quicker than anything else? "FREE." Put that word somewhere in your title and make it big. Making sure the event is "Free and Open to the Public" will bring many brand new families from your community to experience God's love for them in a tangible way.

Utilize your VBS and other summer programs contact lists to invite these families back for this event. Not only will the entire family be back on your campus, they will hopefully reconnect with their summer ministry leaders and further those relationships in positive ways!

Don't be limited to having the event on your church campus. This may not work for every situation. Remember, you are introducing people to the body of Christ, not a pretty brick building. Find an abandoned store parking lot, spend a day cleaning it up, rope off a safe area, and voilà — a temporary fairground! Go into the community. You may be able to find a low-income apartment complex and speak with the property manager. Most would love the fact that you are offering a safe event for the entire family. I have also heard of churches taking over a golf community Clubhouse for a few hours. Don't be afraid to go ask — businesses love people, they bring them more business.

Now, here's a real test as to whether or not your ministry is kingdom minded . . . partner with another local church and bring more resources to the table! Gather a few smaller churches together and really work together at reaching the next generation. It really does not matter where our families attend, as long as they are going somewhere that teaches the Word of God and his plan for their lives!

C — **Capture the Community of Christ.** (Hey, that was pretty good on the "C" I might add!) As your team prepares for this event, make sure you get the entire church involved. Meet with all the Sunday School teachers and/or small group leaders in your church at the beginning of the year, while they are in full swing and looking forward to serving others. Building their excitement early on also takes the last minute planning pressures you might have during your busiest time of the year. Bring the youth pastor on board early as he or she can use this as regrouping time as well.

food and game booths, providing all the necessary items. The church averaged about 450 on a Sunday and saw over 1,200 each year to the Fair. Many families become involved in their Awana Clubs and Upward Basketball programs throughout the year. It was a great way for the adults and empty nesters to see the harvest of the next generation and be willing to step up and help in other areas of the children's ministry throughout the year.

Have the pastor announce it early and often. Put it in your newsletters, bulletins, e-mails. Give the congregation plenty of time to have that date open. Please do not wait until one month before the event to begin asking for help and resources. Trust me, it won't work very well. The Big Event will end up being a one-man circus and no one will ever come back next year. With each announcement, make sure you are communicating the "why." People want to serve with a purpose. They will help "work" a booth once — they will "serve" God each time as they see the faces of kids and families receive God's love through them and in such a fun way.

K — **Keep it simple.** Now what does this event actually look like? Well, that's your part — and God's! Pray with your team. Pray big. I mean really big. Pray for a Ferris wheel, pony rides, and cotton candy machines. Oftentimes we settle for what our already miniscule Children's Ministry budget can handle — a rented movie and a bag of popped popcorn from the discount store. Not that this is bad, but you want this event to be a "Wow, God's people are fun to be around!" You want to do something out of the ordinary. Rent a snow-making machine if you live in Texas. Contact your local Antique Car Club. Dust off the senior citizen's hand-cranked ice cream churns. Bring in your fancy restaurant's chef and have them put on a mini-cooking demonstration. Invite your fire and police responders — all kids love the fire trucks!

> Remember the biggest kick-off event ever? Creation! God kicked it all off extremely well, so we want to make sure he is involved in every part. Stop and pray right now. Pray for direction and excitement.

The main point is to delegate, delegate, delegate. Have different groups take on different parts. One church in Durham, North Carolina, had a Free County Fair every first Saturday in October. The Sunday School classes took on the different

Map out a one mile fun run and a 5k run course and have the biggest finisher's party ever for that distance. Find one theme or one idea and go big. Here are five key pointers to remember as you begin this process:

1. Be organized in every way. Spreadsheets, maps, nametags all communicate "We know what we are doing here" — even if you don't!

2. Three hours is a great length of time. You want people wanting more, but not too much. Be sure to check your local schedule and not plan it during baseball games or a major concert in town.

3. Have families serve for thirty-minute slots — this gives them plenty of time to enjoy the event as a family as well, while still being able to keep the servant's heart beating.

4. Recruit separate set-up and clean-up crews. It makes for a very long day for those who served and have to either come early to set up or stay later to clean up.

5. Capture people's contact information. You want to be able to communicate further ministry opportunities with families. That last point is probably the most

important. One great way to do this is by having a door prize. Make it big enough that everyone will want to enter. A free hot-dog meal at a free event is not enough. A Wii™ or free weekend car rental is much better!

OFF — Off you go!

After the event is done, rest your weary feet and watch your taped episodes from Shark Week. Praise God for a great turn-out and remember to thank your servants. A simple note to your pastor and all of your resource suppliers goes a long way in planning for next year. Brag on God all next week.

The key is to make it your own. Let God guide you through every step and be ready for a huge blessing. This could be an annual event, perhaps even quarterly for the over-achievers. Each time should get easier and easier as you learn from your mistakes and victories.

Maybe in a year or two, the Free Family Fun Fall Fair Festival will be number eight on your top ten stressful things to do in a Children's Pastor's year!

_____

Philip Biles is the Children's Pastor at Lake Hills Church in West Austin, Texas. pbiles@lhc.org

> Let God guide you through every step and be ready for a huge blessing.

The Inside Scoop

Fall Sunday School Kick-off at our church has been a big event. Well-known children's ministry performers have been invited over the years on the Sunday when the children are promoted to their next grade level. The celebration takes place during a late afternoon party that includes the children, their parents, and many other members of the church. We have food, games, and always a surprise element.

This particular year we decided to make it a Lift-off, instead of a Kick-off. A local hot air balloon company was contracted to "take off" from a corner of the church parking lot. Before the assent, the children and parents could see and touch the basket of the hot air balloon and ask the balloon pilot questions. There would be a drawing for a free balloon ride that would take place at a time convenient to the family of the winning child. You can imagine the excitement that had built for this event.

The food venders were in place. The inflatable games were set up, and safety monitors were at their designated post. Our staff members were in strategic stations on the church parking lot and were prepared to recruit more volunteers and sign up children for the Wednesday night programming. But, where was the hot air balloon? We were trying to maintain calm as phone calls were made to the hot air balloon pilot. Just as I was losing hope, I saw my assistant walking across the church parking lot toward me. With her was a woman in a uniform . . . it looked like something that a hot air balloon pilot might wear. As I reached out to shake her hand and welcome her, my assistant spoke. "Judy, this is Penny. She is a hot air balloon pilot, but not the one that is supposed to be here. He decided that it was too windy to bring his hot air balloon." So how did Penny know to show up?

It seems that Penny and her husband had attended one of the Sunday morning services. This was their first Sunday at our church. They read in the bulletin about the Sunday School Lift-off and thought it might be fun to join the celebration by bringing their equipment to the church. Yes, it was too windy to lift off, but they could tether the basket of their balloon and let inquisitive children see what it was like. Later it would become apparent that the dads were really interested as some of them got permission to get inside the basket.

These people were far more a blessing than they could imagine. Not many in the crowd were aware that we had been wringing our hands awaiting the arrival of our special guest. Some of us celebrated more than others as we experienced God's kindness as our need was met.

Judy Comstock, writer and editor

Family Events

As for my family and me, we will serve
the LORD.

(Joshua 24:15, GNT)

Successful Family Events

by David and Teesha Laflin

One of the most difficult challenges that today's families face is simply spending time together. Throughout the week, individual family members are stretched between work, school, sports, music, recreation, and more. Sometimes, almost miraculously, an entire family is able to climb into the same vehicle and go to church together!

The only thing is, once the family reaches the doors of the church they often, once again, go their own directions. Younger kids go to the children's ministry, the teens to youth ministry, parents and senior adults to their own classes, and so forth.

Of course, this can be very good. It is obviously important for each of us to be taught in a way we can understand and to interact with others going through similar life experiences. At the same time, it is very important for families to laugh, learn, and worship together. When parents and children experience and learn together, windows of opportunity are open for communication, and families grow closer.

Most people love the idea of a family event, especially if this is an event specifically designed for the message of Jesus Christ to be shared. In fact, for many Christians this is the premier way in which unchurched friends and family members are invited to church. Research by George Barna shows that in the past year about forty per cent of Christians shared their faith in Christ by taking a non-Christian friend to church so they could hear the Gospel. In some ways the idea of a family event seems simple. But, what does it really take to make it a success?

In the past eight years we have had the privilege of partnering with churches all across the United States and around the world at over 1,000 different events. Through this experience we have made many mistakes, been a part of some "wildly successful" events, and learned more than we ever imagined we would. One of the most significant things we have learned is that no matter how identical different events seem in the planning process, no two events are exactly the same. In spite of this, there are definitely many elements that consistently go into putting together a positive experience for everyone involved.

The first step in planning a successful family event is to identify your purpose. Why are you doing what you are doing? Is the goal of your event to clearly share the message of Jesus with your community? If so, your planning should reflect this. A comedian whose humor revolves around "church life" might be perfect for the members of your church, but for someone visiting for the first time it could make them feel out of place when they do not "get it."

Is this event a closing celebration for a special program or a week of VBS? Would you like to design an event specifically aimed at encouraging those who already attend your church? Are you kicking off a building campaign? Maybe your goal is to simply provide a fun event the family can enjoy together.

Having a clearly stated purpose will give your staff or team direction, shape your promotion, and eliminate unnecessary activities. If the objective of your event is to recognize your children's ministry volunteers and their families, you likely do not need to advertise on the TV and radio, put up posters in local businesses, or rent a billboard. On the other hand, if outreach is your desire, these types of promotion may become an integral part of your plan.

After identifying your purpose, you will be better able to brainstorm and gather information. Where will this event be held? Will this be an indoor or outdoor event? If you will be hosting an event outdoors, there is much to think about providing. It is easy to overlook the necessary items that are naturally provided at indoor events. This includes things like bathrooms, trash cans, signs, access for suppliers (food, water, and so forth), child check-in and security, volunteer space, storage for equipment, emergency vehicle access, and a bad weather plan. These are all important details that must be considered when planning an event.

Once you have decided on the type of family event you would like to create and established a timeframe, you can begin to formulate a more formal plan. The further out you plan, the more likely you will be able to secure all the items you desire (facility, entertainment, and so forth). You may need to have some flexibility in this process to get everything to come together. Double check church and school calendars as well as other community events.

Be sure to confirm that your selected location has all the necessary specifications. Some of the requirements to consider (if necessary for your event) include audience size, sound and light needs, adequate parking, any special permits, and if food and drinks are allowed. If you will be having entertainment and/or a speaker, make sure they are a good fit and will represent you well.

It is always a great idea to confirm all necessary details for the event in writing. If you will be renting a facility, hiring a caterer, or booking a speaker, you should definitely have a written agreement and pay a deposit. This will help prevent last-minute details from falling through due to miscommunication.

> As you develop your timeline it is important to pray, start planning early, line up key volunteers, establish a promotional plan (know when you will start publicizing), and ask any questions that may come up.

Keep in mind, you may not need to bring in anything from outside your church for the event to be a success. Many of the best family events happen right there within the doors of your church using the facilities and resources you already have on site. Do not be afraid to use the gifts and talents God has given to you and your church family!

As you develop your timeline, it is important to pray, start planning early, line up key volunteers, establish a promotional plan (know when you will start publicizing), and ask any questions that may come up. In the process of planning your event, it is recommended that two separate timelines are created, one for the time leading up to the event, and a second timeline for the day itself.

As you think through everything that needs to be done leading up to the event, it can be easy to become overwhelmed. Be sure to delegate. Allow others to play to their strengths. Some will love to create signs and advertising to help with promotion, others will enjoy the behind the scenes detail work. Depending on how big and elaborate this event will be, you may want to create teams to help with different elements of planning. A promotional team, technical team, crowd control team (security), hospitality team, facilities team, counseling team, and a follow-up team are all important to consider.

When the big day finally arrives, it is common to be a little nervous. You will likely feel that you are forgetting something, and sometimes you will be right! You may wonder if anyone will actually show up for the event. While it is perfectly normal to feel a little extra stress, much of this can be alleviated if you have a solid team and a good plan.

In addition, be sure to arrive early and confirm the details of the day. Make sure signs are clearly posted and that volunteers know where to go when they arrive. Pray together as a team, and enjoy yourself! If you are excited for the day, others will catch your enthusiasm. If, on the other hand, you display an example of tension and stress, others will follow suit. Be sure that you help create an environment of excitement for the day.

One of the most important, and often overlooked, aspects of family outreach events is follow-up. Once your concert or carnival has come and gone, it is easy to feel like all of the work must be over with. Maybe it was a success. There were no major catastrophes, attendance met your expectations, and people had a good time. The truth is that this may be just the beginning. Are you prepared for the success you had hoped for? If people came and made a decision for Christ, is anyone following up with them?

If, during the event, there is an opportunity for a decision to be made, be sure someone is there to follow-up. Have decision cards, counselors, and resources available for those who want more

information on what it means to be a follower of Christ. Consider providing follow-up discussion resources for families. And, after the event, touch base with any first-time visitors and those who made a decision for Christ.

Finally, assess your success. What was good about this event? What could be improved? Take the time to recognize and thank your volunteers for their hard work. Also, give your volunteers the opportunity to share their suggestions for next time. You might even use this time to begin planning for the next event.

In spite of all the work and attention to detail that goes into planning a successful event, it is well worth the effort. So be creative, enjoy watching families share this special time together, and have fun!

_____

David and Teesha Laflin are illusionists specializing in outreach events and family entertainment. Their programs have been featured on Daystar Christian Television, stages all throughout the United States, and in seven foreign countries. Thousands have been impacted by the unique and passionate way they present the Gospel though the art of illusion.

Your Child's Baptism

by MaryJane Pierce Norton

> J esus came from Nazareth in Galilee and was baptized by John in the Jordan. As Jesus was coming up out of the water, he saw heaven being torn open and the Spirit descending on him like a dove. And a voice came from heaven: "You are my Son, whom I love; with you I am well pleased."
> (Mark 1:9-11, NIV)

There's something wonderful about a baptism. Perhaps it's the sound of water falling from the pastor's hands as the water is lifted out of the bowl. It may be the look of love on the faces of family members surrounding the child or the expressions on the faces of those in the congregation who experience wonder and gladness on this new life brought to the front of the church. The presence of God's love is felt through this simple ceremony. Even before we can say yes to God, God says yes to us. That's the picture we have with infant baptism. And that's the message we are charged with giving our child.

Frequently Asked Questions

1. How do we know what our church believes about baptism?

While baptism is a sacrament of the Christian Church, different denominations view baptism differently. The pastor or director of children's ministry can define your church's beliefs. Many churches distribute leaflets that explain baptism and schedule a time to talk with parents before they make a decision about having their baby baptized.

2. How does baptism differ from christening?

People in the church often use these terms interchangeably, but they are very different. A christening is a ceremony only for babies. It recognizes that the infant is a gift of God. Baptism often includes a commitment on the part of parents to bring up the child in the church.

Baptism is a sacrament, properly referred to as "the Baptismal Covenant." Covenants are relationships between two parties. In baptism, God enters into a covenant with us by claiming us for a life of grace in Christ. Parents make the decision to bring their baby before God for baptism. And at that moment the baby becomes a baptized member of the church.

3. When is the best age to have our child baptized?

Sometimes this decision is based on when extended family can be present for the service. The decision is even shaped by the fact that there is a family baptism gown and they want the baptism to take place before the baby outgrows the gown. Generally, most parents do wait until the child is over two months old. Toddlers and older children may be more apt to voice displeasure during the service.

The Baptismal Covenant

In many denominations there is a belief that people of all ages may be baptized. During the baptism we celebrate our covenant relationship with God, a relationship where both parties make promises and assume responsibilities.

These words are read during the baptism to confirm our belief about baptism:

Through the Sacrament of Baptism we are initiated into Christ's holy church. We are incorporated into God's mighty acts of salvation and given new birth through water and the Spirit. All this is God's gift, offered to us without price. (*The United Methodist Hymnal*, page 33)

In baptism, God's side of the covenant is established. God claims us and names us as a child of God. Because God is faithful, this side of the covenant is never-ending. In baptism, your baby is claimed as God's own. It is a gift that we do not earn. This gift doesn't rest on the capacity of the baby to respond in any way. It rests on the action of Christ through the church. We are loved and accepted by God when we can do nothing ourselves. This is true for all — no matter what age.

Our side of the covenant includes a promise to grow in faith and to live as God calls us to live. We promise to follow the example of Jesus and to increase in our ability to love God and to love others. We promise to be nurtured, shaped by the community of faith, taught, and live those teachings. These promises obviously cannot be made by the infant. Parents and other adults, along with the community of faith, promise to form this child as a Christian.

> In baptism, your baby is claimed as God's own. It is a gift that we do not earn. This gift doesn't rest on the capacity of the baby to respond in any way. It rests on the action of Christ through the church. We are loved and accepted by God when we can do nothing ourselves. This is true for all — no matter what age.

In the baptism of their baby, Christian parents reaffirm their own place as a part of the family of the faithful within the household of God. The people of God, in turn, receive the infant, who is their rightful responsibility. The congregation acknowledges that they will teach this child about God, lead this child in words and actions to know the ways of Jesus Christ, and provide a place in the family of God through their congregation.

There is mystery surrounding the sacraments of the church, but not magic. Some traditions of faith might feel that a child who is not baptized is condemned to hell. This is not why we participate in baptism. As a sacrament, baptism is one of the ordinances instituted by Jesus that he commanded his followers to continue. The people of God are reminded once again that God takes the initiative in claiming the child and including the child in God's family.

Bringing Up Your Child

The administration of the sacrament by the pastor is a public sign of God's grace freely given to your baby. It is also used by God as a means of grace for parents and the congregation as they are reminded again that they too are God's children. Parents and the congregation are charged with the responsibility of teaching, loving, and caring for the child in such a way that the child grows in faith.

In this service, parents assume special responsibility for their child through the vows they take. In guiding a child, adults learn. And in fulfilling the promises made at baptism, adults are reminded of the responsibility they have for other children in their Christian community as well.

Confirmation

A covenant has two sides. God's part of the covenant is signified in baptism. We are to respond by accepting God's gift of grace. For those who are baptized as infants, this response is celebrated in the service that the church calls confirmation.

Confirmation most often is offered to boys and girls from sixth through eighth grades. When boys and girls come to be confirmed in the church, they publicly confirm the vows taken by their parents at the time of their baptism. They then profess their beliefs and make their vows of membership in Christ's church.

Requirements for Baptism

The sacrament of the Baptismal Covenant takes place in the church in the presence of the faith community at a stated hour of worship. It is not meant to be a private ceremony. And it takes place in the congregation where the child will be raised. When a child is baptized, the whole faith community pledges to surround that child with God's love.

We read these words:

"With God's help we will proclaim the good news and live according to the example of Christ. We will surround these persons with a community of love and forgiveness, that they may grow in their service to others. We will pray for them, that they may be true disciples who walk in the way that leads to life." (*The United Methodist Hymnal*, page 40)

There is also a requirement that the parent(s) or sponsors of the child who will be baptized are members of Christ's holy church. No others are in a position to assume the vows on behalf of the infant and to fulfill the pledges made to God, to the church, and to the child.

An adult who by choice has not entered into faith in Christ cannot pass on to the child what he or she does not have. A child's baptism is a means of God's grace not just at the moment when the pastor lays hands on the child but throughout the child's life.

The physical act of baptism is not magic. It is the conscious acceptance of the grace of God and a commitment to live life according to God's commandments. It is the outward and visible sign of the inward and spiritual grace received from God.

The Baptismal Ceremony

The pastor dips his or her hand into the water of the baptismal font and, gathering up this clean water, pours it gently onto the head of the child. In this act, we are reminded of the words of Ezekiel, who said, "I will sprinkle clean water upon you, and you shall be clean" (Ezekiel 36:25a, NRSV). After the water has been sprinkled or poured, the pastor lays his or her wet hand on the child's head. In this ancient ritual of blessing, the physical act of laying on of hands represents the transmission of God's love from one living Christian to another. The pastor also blesses your baby in God's name, remembering that it is God's action symbolized here.

The physical act of baptism is not magic. It is the conscious acceptance of the grace of God and a commitment to live life according to God's commandments. It is the outward and visible sign of the inward and spiritual grace received from God.

Another meaning of the symbol of water comes from the connection between baptism and Jesus' death and resurrection. In some of the Orthodox traditions, this symbolism is emphasized in the service through total immersion of the naked child, then clothing of the child in white garments for new life.

Baptism witnesses to newness. Renewal is a new and clean life, a new dedication, a new mind, a new heart, and a new joy. To celebrate this joy, in many congregations the child is carried up and down the aisles so that all may see their new brother or sister in Christ. Many congregations use a hymn of welcome that is sung as the baby is carried through the congregation. It's a time of laughter and joy and tears. We all are renewed again as we participate in the sacrament of the Baptismal Covenant.

Sponsors for Your Baby

One of the biggest honors is to be asked to be a godparent for a child in the congregation. It is an honor to take on the responsibility to be a friend in faith for the entire life of the child—not just for the day of the baptism. The sponsors are challenged to keep growing in their own faith to be a good example for the child.

Celebrate This Day!

To mark this day, the church may present a gift to the child. This gift might be a baptismal candle that you can light year after year on each anniversary of your child's baptism. The gift may be a Bible or a cross to keep until the baby is old enough to enjoy the Bible or cross. Presenting a Certificate of Baptism that can be framed and displayed in their home is another way to celebrate the day.

Here are some ways that parents can talk to their child about his or her baptism as he or she grows:

- Take pictures of the baptism. Prepare a special photograph album with pictures and memories of the day.

- Have a party after the service. Invite friends and relatives to share a meal after the baptism.

- Select special clothing for the child. It does not need to be a "baptismal gown" unless this is something important to the family. Even if the clothing will be worn often, the parents may want to save and label the outfit. As the child grows, showing the child these clothes can be an easy way to talk again about the baptism day.

- Tell the child the story of his or her baptism. Parents can include their thoughts and feelings about the day. Tell who was present. State what the church did. Write the story so the details are not forgotten as the child grows older.

- If there are other children in the family, involve them in some way during the service. This could include placing their hands on the hands of the pastor as the water is poured, holding something special, such as the baby's cap, during the baptism, and standing close by so they can clearly see what is happening.

Adapted from *Your Baby Is For Loving* © 2005 by Abingdon Press

---

Maryjane Pierce Norton is the Associate General Secretary for Leadership Ministries at the General Board of Discipleship of The United Methodist Church. She is also a nationally known workshop leader and consultant in The United Methodist Church and is an ordained deacon in the Western North Carolina Conference. She and her husband have three children and live in Nashville, Tennessee.

A Planning Guide for Baptism

Date to contact pastor for scheduling baptism:

Pastor visit to discuss baptism:

Date scheduled for baptism:

List of those to invite to the baptism:

Clothing for the baptism:

List of pictures to take after the baptism:

Plans for celebrating the baptism:

Our Baby Is Baptized

Name

Child of _____

Born at _____

On the_____day of_____, 20_____

Received

The Sacrament of the Baptismal Covenant
As a sign and seal of God's grace

At

_____

Minister_____

Sponsor(s)_____

Relatives_____

Friends_____

Sample Letter to Send Announcing the Baptism

Dear _____

We are so pleased to announce that our son/daughter _____ will

be baptized on Sunday, _____(date)_____ at the_____(time)_____

Service at_____Church,

(address)_____.

This is an important moment for our family. Through baptism we know that God claims

each of us as God's own child. And we know that even before our child can accept this

gift from God for himself/herself, he/she is claimed by God. We also will be affirming

our faith and promising to bring up our child in the ways of the faith. We ask that you

also pledge to help us with this task.

We would love for you to join us for the service and for a reception afterward to be held

at_____.

If you cannot be present, we ask that you hold our child and our family in your prayers.

Blessings to you,

(signature)

© 2010 Abingdon Press

Entering the Waters of Baptism

Celebrating and Preparing for Believer's Baptism

by J. Otis Ledbetter

> Thank you, Lord, for the gift of salvation in this young life. As she follows you into the waters of baptism, let the river of your love flow, deep and wide, within her heart.

"They kicked me out of the house," said Sherry. "Actually, they kicked me right out of the whole family!"

She's a close friend of mine who was raised in a non-Christian religion. Although Sherry's parents were devout in their faith, Sherry chose not to follow in her parents' beliefs but instead began attending an evangelical church. Her parents were disappointed, but they allowed her to continue to attend. Even after coming home one day and telling them she had accepted Jesus, they still allowed her to be heavily involved at the church.

But then she announced: "I'm going to be baptized tonight."

Her parents walked, stern-faced, to another room, talked it over, and handed down their solemn verdict: "If you go through with this baptism, you can no longer live in our home."

That very evening, after her baptism, Sherry's possessions were waiting for her on the front porch. You see, for Sherry's parents and many others like them, baptism represented a critical point of no return. Professing Jesus was okay; identifying with him was just too much. Even those outside Christendom recognize the gravity and significance of baptism, even to the point that family and culture often spurn those who submit to it. Why such a wrenching, deep-seated reaction? It's because participating in baptism is so much more than a nice religious activity with little significance. It is identifying with, and entering into, an action that was modeled by God Incarnate. By imitating him, the participant is saying, "This is my first step of obedience in a brand new way of existing — living as a citizen of God's kingdom." It's an outward demonstration of a radical inward change of one's entire being. We are buried with him in baptism and raised to walk in a new life.

Milestone-At-A-Glance

The Testimony: Entering the Waters of Baptism: This is the Christian ceremony of public witness to one's personal salvation. It also sometimes serves as the initiation rite of the church. It is important as a step of obedience to Christ and public identification with him.

The Goal: Your parent/child discussions should help to prepare your child spiritually and intellectually for his or her decision to be baptized.

Recommended Age Range: There is no "set" age at which a child is ready to make a personal salvation decision. This Spiritual Milestone can begin when your child can comprehend the most basic meaning of "accepting Jesus as my Savior." Naturally, your child will continue to grow in understanding and commitment as he or she matures.

Symbol Idea — The Baptism Certificate:
Usually this certificate will be issued by the church and signed by the pastor. It will remain in the family and be cherished for generations. Even after death, this symbol can indicate to surviving family and friends the date their loved one gave public testimony to receiving Christ.

Relational Emphasis: Parents who consistently provide loving instruction in a safe environment are building a foundation for faith. Your role in this Milestone is both as *protector* and *teacher*.

New Privileges: Your child may enjoy a new level of fellowship as a confessed believer in the congregation. Consider increasing your child's participation in family devotional times, perhaps offering a prayer or reading a verse of Scripture.

The Ceremony: Before the actual ceremony, take a field trip to the place where the baptism will be held to familiarize your child with the surroundings. Try to attend a service where a baptism is taking place and explain the steps as they unfold. (Some parents even practice the baptism in the bathtub at home to give the child a "feel" for what will take place.) Be prepared to answer questions like, "How long will he hold me under?" and, "What happens if he drops me?" or "Will the water be too cold or too hot?" Maybe even, "Will everybody laugh?"

On the day the child is to be baptized, invite all the grandparents, uncles, aunts, cousins, and any other interested persons. Hold a celebration afterwards, with cake, ice cream, and a gift. Make this occasion special and memorable. And remember that children who have accepted Christ at an early age sometimes struggle with their faith as they grow older. By making this time special, they will remember it and use it as a point of reference when doubts arise.

Here are a few more quick tips to help prepare your child and yourself for the baptismal service:

1. Discuss baptism on a family night. As a teaching analogy, have each person write down personal "clues" on a slip of paper. Randomly draw the slips from a bowl, reading one clue at a time until the individual can be "identified." (*Clues might include physical features, special talents, or character traits. You might also point out that the people we are identified with — family members and friends — also help define who we are. Use this analogy as a way of leading into the discussion on baptism and being identified with Christ.*)

2. Take your family to a baptismal service. Encourage everyone to talk about the event and share his or her observations.

3. If your child will be baptized at a church, get permission from the church to visit the baptismal dressing rooms. Help your child become familiar with all aspects of the location and, if possible, meet with the pastor for a brief question-and-answer session.

4. Thoroughly plan the day of the ceremony with your child. Let him or her help you decide how you will celebrate. Encourage your child to be creative.

5. Have your camera ready to record this historic tradition!

Background Information for Parents

There are several Bible passages to consider as you prepare to discuss the Spiritual Milestone of baptism. In Acts 2, after Peter preached his famous Pentecost sermon, those who responded positively were baptized, signaling the beginning of an ongoing process of spiritual growth (v. 42). Eventually these believers became the charter members of the first church established by the Lord and his disciples.

When Peter had finished speaking, the people of Israel in the crowd asked, "Men and brethren, what shall we do?" (v. 37, KJV) The apostles responded with a list of "suggestions" designed specifically for those asking the question! These brethren were repentant Children of Israel, ready to receive the ancient promises belonging to them. So "they that gladly received his word were baptized" (v. 41, KJV).

This passage can best be understood from the Jewish point of view, because it flows with the language of the Messianic kingdom, not the language of salvation by grace. What Peter and the apostles are suggesting here is preparation for receiving Christ's earthly kingdom. Peter is saying: (1) repent — change your mind about Jesus, the one you crucified, acknowledge him as the eternal Son of God and your Messiah; (2) be baptized — identify with him and his kingdom; and (3) review — recall the ancient promises made to you and your children concerning your Messiah and his kingdom.

We see a shift from "offering the kingdom" to "presenting the plan of salvation," as the Gospel of Jesus moved from the Jews who rejected it to the Gentiles who embraced it. An example of this shift is found in the story of Philip and the man from Ethiopia. Although the Ethiopian is reading from Isaiah when Philip approaches, notice that Philip didn't preach the Christ or Messiah, which would be kingdom language. He preached "Jesus," which was his Savior's name, according to Matthew 1:21. This is redemption language.

We have two more salvation stories, one in Acts 10 and the other in Acts 16. Both times the Gospel is offered to Gentiles: Cornelius and the Philippian jailer. In the case of Cornelius, the message was that peace was to be preached by "Jesus Christ" (10:36), which is the salvation name. Add to that the words in verse 10:43, "To him give all the prophets witness, that through his name whosoever believeth in him shall receive remission of sins" (KJV). Now we know that Peter was leading Cornelius and his family to faith. That became a reality as demonstrated by their reception of the Holy Spirit. Then they were all baptized. This same process was repeated in Acts 16 with Paul, Silas, and the Philippian jailer, with the same results.

Here is the point: In all cases, whether it was the Jews preparing for the coming kingdom or the Gentiles accepting Jesus as their Savior, immediately after their belief and confession of faith, they were baptized. So the "what?" of baptism is that it is reserved for those who have already received his name, who have accepted the Lord Jesus Christ as their personal Savior. Whether it was one believer on the Day of Pentecost, the man from Ethiopia, Saul of Tarsus, Cornelius, or the Philippian jailer, they were all saved prior to being baptized.

Parent & Child Discussion Guide

Begin each discussion time with prayer, inviting God to be part of your time together.

Step 1: Talk about the What

Thankfully, God has provided a meaningful way parents can participate in acknowledging our children's spiritual transformation in Christ — the waters of baptism. Though it's the first Spiritual Milestone we'll be exploring together, it's really the culmination of a process begun often before your child's birth!

Parent: Open with prayer. Thankfully, God has provided a meaningful way parents can participate in acknowledging our children's spiritual transformation in Christ — the waters of baptism. Though it's the first Spiritual Milestone we'll be exploring together, it's really the culmination of a process begun often before your child's birth!

Many Christian couples who are anticipating parenthood will enlist the spiritual support of their church by: (1) participating in a pre-birth dedication, offering the baby-to-come into the Lord's love and care; (2) having a baby-and-parent dedication service soon after the birth; and (3) acknowledging when the child receives Christ as Savior by celebrating his or her becoming a member of God's family. When the time is right, and after an instructional process like this one, you can plan for Milestone #1: The Testimony of Baptism.

(Note: Different churches have different views on this act of obedience. If you are part of a denomination, we encourage you to learn its position on baptism and work through your church. This Spiritual Milestone is offered to complement the traditions of your church or to establish a new tradition in your family.)

Step 2: Discuss the Reason Why

(Note: For this portion of the study, gather three things: A small posterboard with the word "obey" printed on it in large letters, a wedding ring, and a photograph of someone familiar to your child.)

Read Together: Acts 2 (focusing on 2:37-41)

Discussion Question #1: Why should a Christian be baptized?

Possible answer: You might want to emphasize that baptism is a command, the first act of obedience a new Christian can perform. Show the posterboard with the word "obey" written on it. Write around the word acts of obedience you have observed in your child recently. Emphasize that obedience is required behavior. Therefore, the question should not be, "Why should I be baptized?" It ought to be "Why shouldn't I?" or maybe, "When can I?"

Your Insights or Stories:

Discussion Question #2: Are there any other reasons to be baptized?

Possible answer: Before responding directly, hold up the wedding ring and ask, "What is this?" Give your child time to respond and make any comments that come to mind. Then ask, "What does this ring mean?"

Emphasize that the ring means you are married to someone, and that you want everyone to know you're married and not ashamed of it. It means that you publicly identify with your spouse and give testimony to your married status. Along with pure obedience, then, this is another aspect of baptism: it is a willing, public identification with Christ, something we will naturally want to do because we love him so much.

Your Insights and Stories: *(Suggestion: This would be a good time to talk about the reasons why you, yourself, were baptized. Share details such as how, when, and where, as well as what it meant to you. If you have not been baptized, be prepared to answer questions about why.)*

Discussion Question #3: Why is the act of baptism considered symbolic?

Possible answer: Read aloud 1 Peter 3:21 (KJV), where baptism is referred to as "the like figure." Baptism is a like figure, or symbolic representation, of our salvation.

Now hold up the photograph and ask, "Who is this?" (Don't ask, "Who is this a picture of?" or you will spoil your illustration!) Since the person is known to him or her, your child will likely say, "It's Dad," or "Mom," or whoever. Each time she answers like this, say, "No." Soon she'll become puzzled. Then you will say something like, "It's not Dad . . . it's a picture of Dad. Over there is Dad, the real Dad. This is only a picture of him."

Then apply this same idea to baptism. Baptism is not salvation. It is only a picture (like figure) of salvation. So I'm baptized to show everyone what really happened to me. I died as a sinner and was buried, and then I arose as a new person in Christ. My baptism pictures this reality.

Your Insights or Stories:

Step 3: Convey the Power of How

Read Together: Luke 3:15-16, 21; Romans 6:3-7

Parent: Talk about how the action of baptism represents what Jesus went through so that we could be free from our sin nature. Therefore, when a person is baptized, the ritual is symbolic of the "good news" message of Jesus' death, burial, and resurrection.

Discussion Question #4: How will I be baptized?

Possible answer: *(Christians differ on exactly what method to use when baptizing someone. A good way to approach the issue is to simply study the Scripture passages regarding baptism. You may want to use a*

Bible commentary or other reference book. Or, you may wish to discuss the means of baptism with your church leadership before explaining it to your child.)

Set aside plenty of time to talk with your child about the baptismal process, especially the ritual and method to be used (see the Ceremony preparation ideas above).

Your Insights or Stories:

When you feel that you have adequately addressed your child's questions and concerns regarding baptism, pray together in closing. You may wish to share these final thoughts with your child: This will be one of the most spiritually rich milestones you will experience because of the eternal choice it represents. The old is dead and buried — a new life in Christ begun. You have chosen this new life in Christ and now want to publicly identify yourself with him and his people. Congratulations!

You and your child are now ready to celebrate this Spiritual Milestone!

Being baptized, she has witnessed to your goodness, Lord. Now let her live a good life — out of pure gratitude!

Content used by permission from the Heritage Builders book *Spiritual Milestones* by Jim Weidmann and J. Otis Ledbetter. For more information please visit www.Heritagebuilders.com

J. Otis Ledbetter, Ph.D. resides in Clovis, California, where he is the senior pastor of Sonrise Church and Chairman of the Board of Heritage Builders Association, a ministry in partnership with Focus on the Family, and a cooperative network of families and churches committed to passing a solid heritage to the next generation. He earned his Ph.D. from Louisiana Baptist University in 1984. His books include Your Heritage, Family Fragrance, Family Traditions, Extending Your Heritage, Spiritual Milestones for Your Children, *and his most recent book,* In the Secret Place, *a Small Book / Big Change release. He and his wife, Gail, have three grown children and nine grandchildren. He is a frequent conference speaker, and has written numerous articles for magazines. He specializes in Heritage Builders workshops, which teaches parents and grandparents the spiritual, emotional, and social components of the heritage they are passing to the next generation. He has been featured on radio and T.V. broadcasts including The 700 Club, Thomas Road Baptist's T.V. Angel Network Show, Moody Broadcasting Network, CASA Radio Broadcast, and other call-in shows where parents and grandparents frequent with their questions. His book* Your Heritage *was distributed as a premium offer on Billy Graham's Hour of Decision.*

Father-Daughter Cake Decorating Contest

by Kal Otis

Family Time! A church's guide to planning a fun family event! (This event can be doubled up as a fundraiser.)

Why Family Night?

It is vital for us to provide opportunities to strengthen and encourage families in your churches and community. Time is a valued and rare commodity. Unfortunately, family time is too often planned by "TV Guide," and parents are more aware of what is happening on prime time than in their kid's life!

Maybe it's not television. It might be baseball or gymnastics or music lessons, but there are just a lot of distractions for families today. Are families investing their time where it best serves their needs, or are they letting school, community, and sometimes even the church and other demands pull their time and attention away from home?

When family members spend time together, it creates a sense of security and good feeling about each other and themselves. Time together creates a reserve of tremendous emotional bank account that each member can draw on in their daily lives with less effort and without feeling stressed. Church leaders should help families reclaim "family time"!

How Does A Family Night Work?

Basically, the church sets a night aside, whether that is once a week or once a month, where the family is together for a *meaningful* experience together. Since the key to a successful Family Night at your church is to provide as many opportunities as possible, it is important that you keep a few basic principles in mind while planning. Keep it simple and fun! Remember, the family give-and-take, the laughter, the conversation, and the fun — strengthen family bonds.

Set a Time: Families are busy! It is important that you have a standard time set aside for Family Night. It could be on a weekly, monthly, or quarterly basis. Schedule it on the same day (or night) of the week.

Once you set this time aside, keep it there! Advertise it. Don't be discouraged by fluctuating numbers in attendance. Your event serves a purpose for every family that attends. Encourage your families to commit to Family Night.

Time is spent together: One of the primary goals for having Family Night is to provide opportunities for family members to interact and spend time together doing the same thing. That means you want to reduce what happens naturally . . . all the moms socializing with moms, dads with dads, teens with teens, and kids with kids.

Family Night, unless planned for networking purposes, should make members of the same family spend time together, not apart! That is the goal for having Family Night. The planned activity or focus will result in family members interacting and spending time together doing the same thing.

No Heavy Stuff: Plan carefully to avoid having issues with discipline and family arguments. Make the event light, fun, and engaging! A little variety helps a lot.

Plan Purposefully:

- Understand the culture of adults, teens, and kids. It will help you plan!

- Make sure that the event lends itself to one hundred percent participation.

- Maintain a family events database.

- Select a theme.

- Select a target audience: Events for the whole family, ages 6 to 96, father-daughter, mother-daughter, father-son, and mother-son. Single parenting is a fact of today's society. Be sensitive and accommodating of this fact. Provide mentors.

- Promote in advance. If possible, advertise all the events and dates for a whole year!

- Plan and prepare before the event.

- Some events do require pre-registration for better planning.

- Start and end on time.

- Follow up!

- Make sure you have enough staffing. Avoid using those who might attend with their families.

- Have fun!

Father-Daughter Cake Decorating

Father-daughter teams have a great time creating and decorating a scrumptious unique cake! In the process they spend time planning, talking, laughing, and enjoying their time together. You can also plan this event for mother-son. Make this an annual event.

Target Audience

Fathers (or adopted father: uncle, grandpa, brother, or possibly a male neighbor if father is unavailable) and their daughters.

Promotion

- Advance promotion and pre-registration for this event is important.

- Contest guidelines and rules need to be given out to all participates.

- Posters and invitations (shaped like a cake or box of cake mix) would include: time and location of event, date, theme, guidelines to enter, and cost.

The Basic Setup

- Teams should pre-register to enter the contest.

- Assign numbers to each team as they register so that the names stay anonymous for judging purposes.

- The team needs to design, create, and bake a cake without the help of a mother or other females.

- Father-daughter team must bring in their caked baked, but UNDECORATED.

- A cake mix may be used, but NO store bought cakes.

- All cakes need to arrive on a "Give Away" tray or board with the team number written on the board so that it is visible.

- Set a theme (red, white, & blue, Easter, favorite Bible story, and so forth). All cake entries must relate to the theme.

- Different combinations of size and shape are encouraged. Teams come prepared with all frostings and additional decorations prepared ahead of time and ready to be used at the start of the contest.

- Select a panel of judges and give them criteria to judge the cakes by. For example: use of theme, creative use of theme, appealing to the eye, neat presentation, best use of color, best use of frosting, use of other items to decorate cake, and so forth.

Remember, cakes are to be judged for how they are decorated, not taste!

• Consider different entry levels based on the age of the daughter.

How It Works

Allow thirty minutes for the decorating. Then have games prepared for the father-daughter teams to play while the judging goes on. Invite moms and other relatives to come and see the cakes on display. Cake and coffee or punch can be served as the meeting winds down.

Award cupcakes as trophies. Create multiple categories and levels of awards so that everyone should go home with a trophy. You can plan an auction or fundraiser after the contest.

This excerpt is taken from *1...2...3...Family Time! Your Guide to Seven Outrageously Fun Family Events For Churches* by Kal Otis-Gilchrist. Copyright 2010, Creative Ministry Group Consultants LLC. All rights reserved.

Kal Otis has over 24 years of team building experience in both secular and ministry settings. In her current position as a Family pastor, she leads high performance teams that are both multigenerational and multifunctional. She has been instrumental in leading the charge of envisioning and implementing an integrated approach to Family Ministry at her church. She is passionate about equipping others to "think outside the box." A published author, she has been involved in evaluating church systems and assisting leadership to creatively align and synchronize all areas of ministry towards a common vision.

SAMPLE JUDGING SHEET

Welcome! Thank you for offering to judge our annual Father-Daughter Cake Decorating Contest.

Prizes will be awarded in these different categories (create more categories if you need them):
- Best use of theme
- Best use of color
- Most appealing to the eye
- Best use of decorating items

Please use the NUMBER of each cake to record your votes. Please put them in ranking order.

Please list your three favorite cakes that represent **Best use of theme:**

1. _____

2. _____

3. _____

Please list your three favorite cakes with **Best use of color:**

1. _____

2. _____

3. _____

Please list your three favorite cakes that are **Most appealing to the eye:**

1. _____

2. _____

3. _____

Please list your three favorite cakes that had **Best use of decorating items:**

1. _____

2. _____

3. _____

THANK YOU FOR BEING A JUDGE!

Permission granted to copy for local church use. \ This page is on the CD-Rom.

Five Models of Family Ministry

by Denise Muir Kjesbo, Ph.D.

I believe Family Ministry holds great promise to help us reach this generation of children and parents. If we want to see the roots of faith grow deep into a child's life, we need to help parents create a culture of spiritual formation within the home that both initiates faith conversations and responds to teachable moments. Yet, many of today's parents feel ill-equipped to provide spiritual formation for their children. The church has an amazing invitation to step into the gap and equip parents and thereby increase the impact of children's ministry.

So what does family ministry look like? It is definitely not a "one size fits all" endeavor. Let me invite you to consider five models of family ministry with an eye to assessing your current ministry context and possibilities for the future.

1. Educational Model

Philosophy: Family Ministry is to provide education and training in a preventive, proactive way to support marriages and family. The goal is to train and equip so that people will be prepared, or to offer skill development so that current issues can be remedied.

Biblical basis: 2 Timothy 2:2: "And the things you have heard me say in the presence of many witnesses entrust to reliable people who will also be qualified to teach others" (TNIV).

Examples: Publishing companies and parachurch agencies are active in this model since they are able to provide curriculum resources as well as retreats, DVD-based training, and speakers for educational gatherings.

Focus of ministry: Seminars, workshops, classes, retreats, small groups, and mentoring networks which provide education, support and training for couples, parents, grandparents, and children.

Advantages:
- Appeals to the healthy family and seeks to strengthen the family in a proactive fashion.

- People find support in others at same age/stage of family life cycle.

- Can provide helpful outreach into the community with workshops.

Disadvantages:
- This model can degenerate into an information-driven experience without transformation of the heart or actions.

- This model can become very seminar focused without depth of relationships forming among participants, which offer long-term support and accountability.

- Attendance at classes/seminars/workshops may be lacking and by necessity can only target a segment of the congregation.

- It may minister to the head but miss the heart!

2. Counseling/Therapeutic Model

Philosophy: Family ministry exists to come alongside people in their time of great need — it is a hospital for broken people. The underlying thought is that if people are on a pathway toward greater emotional and spiritual health they can function more effectively in home, church, and community.

Biblical basis: In Luke 4:18-19, Jesus declares the focus of his ministry to bring hope in desperate situations: "The Spirit of the Lord is on me, because he has anointed me to proclaim good news to the poor. He has sent me to proclaim freedom for the prisoners and recovery of sight for the blind, to set the oppressed free, to proclaim the year of the Lord's favor" (TNIV).

Examples: Parachurch organizations help families in crisis through programs such as 12-Step groups or divorce support and through resources for adults and children. In addition some churches have hired counselors who serve on their church staff or host a counseling center within their church facility to provide care for families in crisis.

Another approach that churches take is to develop a clear network of referrals that they have trained all of their staff to provide when a person or family in crisis is identified. Churches may underwrite the cost of some of the counseling services, or counselors may contract for reduced fees in conjunction with a sliding scale fee structure for referrals that come through the church.

Focus of Ministry: Providing support groups, therapy, crisis intervention, and therapeutic referral networks to help people on the path to becoming whole and holy.

Advantages:
- This model responds to the "felt needs" of our culture with the various dysfunctions that are present today.

- The Counseling Model has amazing community outreach potential. For example, people will come to a divorce recovery/grief recovery/substance abuse recovery group who would not come to a worship service.

- This model provides balance of accountability and support.

- People who are moving along the path to healing are better able to function in the family, and there is the potential for a healing impact on the family system as a whole. If God changes a member of the family system, the system as a whole changes.

Disadvantages:
- This model may put an overemphasis on restorative ministries to the neglect of preventive/educational ministries.

- Church people may not want to "own up" to their problems and get the help needed until they hit rock bottom. Shame issues may keep them from seeking help from the church which may be perceived to be filled with people who "have it all together!"

- The church may lose its focus and become unbalanced as a therapy clinic/support network with little emphasis on evangelism and discipleship.

- This model attracts a high percentage of "needy" people. Churches must be ready for this with an infrastructure that can support those who come with great needs. The church will need to have several layers of leadership ready to avoid leadership burnout.

3. Nuclear Family Model

Philosophy: Parents are the primary faith nurturers of their children, and the church is called to equip and support parents in this calling.

Biblical basis: The Old Testament has several passages that undergird this model. Deuteronomy 6:6-9 is a good example: "These commandments that I give you today are to be on your hearts. Impress them on your children. Talk about them when you sit at home and when you walk along the road, when you lie down and when you get up. Tie them as symbols on your hands and bind them on your foreheads. Write them on the doorframes of your houses and on your gates" (TNIV).

Examples: Curriculum publishers that offer materials to help parents be prepared to reinforce the teaching that occurs in the children's ministry fit this model. In addition, some churches offer family cluster educational opportunities during the children's ministry time so that parents are equipped and supported to teach their children alongside other families that are doing the same thing. Providing resources for families to use at home that combine teaching with experiential learning is another example of this model in action.

Focus of ministry: This model focuses on equipping parents to lead their families in faith formation and ministry in their communities, building strong networks between children's ministry and parent equipping ministries. The church's role is to resource the parents who are the primary faith nurturers of their own children.

Advantages:

- This model follows the Old Testament law.

- It can be individualized.

- The children's minister's role is to train parents more than provide children's programs.

- It encourages the family to minister together within their neighborhood through hospitality and evangelism.

- This model is especially popular among the home school population and families where there are two parents who are heritage Christians who have inherited and desire to pass on a legacy of faith.

Disadvantages:

- Some parents can't/won't take responsibility for their children's spiritual formation.

- This model misses children in non-Christian homes. It also seems to have limited outreach potential for the church.

- There may be an overemphasis on a particular structure of family (two parent family — typically middle class or higher) to the neglect of other family structures.

- Families are extremely busy and pressured. They may feel like this is one more thing that they "have to do" and end up feeling guilty and immobilized rather than empowered.

- The model can degenerate into a cocooning approach which says, "I'll look out for me and mine!"

4. Family of Families Model

Philosophy: The church needs to function as an intergenerational family of families and be

family to one another in today's broken and disjointed world.

Biblical Basis: Jesus redefines family to being the "family of God" in the New Testament. Luke 8:20-21 states, "Someone told him, "Your mother and brothers are standing outside, wanting to see you." He replied, "My mother and brothers are those who hear God's word and put it into practice" (TNIV).

Focus of ministry: Fostering intergenerational connections through family activities, cross-generational family clusters, mentoring between generations, intergenerational worship, and spiritual formation with the emphasis on "being" the family of God.

Advantages:

- This model provides an intergenerational support network to highly mobile family units of 21st century America. The church becomes a place to provide "surrogate" faith family aunts and uncles, brothers and sisters, parents and grandparents, children and grandchildren.

- This model includes everyone — no one is left out! (including singles)

- It follows the model of Jesus by emphasizing teaching through life experiences across the generations.

- It is a highly relational model.

- Children are "splashed" in the overflow of the abundant life in Christ that is experienced by the entire congregation.

- This model tends to be popular among emergent churches, smaller churches, and churches with highly stable populations such as in more rural areas.

Disadvantages:

- Taken to extreme there would be no age-appropriate learning focused at developmental needs at each stage of life.

- This model may face challenges for families with adolescents who naturally seek to establish independence from their family of origin as part of their developmental cycle.

- We live in an age-graded culture, so this is highly counter-cultural and may face resistance from adults, youth, and children.

5. Family in Service Model

Philosophy: The family is the launch pad for service and ministry in the community. The church is to equip, provide opportunity, support, and connect families with other families and help debrief the service experiences.

Biblical basis: Matthew 25:31-46 says that to feed the hungry, clothe the naked, extend hospitality to the stranger, visit the sick and the prisoner is the mark of the true believer who will spend eternity with God. Mark 10:45 offers families the model of Jesus: "For even the Son of Man did not come to be served, but to serve, and to give his life as a ransom for many" (TNIV).

Focus of ministry: The church prompts, equips, networks, provides opportunities, and then helps families debrief service opportunities.

Advantages:
- Family in service together builds the cohesion of family unit.

- Merton Strommen (Search Institute) and Dick Hardel (The Youth and Family Institute) note family in service during childhood and adolescence as one of the top factors that encourage young adults to sustain faith on their own when they left home (others were faith conversations with mother and/or father and family devotions).

- Eric Swanson and Rick Rusaw, of the Externally Focused Church movement, speak of people offering good deeds, which creates good will, which becomes the bridge across which the good news can travel into the community. The Family in Service Model believes that families are a key component of this approach.

- This model tends to be present in externally focused and missional churches.

Disadvantages:
- Families are busy and service can degenerate into one more thing to do!

- Without appropriate preparation and debriefing in a church culture of service, service can become simply humanitarian acts of charity rather than spiritual experiences.

- Faith can become about "doing" versus "being." There must be continued attentiveness to developing one's faith journey to accompany the acts of service.

It is uncommon for one church to have all of these models in place. On the other hand it is unusual for a church ministry to have only one of these models as their exclusive approach. Most churches will do best to have a "mix and match" approach, which takes into account their overarching ministry vision and mission, the resources of leadership, people and facility that are available, and the calling of God for that particular body of believers in the area of family ministry.

Questions for Reflection and Conversation:

1. Which family ministry model(s) do you currently have in your ministry context? What is working well in your model(s)? What might you be missing in your model(s)?

2. How can you accentuate the advantages and address the disadvantages of your current family ministry model(s)?

3. Which model(s) of family ministry are you most drawn to? Why? Which model(s) is most appropriate for your setting?

4. What might the unique blend of the models look like in your ministry setting?

5. Where might God be leading in the future of family ministry in your ministry setting?

Denise Muir Kjesbo, Ph.D., Professor and Lead Faculty, is the Children's and Family Ministry Director at Cory Center for Children's Ministry Bethel Seminary, St. Paul, Minnesota.

The Inside Scoop

While I was serving at a medium-sized church in Durham, North Carolina, each pastor was assigned a day to make hospital rounds. Even though I was the children's pastor, it was good to get to know the older members of our congregation, as they were the majority of my visits.

One day, I was visiting an elderly aunt of one of our volunteers. As I approached her room on the third floor, I could tell by all the commotion right outside her door that this was going to be a tough visit. Upon reaching her room, I was informed by the doctor that she had just passed away. After saying a prayer over her body, I exited the room to find her sixty-five-year-old brother, George, walking towards the room, unaware of what had just happened.

As I began to share with him the news, he passed out. His nearly seven-foot tall, 250 pound body quickly began to collapse on my five-foot, 130 pound frame. With the help of some nurses, we managed to get him to the floor and then down to the ER. I spent the next three hours between the ER and the aunt's room receiving family, not knowing exactly what to say or do, just praying for wisdom. Thankfully, George was released in just a few hours.

A few days later, the family called and wanted me to officiate at the funeral. I had taken a small part in a child's funeral a few years earlier, but this was my first one to lead entirely. As I was meeting with the family that night at the funeral parlor, another sister of the family passed out! The rescue squad was called, and she was carried off to the hospital. I finished getting all the personal information I needed about the deceased and headed to the hospital to check on the sister. All was well, but I learned that she would miss the funeral and be kept in the hospital for several days.

On the day of the funeral, I was very nervous and asked the other pastors all the proper funeral service etiquette and made sure I had my list of what exactly to do at each moment. All seemed to be going well throughout the service until the last song. As I asked everyone to stand as the casket was being wheeled out, George fainted again and fell into the aisle.

After what seemed like eternity, they were able to revive him, and I began to escort everyone out to their cars for the drive to the graveside. As I approached the tent area over the grave, a young girl was running past me to her mother, tripped over the guide wire and began to cry uncontrollably. I looked around for others for help, but they had all turned to look at another elderly friend who had just fainted! Was this ever going to end?

I read some Scripture at the head of the casket, prayed, and began to walk toward the seated family and friends. I took two steps towards the family, when all of a sudden the green carpet gave way under my foot — I stepped into the grave with one leg, the crowd let out a resounding gasp. I felt the funeral home director's hand grab my arm and pull me back up, keeping me from falling completely in! I wished I had just gone on into the hole for the day and called it quits! Instead, I dusted myself off, spoke to each family member, and quickly escorted myself to my car. Now that I know what to do and where not to step, my experience officiating funerals has gotten much better!

Philip Biles
Lake Hills Church in West Austin, Texas
pbiles@lhc.org

Fundraiser Events

As for those who in the present age are rich, command them not to be haughty, or to set their hopes on the uncertainty of riches, but rather on God who richly provides us with everything for our enjoyment. They are to do good, to be rich in good works, generous, and ready to share, thus storing up for themselves the treasure of a good foundation for the future, so that they may take hold of the life that really is life.

(1 Timothy 6:17–19)

Fundraising

by Kevin Reynolds

> Scripture teaches us that "The earth is the LORD's, and everything in it"(Psalm 24:1, NIV), that "'The silver is mine and the gold is mine,' declares the LORD Almighty" (Haggai 2:8, NIV), and that "Every animal of the forest is mine, and the cattle on a thousand hills" (Psalm 50:10, NIV).

We all know that it takes finances to facilitate ministry in today's culture. And if all the finances belong to the Lord and we all work for him anyway, then why does the money seem to come easier to some than others? This article, along with faithful prayer for the Lord to "sell some cows on your behalf," will give you solid practical tips, advice, and a "Must Know" list to help you in planning and providing fundraising strategy and events.

Although this article does provide specific action steps when implementing fundraising strategy and events, it is important to note that the purpose is not to provide a list of the latest and greatest fundraising ideas. There are many resources available online and in book form for fundraising ideas.

To begin, the most basic and fundamental thing to remember is that fundraising is not about money, it's about people.

Having said that, number one on our "Must Know" list is —

1. Our Ministry to the kids will never grow beyond the system that supports it.

Investing and building into the lives of children is like any other endeavor involving structure, whether that is building a bridge or skyscraper, pulling together a professional sports team, or even learning a new language. The actual thing being built can never exceed the system that supports it.

In ministry to children, aside from the leading of the Holy Spirit, there are two parts to this equation: the first is the actual program that involves our interaction, instruction, and communication with the children. The second is the support system that facilitates this process such as staff and volunteers, facility and resources, and money. This much is obvious, but how much of our time and energy is focused on the second half of that equation, specifically concerning money?

Many times in children's ministry we simply take the figure we are given in "our" line item of the budget and work from there. Well, it stands to reason that if the figure is adequate, then we simply work with what we have. But what if it is not adequate for what we feel the Lord is calling us to do?

Although great effort should be made to not move outside of the blessing and authority of those in authority over us, there are things we can do to generate additional finances for our ministry work without having to make an appeal from the pulpit on Sunday morning or put a notice in the bulletin. The effectiveness of our actual program and work with the children requires that we focus concentrated effort on the support system.

Number two on our "Must Know" list is —

2. Money Follows Relationship.

The most basic and fundamental thing to remember about fundraising is that fundraising is not about money, it's about people. This truth that money follows relationship is both conditional and predictive. It's conditional in that, in order for money to flow from one person to another, some sort of relationship is required. If I don't know you or anything about your needs, there is no chance for me to partner with you in meeting those needs. It's predictive in that where there is relationship there is at least some sort of certainty that money can and will flow from one person to another. If I know and care about you and your needs, I will want to partner with you in meeting those needs, at least in part, *because of you!*

For example, let's suppose you are out to lunch and you forgot your wallet or purse. If I don't even know you and am not aware of your situation, there is no chance that I am going to help you. But, on the other hand, if you and I are friends and we are together it would be completely natural for me to cover for you and let you return the favor next time. You would do the same for me because that is something friends do for one another.

Because fundraising is not about money but people, it translates into our discussion in several ways. One, the more relationships we have, the more opportunities that will exist for money to flow. Two, because fundraising is about people not about money, the relationships we have are not based on asking for money. That is secondary. People are naturally interested in what the people they have relationships with are interested in.

One of the last things I am ever interested in is someone who is talking to me in order to get money from me. But if someone that I have a relationship with is talking about something they are passionate about, and in the course of our conversation their needs come up, I naturally evaluate my ability to help them meet those needs.

Taking this understanding and developing it further brings us to the concept of webs of relationships. To put it simply, every single relationship that you and I have connects us to all of the other relationships that individual has, then all the relationships that all those individuals have, etc, etc.

The more times we can communicate what we are passionate about to the people with whom we have relationships, the more opportunities we can develop for money to flow to meet those needs. Single relationships can influence broader circles of relationships, then you and your need have made a connection to more individuals, allowing the opportunity for communication and money to flow.

People often say that they are uncomfortable speaking to people about money. *It's not about money!* You don't have to talk about money, in fact at first you should not even talk about money. Keep in mind that if your relationship is based on money (or even if the only communication is about needs), then whatever money flows may be a result of guilt and obligation. Now let's turn our attention to some practical ways to communicate our passion about children's ministry and share our needs in this next section.

Number three on our "Must Know" list is —

3. Faith moves the hand of God. Passion and vision move people.

This may come as a shock to some, but need does not seem to move the Lord to action. In the economy of God as he designed it, faith is what moves his hand, not need. If need moved the hand of God then there would be no need. He, being God, would have seen it, been moved to action by the need, and then met the need. Because there is unmet need we must assume that need is not what moves God to action.

I believe that what moves the Lord to action is faith. He even said that without faith it was impossible to please him. Scripture is full of examples of those who stepped out in faith only to find the Lord providing whatever it was that they needed.

Here is a secret: people are not moved by need either. If people were moved by need, then we could stand up on any given Sunday morning and communicate our need for, let's say, more nursery workers, and people would line up to volunteer. As it is (and we've all been there), when we simply make an announcement about something like needing nursery workers, people all over the room are reading their Bibles, searching through their purses, and trying to avoid eye contact.

Just as the Lord is moved by faith and not need, people are not moved by need but vision and passion. Everyone wants to be a part of something bigger than themselves, and when you and I communicate our vision with passion to those with whom we have relationships, people are much more inclined to share in that vision. Simply said; "Share your story!"

Now let's talk about how to do this. Here are what I call the 3 T's of fundraising: Tell Your Story, Touch Points, and Time Sensitive.

1 — Tell Your Story

Tell the story (don't talk about money) of your project or ministry to as many people in as many ways as you possibly can. To go back to number one on our "must know" list, doing so requires concentrated time and focus — this is part of the system that supports your actual program. This

means verbally talking to people obviously, but again, don't talk about money or your needs initially, let them bring it up. Going back to number two on our "must know" list, the people with whom you have relationship will pick that up and it will naturally flow to their relationships *if it's not about the money!*

I once heard John Maxwell say that whenever you talk to people always give them three things:

1. Something to know, engaging their mind and intellect;

2. Something to feel, engaging their heart and emotions;

3. Something to do, presenting them with opportunity to get involved.

So, whenever you tell your story, start with something like an interesting fact or statistic. Next communicate something from the heart with a story that brings that interesting fact or statistic to life. Only then do you provide an opportunity for possible involvement such as a sponsorship, gift, or whatever.

> Everyone wants to be a part of something bigger than themselves, and when you and I communicate our vision with passion to those with whom we have relationships, people are much more inclined to share in that vision. Simply said; "Share your story!"

2 — Touch Points

Pray and think of ways to creatively broadcast the passion and vision you have for what you are doing. Verbal communication is simply one of many ways this can be done. You can also use newsletters, flyers, handouts, bulletin boards, bulletin inserts, e-mails, web pages, and yes even announcements, and so forth. There is a reason the advertising world does what they do so well. They know people and they know that people have to hear something numerous times before it really gets into their system.

Regularly evaluate all the ways that you are communicating your passion and vision. With each of them go back through the John Maxwell outline and make sure you are addressing each point in turn. Every one of these ways creates opportunities for people to partner with you and reinforces your obvious passion and vision.

Getting back to the concept of webs of relationships, consider making a list or diagram of all the people with whom you have relationships. Then prayerfully consider all their relationships and how you might gain an opportunity to open up a Touch Point with them.

One of the most effective Touch Points we have found is something we call a HOF (House of Faith) 101. Once a month our ministry hosts a one hour sandwich lunch where people can come to learn more about our ministry. During that one hour we use a simple slide show to communicate about our ministry, keeping in mind the simple three-stage outline from John Maxwell. While the purpose is to facilitate relationships and communicate to people, it has been amazing to watch how many times people get plugged into one of our Touch Points during these 101's.

3 — Time Sensitive

For one thing, remember that fundraising takes time, but using this approach will cause your effectiveness in fundraising to build over time, like interest. And for another, there is a limited window of time when people are more likely to partner with you. It's like visitors at church. Research has shown that people who visit a church are more inclined to return if they are contacted within a 24-hour window of their visit. The same window exists in fundraising. People are more likely to partner with you (or at least commit to it) within a short time of you having shared your passion and vision with him.

May the Lord bless and keep you in him as you seek to take Jesus to neighborhood children!

Kevin Reynolds is Co-Founder/Co-Director of House of Faith, a ministry that works with over 3500 neighborhood children and youth in San Angelo, Texas. Kevin is also a speaker who travels throughout the United States and internationally, training others to reach neighborhood kids.

Kevin@hofministries.org
www.hofministries.org
www.handsandfeetbook.com
www.echoexperience.com

Putt Putt Golf Marathon

by Rich Vinson

Putt Putt Golf Marathon is a unique way to raise money for a given need. The idea is to have the children play 90 holes of golf in one day. The children ask for sponsors to support their effort. But, what is more important, the children are doing the work to raise money for the needy.

Define Your Purpose

Any fundraiser must have a clearly defined purpose. Take time to define the purpose for the event. Are you raising funds for missions, equipment for the church, or to support a local outreach?

Give a Biblical basis for the event. This is critical because it will provide a sound reason for the event, build up the child's knowledge of God's Word, and give a practical application to the faith.

As you work on defining the purpose, remember to do it from a child's perspective. The children have to have a sense of ownership. They also have to be able to explain the event to adults as they look for sponsors. You want the children to be inspired and motivated to participate in the event. Remember, this is a children's event.

After you define the purpose, the next step is setting a monetary goal. The goal should be reasonable for the children to achieve. It should also stretch the child's ability, so when they do reach their goal, it is special. So, inspire the children with a reasonable goal that will stretch them at the same time.

As a leader or as a team, you will need to provide some incentives for reaching their goals. You will be amazed at what the right incentive will do to inspire the children. The incentives are not limited to the following, but here are a few suggestions:

- Match dollar for dollar up to a fixed amount.

- Shave your head.

- Have your hair brightly colored for a period of time.

- Take the participants out for pizza.

- Reward the top three children who raise the most money.

The next step is to locate a Putt Putt Golf Course. When you call or visit the business, make sure you talk with the manager or event coordinator. Take a few minutes to briefly explain to the management the purpose of your event. Be bold and ask if there is a discount or if you can start early in the morning to avoid crowds. Discover what dates are available. Let them know that their business will be promoted in the church communication strategies. Businesses love free advertising!

After talking to the Putt Putt Golf Course manager, set a date and time for your event. Review the church calendar, the local school calendar, and consider any holidays that could impact your event. Consider the weather and the time of the year. If school is not in session, consider an early starting time to avoid crowds of other golfers. This will make the event personal. The date and time is critical to having a successful event.

Present the Event To the Children

You have worked to define the purpose, goals, incentives, and to select the date and time. Now it's time to tell the children. The week before you present the event to the children, inform the parents via mail or e-mail about the upcoming event. This will insure a higher rate of participation when the parents are informed. The presentation of the event should be exciting and motivate the children to participate. This presentation is the key to getting the children motivated to go out and sign up sponsors. Explain the purpose and goal, along with the incentives. Hand out the sponsor forms and explain how to use them. The forms should have the following information:

- Name of the child participating in the event.

- Date, time, and location of the event.

- A brief description of the purpose of the event. This will assist the child's presentation.

- Name and contact information of each sponsor that the child signs up.

- Define how the sponsors can donate:
  One time gift
  Number of holes played
  Number of strokes taken to complete the marathon
  Use your imagination for how you will donate

- Set a deadline for turning in all of the donations.

Until the Day of the Event

Each week ask how the children are doing in signing up sponsors. Focus on the one or two driven children who are way ahead of the other children. Use them to encourage others and share ideas. Mail or e-mail home postcard updates telling parents what other children have accomplished. The postcards will remind parents about the event and encourage others to attend. Parents are also a great source for help during the event. Communicate effectively between the announcement and the actual date of the event.

The Day of the Event

The day has arrived and the children are ready to start the Putt Putt Golf Marathon. Have the children form groups of four with one adult assigned to each group. Use the "shotgun" start to begin the marathon. That means, each group will start on different holes on the putt putt course. Set a start time so all groups begin together.

If you are playing 90 holes, then try this approach: Each child will either have one ball or five balls. If the children have one ball, they play that one ball five times at each hole. If they have five balls, then they play all five balls at each hole. The concept is they played each hole five times at one setting, versus walking/playing 18 holes five times. When they have finished playing 18 holes, they will have played a total of 90 holes of golf, $18 \times 5 = 90$.

Celebrate the Results

When all the money is collected by the established deadline and you determine who your top three winners are, set a date to celebrate the results. On the day of celebration, announce the total that was raised, recognize the top three winners, hand out prizes, and show a video or PowerPoint® presentation of the event. The celebration will give the children a sense of accomplishment and motivate them for the next event.

This fun event will ultimately help in raising funds for your desired purpose. We use ours to raise funds for missions.

Richard R. Vinson, M.Div., is the Children's Pastor at Northland Cathedral Church, Kansas City, Missouri. He is a graduate of Gordon Conwell Theological Seminary and an ordained minister in the Assemblies of God Fellowship. Richard has served in children's ministry for ten years.

The Inside Scoop

I was the children's director for a large downtown church in Midland, Michigan. We had just finished a week of VBS on John Wesley, the circuit riders, and United Methodist History. We had transformed the fellowship hall into a village from the late 1700's. A circuit rider had come every day to tell the children Bible stories.

As part of the activities, the children had decorated quilt squares. I had taken the squares home and sewed them together into a quilt. On the last night of the event, parents were invited to celebrate and experience some of what the children had learned. We displayed the quilt and raffled it off to raise money for the week's mission project. Of course I bought a ticket — one ticket.

When the raffle ticket was drawn, I was dismayed to realize it was mine! I wasn't supposed to win, I was the paid staff member. Embarrassed, I accepted the quilt to the laughing comments of "this raffle was rigged." Then I presented the quilt to the volunteer who had coordinated the event.

Moral of the story: You can buy raffle tickets to help the fundraiser, but don't put the tickets in the drawing.

Daphna Flegal, Lead Development Editor
The United Methodist Publishing House

Ten-year-old Mackenzie had been saving her money for years to purchase a bicycle. On this particular Sunday, she actually brought her accumulated one hundred dollars to church. It may have been that she was planning to contribute to the offering all along, but her parents didn't know anything about what happened until after church. The focus in children's church was on missions, and the kids were challenged to give in the mission offering. Mackenzie gave it all . . . all one hundred dollars.

After church, she told her mother what she had done. Her mother and Mackenzie came back to the children's church room to talk with me, the children's pastor. Together we determined that Mackenzie would decide. I was willing to return the money to her after learning how many years she had been saving for a bike and knowing that the family was not financially well off. Mackenzie didn't want the money back. She felt that the Holy Spirit had spoken to her heart about the mission need.

Now, this kind of thing doesn't always happen, but an unforgettable memory was made that afternoon. Mackenzie and her family went to a restaurant for Sunday lunch. The restaurant had a gumball machine in the entrance. Mackenzie asked her mother for a quarter, and everyone's attention was captured when the gumball rolled out with the sound of bells and whistles. They soon learned that Mackenzie had won a grand prize. Her gumball was the one hundred dollar gumball. Wow!

Like I said, giving to God doesn't always result in this kind of experience, but I am convinced that Mackenzie will never forget when she learned that you can't outgive God.

Curt Zastrow, founder and director of The Children's Heritage Foundation
Former children's pastor in Midland, Michigan

Mission Events

"For I was hungry and you gave me something to eat, I was thirsty and you gave me something to drink, I was a stranger and you invited me in, I needed clothes and you clothed me, I was sick and you looked after me, I was in prison and you came to visit me." Then the righteous will answer him, "Lord, when did we see you hungry and feed you, or thirsty and give you drink? When did we see you a stranger and invite you in, or needing clothes and clothe you? When did we see you sick or in prison and go to visit you?" The King will reply, "I tell you the truth, whatever you did for one of the least of these brothers of mine, you did for me."

(Matthew 25:35-40, NIV)

Junior Mission Retreat

by Mary Lou Bishop

Emphasis: Missions

Purpose: Junior Missionary retreat is a 24-hour intense time for tweens to learn about missions in another country.

Calendar: January or February or the slowest time on the church calendar.

Personnel: Everyone in the church. Anyone could help with anything.

Timeline: 6–12 months before — decide on country and find a missionary
3–6 months before — decide on personnel and assign jobs
1 month and closing — finalize all the details

Hosting a Junior Missionary Retreat (JMR) for fourth through sixth graders can be a memorable way to increase your student's understanding of a mission trip. The retreat can be designed to fit a variety of circumstances depending on the church. Retreats that we have planned have really given the children a vision for the mission field not only abroad but locally, as well.

Our church is quite small, so to make the numbers a little larger we have the children bring a friend for a reduced rate. Fifteen children would be the least that would work effectively as you need at least three groups of five children. You can have as many groups as you need, keeping in mind you will need that many counselors to commit to stay with the children overnight.

Each child and counselor is provided with a bound booklet. The booklet is made to help the children on their journey. It is important that the schedule is tight to keep the children focused on

their mission. Even after having JMR for the last nine years, we are still fine tuning it to fit our situation. In the front of every booklet are security check cards and the four stages of culture shock cards.

The country is chosen by connecting with members of our congregation who had gone to a mission field through our church's Work and Witness program, or we focus on a country where we will have missionaries visiting our church during the program. One year, a couple in our church was adopting a child from Nepal. We provided them with about one to two hundred dollars to buy native trinkets from Nepal that could be used in the market.

We usually plan the Junior Missionary Retreat during January or February. It is usually a slower time of the year for our church, so we are able to gain a lot of volunteer support and it becomes a whole church undertaking as apposed to competing with other events during the year.

Through setup, planning, and the actual night of the event nearly everyone in our church is included. Our congregation is small, and this event really becomes a whole church effort. Anyone can help.

The 24-hour trip

The passengers must arrive by 5:30 PM and be checked in. They must have their "passports" filled in with all their information and a roll of dimes (fine money) to receive their tickets.

They weigh their luggage, which must weigh less than thirteen pounds (including their sleeping bags, overnight stuff, Bible, and so forth), or they are fined for each pound they are over. They proceed to the scanning area where they are scanned and their luggage is checked.

They go to the nurse's station to make sure that their vaccinations are in order. The nurse will give them a "shot" and some "malaria pills" for their protection. Then they wait with their luggage in the waiting area until the plane is ready to board.

On the plane they will receive a sack lunch with a sandwich, chips, cookies, and a mint. The stewardess shows them all the safety information that you usually get on a flight and then passes out the lunches and drinks.

When they get off the plane they proceed through customs. Customs includes going through their luggage looking for contraband — Bibles — that are not allowed in the country.

The passengers then pick up their luggage and continue to their hotels. After check-in and receiving a room number (areas taped like rooms in the sanctuary with masking tape), they make their beds.

They then gather with their teams to make a flag, choose a name, choose a Bible verse to go along with their team motto, and prepare a skit.

The teams present their team names, mottos, verses, skits, and flags to an adult mission board. Points are given on the creativity, neatness, and appropriateness of their presentations.

While the mission board calculates the results, the teams experience their first cultural snack.

The team begins memorizing the security codes and practices speaking the language of the country. Throughout the night, money from the country being highlighted will be given to the junior missionaries for memorizing, listening, being good missionaries, and so forth.

Later in the evening the money will be used to purchase the trinkets that were brought by the missionaries. Then the missionary gives an overview of the country — its government, language, scenery, schools, and so forth — all the information that is important to know about a country you are going to do ministry in. The

T he hunger banquet is usually the climax of the experience. Children receive just a small bowl of chicken broth and rice for dinner. They are challenged to not eat until the next morning when, at Sunday School, a breakfast will be provided.

final points for the presentations are then announced at the end of this session.

The evening will close with devotions in teams with the adult counselor. While the passengers are getting ready for bed, the counselors can catch up on the point system for each of the individuals on their team as well as calculate the team points.

Fines can also be given after lights out. Every time someone talks they can be fined. After the third fine for the evening, parents are called and the child sent home. We always want to have the child participate, but we also want the children to learn that service includes obedience. Over the past nine years, we have never had to send a child home.

The next day begins with a wake-up call and breakfast from the country. Classes on the culture, language, and crafts begin right after breakfast. These activities can be changed for the number of teams and children that are at the retreat. Any time that there is "down time," kids can be memorizing the security codes and language. Keeping up with the point system can be a challenge for the counselor, but it is worth the diligence.

A mission training could be part of the classes given in the morning session. But as always the schedule can be flexible to your needs. Mission training was the class where the missionary would tell about her or his call to the mission field. Since we didn't always have a missionary, we asked a lay person that had gone on a mission trip. We also asked someone who had a testimony of being called to ministry.

We improvise wherever we need to. For the music section, we had a Skype connection with missionaries from the country and they taught us a song that they sung at summer camp. It was really an effective way to use technology to help bring kids right into the culture of the country.

For lunch, a menu is printed with a list of all the food that will be served, but it is written in the language of the country. There is a blank by each entry. The child will write a one by all the things that are the first course, two by all the things that are the second course, and three by all the things that are the third course. So it is important that they learn the language in the book or they won't get their utensils first. It can become a little chaotic with a large group, so your waiters and waitresses will need to be well informed and on their toes.

The missionary speaker will tell about his or her work in the country, and the children will have the opportunity to have a question and answer time.

After the missionary speaks, the teams participate in a scavenger hunt where the children find "trash" and make a display which promotes missions and/or their theme Bible verse. In inclement weather we have gathered a bag full of trash with each bag being the same

for the children to use in their displays. A mission board of adults will judge them during afternoon snack, and winners are announced after that. The First Place Team will be able to go to the market first, and the other teams follow in turn. We make sure there are enough prizes from the country that each child can take home a souvenir to pray for that country.

The culmination of the retreat is Communion with the pastor. The children start this time by having a Bible study using the Thinking and Thanking section in their booklet. We encourage the children to spread out until they are in their own space. When they feel they are ready, they can participate in Communion with the pastor. We encourage the children to really connect with God. This is always the most spiritual part of the weekend.

The hunger banquet is usually the climax of the experience. Children receive just a small bowl of chicken broth and rice for dinner. They are challenged to not eat until the next morning when, at Sunday School, a breakfast will be provided.

The retreat for the children could be planned in conjunction with a missions weekend for the church. Missionary speakers and the impact that their experiences can have on whole families could radically change how your families view missions.

Junior Missionary Retreat (JMR) was introduced to the author through the children's ministry at Denver First Church of the Nazarene. The Children's Director at the time was Liz VonSeggen. Liz and her husband Dale are the founders of One Way Street.

> **M**issionary speakers and the impact that their experiences can have on whole families could radically change how your families view missions.

Mary Lou Bishop works in the Finance Department of the International Network of Children's Ministry. She has a B.A. in Religious Education from Rockmont College and a B.A. in Elementary Education from Kearney State College. Mary Lou also has a Masters of Arts in Curriculum and Instruction. She is also a Preschool Teacher at a local church. Mary Lou is a lifelong Coloradoan and lives just outside Castle Rock, Colorado.

Mission Adventure Teams

by Dr. Roger Theimer

It's Wednesday night. It's midweek at church. But something is different. Children aren't sitting through another version of Sunday school. They're preparing for an adventure. They're on a mission. And they are excited.

A team of six elementary-aged students will soon be prayer-walking an inner city block where a new storefront mission will be planted. A team of young puppeteers and gospel illusionists are packing their suitcases for a visit to the women's shelter. The blanket-making team is preparing to hand-deliver their prayerfully crafted blankets to the Open Door Mission.

Elementary children are plugging into Mission Adventure Teams (MAT) at King of Kings Lutheran Church in Omaha, Nebraska. Preschool-aged children are serving as well, but they don't leave campus. Their midweek program is called Mission Adventure Club, where they learn about serving — and actually serve — through hands-on activities.

Impact of Ministry

Kids are ministers too. That's the slogan for Mission Adventure Teams. It's all too easy to design a program where kids look cute and have a good time but end up with a light encounter in the kingdom of God. Mission Adventure Teams allow kids to experience what God is doing to bring people to himself. Leaders focus on helping kids discover firsthand what it means to be a disciple of Jesus — to trust him as Savior and then follow him by sharing his love with the world.

A few years ago, one of the members of King of Kings opened a storefront mission in a high crime and poverty area of the city. The kids'

prayer team spent a Wednesday evening visiting the site. They decorated the walls with some of their handmade art as they learned about the ministry needs. They prayed that the Holy Spirit would fill the lives of the people entering this building that had previously been used as an illegal gambling operation. They walked the sidewalk and prayed for the broken lives of people who were living life far from God. They prayed against crime and violence and drug dealers. They prayed for those addicted to alcohol and for families without fathers. They prayed that this new mission would bring good news and healing to the neighborhood.

So what was the result of their prayers? The next Sunday at worship service the room filled quickly. Previously, the highest attendance had been 18 people. But on that Sunday 48 people crowded in. God asks that we pray expectantly and with faith. Who does that better than children?

Philosophy of Ministry

The philosophy of ministry behind Mission Adventure Teams recognizes that there is more to discipleship than learning the content of the Bible. Certainly, kids need to learn God's Word, encounter Jesus, and trust him as their Savior. But that is not where it ends. That is where it begins.

We live that relationship by serving him. We serve him by serving others. Children should not wait until adulthood before they get that message from the church. Without the challenge of serving, how might a child answer the question after sixteen years of Sunday school: "What does it mean to be a good Christian?" Would they respond with: "Sit there, be quiet and listen"?

How did Jesus describe discipleship? "Follow me and you will see the kingdom of God at work!" Jesus taught his disciples about the kingdom of God as they traveled from place to place serving the needs of people.

Components of the Program

There are three key components to organizing a Wednesday night Mission Adventure program:

- Select a clear focus and communicate it clearly to parents. ("Cast the vision.") Some possible phrases that capture and communicate the vision well might be: "Kids Are Ministers, Too;" "To minister is to serve;" "Kids serve."

- At MAT Kids discover spiritual gifts and experiment with them. No matter what the activity, kids should see the link between serving and spiritual impact in the kingdom . . . the more direct the contact with people, the more significant the impact.

- The third key component is enlisting leaders. Adults who are passionate about serving help ignite a fire in the hearts of the children they work with.

Mission Adventure Club— Preschool Ages

Sample activities:
- Make bookmarks for church library gifts.
- Decorate white aprons to give to church kitchen team.
- Sponsor a child overseas.
- Make doorknob hangers for nursing homes.
- Make thank-you notes for volunteer teams that serve at church.
- Make Thanksgiving or Christmas treat bags for kids living at local homeless shelter.
- Make treat bags for cats and dogs at humane society.
- "Soup in a jar" — put all dry ingredients for soup in a jar — just add water.

Mission Adventure Teams— Elementary Ages

On-Site Schedule

6:40 PM – 6:50 PM	Kids arrive
	Worship and prayer
6:50 PM – 7:00 PM	Announcements / Discussion of upcoming off-site event
	Break into teams
7:00 PM – 7:45 PM	Work in individual teams
7:45 PM – 7:50 PM	Clean up
7:50 PM – 8:00 PM	Return to large group
	Talk about projects / activities done that evening
	Prayer / Closing

Off-Site Schedule

6:30 PM	Leave church to go to off-site locations
6:45 PM – 7:45 PM	Arrive at off-site location Deliver items made or share presentation
7:45 PM – 8:00 PM	Arrive back at church As time allows, share testimonies about evening's events

Sample Five-Week Term

9/15	Kick-off and Select Teams
9/22	Work in teams to prepare for nursing home off-site event
9/27	Off-site to nursing homes
10/6	Work in teams to prepare for homeless shelter off-site event
10/13	Off-site to homeless shelters

Service Ministries/Presentation Ministries

Service Ministries provide a "hands-on" way to minister. The kids get to do something they enjoy, such as baking cookies or putting together a care basket. The most significant impact for the kids, however, is seeing someone blessed by what they have done. They learn how to use their time and love of an activity to show the love of God to others.

Presentation Ministries allow kids to minister to others by using their talents in dancing, singing, acting, and so forth. They are able to lead worship for residents in a nursing home or present a program to children at a women's shelter. Each presentation shares God's message and brings hope and encouragement to the audience. In addition, the kids learn how to use their talents in a way that brings glory and honor to God.

Sample Service Ministries:
- Blanket Making — fleece blankets for homeless shelters or those hospitalized.
- Baskets of Care — Baskets filled with small gifts and words of comfort and encouragement for hospitalized and elderly.
- Jewelry Making / Woodworking / Leather craft — making an item that can be given to a friend, teacher, senior citizen.
- Cards / Letter — to send to soldiers overseas or orphans in other countries.
- Baking meals for a family with a new baby, or one that has suffered a loss.
- Meal bags for homeless — put together a meal that can be handed out to homeless on the street.
- Treat bags for church staff to say thank you for all they do for the congregation.
- Random Acts of Kindness — find ways to make someone smile, such as placing an encouraging message for someone to find.
- Prayer Walking — go to the mall, inner city neighborhoods, or around schools and pray for the area and ask people if they have a need that can be prayed for.

Performance Ministries:
- Dance — add a visual element to a song with dancers.
- Choir — sing for a worship service, Christmas musical, and so forth.
- Puppets — create a skit with the puppets or create a rock band with them to lip sync to a song.
- Gospel Illusion — attach a Biblical truth to a "magic" trick.
- Drama — perform skits for nursing homes, homeless shelters, even your church's worship services.

- Worship team — lead other kids in Sunday School opening worship time.
- Human Videos — kids perform choreographed actions to "drive home" the message of a contemporary worship song.

Family Serve Events

Research tells us that one of the greatest factors for kids staying active in the Christian faith is that they served alongside their parents. Family serve events provide a designated time, such as the second Sunday of every month, in which a family can serve together. This could be serving a meal at the local mission, adopting a grandparent to visit and help with work around their home, reading books to children in a shelter, and much more.

Final Story . . .

On Wednesday, December 5, 2007, the Von Maur department store in Omaha, Nebraska, was the site of a mass shooting. A sole gunman killed eight people and injured five others before killing himself. The next weekend, the fifth and sixth graders of King of Kings left campus after their Sunday school hour to minister to the victims' families and the community. They "prayer-walked" the mall, left notes for family members, and left prayer cards on the mall steps. Those kids will never forget that day. They had experienced that they are the body of Christ ministering to a broken world.

For more information contact dianak@kingofkingsomaha.org

Roger Theimer is the children's pastor at King of Kings Lutheran Church in Omaha, Nebraska. His doctoral studies were dedicated to applying small group Bible study techniques to children's ministry. He has authored two curriculums: Kingdom Quest and Kids Church (www.kidskountpublishing.com <http://mail.kingofkingsomaha.org/exchweb/bin/redir.asp? URL=http://www.kidskountpublishing.com/>). He is co-author of Faith Legacy Series, a curriculum to help families grow spiritually at home. He has taught children's ministry leadership across America, in Europe, Africa, and Asia.

Local Missions for Kids

by Pat Douglas and Ana Mitchum

Service in God's name. We all agree that serving others is important. However, we often struggle with fitting it into our busy lifestyles. Serving God by serving others is what God asks us to do.

Imagine if lifelong everyday service was a part of everyone's life. That may seem like a far reaching goal, but children serving God can change the future. Children naturally want to help others. Through active service they learn that they are active emissaries of God's love, they are the catalyst of change.

The earlier a child becomes aware that there are others who suffer and need help, the more likely it is that they will learn compassion. It is important that they realize that those in need are "just like them" in different circumstances. Provide opportunities to instill a lifelong habit of sharing God's love through service to others. As children give of their time and talents to others, they experience the joy of living in accordance with God's word. Their faith and love for God deepen as the roots for their future.

Sounds good, but how can I put it into action at my church? Here's an example:

Dog Days of Summer

Learn About Local Animal Shelters and Make Dog Biscuits

The purpose of this activity is to learn about animal shelters and their important role as caretakers of God's creatures. Show your love by getting messy and making yummy dog biscuits!

Setup, Prepare, and Conduct Mission Activity

Learn about and contact a local organization that supports and protects animals in your community.

- Obtain free pamphlets, posters, and videos to educate and share with the children.

- Ask if your group can tour their facility and see and learn firsthand about their work.

- Ask if you can bring homemade treats. (Be prepared to list ingredients.)

- Discuss with your group the importance of animal shelters and how they can help.

- Determine where and when to make dog biscuits.

- Gather all the supplies and ingredients to make the dog biscuits.

> You made him ruler over the works of your hands; you put everything under his feet: all flocks and herds, and the beasts of the field, the birds of the air, and the fish of the sea, all that swim the paths of the seas.
>
> (Psalm 8:6-8, NIV)

To make the biscuits:

Dog Biscuit Recipe
    1 package dry yeast
    ¼ cup warm water
    1 pint vegetable or chicken stock
    3 cups unbleached flour
    2½ cups whole-wheat flour
    1 cup rye flour
    2 cups cracked wheat or wheat germ
    ½ cup dry milk
    ½ teaspoon salt, optional
    1 egg
    1 tablespoon milk
    Measuring cups
    Large Bowl
    Rolling pins, several
    Doggie-bone cookie cutter(s) optional
    Baking sheet
    Disposable storage containers

Note: Makes 4–5 dozen. Recipe easily doubled

Preheat oven to 300 degrees. Dissolve yeast in ¼ cup warm water. Add to vegetable or chicken stock. Combine all dry ingredients in a separate bowl. Then, add stock mixture. Knead mixture on a flour surface for about three minutes, working into stiff dough. Roll out dough to a thickness of ¼ inch. Cut the dough into bars or use doggie-bone cookie cutter. Beat one egg with one tablespoon milk. Brush each biscuit with the egg/milk mixture and place on cookie sheets. Bake for about 45 minutes. Turn oven off; leave biscuits in the oven overnight. This makes them hard and crunchy.

As you work with the children to make the dog biscuits, ask these questions:

- Why do we need organizations that protect and take care of homeless animals?

- Why is it important that we take care of animals?

- How is supporting animal shelters doing as God asks us as "ruler over the works of his hands"?

Pat Douglas and Anna Mitchum are the creators and authors of Kids With Purpose, *which they run out of their own faith community in Leesburg, Virginia. They continue to give back to their community in a myriad of ways.*

www.KidsWithPurpose.org

Dog Days of Summer

Learn About Local Animal Shelters and Make Dog Biscuits

"You made him ruler over the works of your hands; you put everything under his feet: all flocks and herds, and the beasts of the field, the birds of the air, and the fish of the sea, all that swim the paths of the sea."

Psalms 8:6-8

The purpose of this activity is to learn about animal shelters and their important role as caretakers of God's creatures. Show your love by getting messy and making yummy dog biscuits!

Set-Up, Prepare and Conduct Mission Activity:

Learn about and contact a local organization that supports and protects animals in your community. Obtain free pamphlets, posters, and videos to educate and share with the children.

Ask if your group can tour their facility and see and learn first hand about their work.

Ask if you can bring homemade treats. *(Be prepared to list ingredients.)*

Discuss with your group the importance of animal shelters and how they can help.

Determine where and when to make dog biscuits.

Gather all the supplies and ingredients to make the dog biscuits.

To make the biscuits:

Preheat oven to 300 degrees.

Dissolve yeast in ¼ cup warm water. Add to vegetable or chicken stock. Combine all dry ingredients in a separate bowl. Then, add stock mixture. Knead mixture on a flour surface for about 3 minutes, working into stiff dough. Roll out dough to a thickness of ¼-inch. Cut the dough into bars our use doggie-bone cookie cutter. Beat one egg with one-tablespoon milk. Brush each biscuit with the egg/milk mixture and place on cookie sheets. Bake for about 45 minutes. Turn oven off; **leave biscuits in the oven overnight**. This makes them hard and crunchy.

Package biscuits and deliver.

Supplies:

Pamphlets, posters, and other materials to educate children about animal shelters

Dog Biscuit Recipe

1 package dry yeast

¼ cup warm water

1-pint vegetable or chicken stock

3 cups unbleached flour

2 ½ whole-wheat flour

1 cup rye flour

2 cups cracked wheat or wheat germ

½ cup dry milk

½ teaspoon salt, optional

1 egg

1 tablespoon milk

Measuring cups

Large Bowl

Rolling pins, several

Doggie-bone cookie cutter(s) optional

Baking sheet

Disposable storage containers

Note: Makes 4-5 dozen. Recipe easily doubled.

Discussion

∞ **Why do we need organizations that protect and take care of homeless animals?**

∞ **Why is it important that we take care of animals?**

∞ **How is supporting animal shelters doing as God asks us as "ruler over the works of His hands"?**

This page is on the CD-Rom.

Reaching Neighborhood Kids

by Kevin Reynolds

There are a number of issues that are unique to effectively reaching neighborhood kids. These issues arise in addition to what is necessary for effective ministry to the kids already involved in our churches. While this is by no means an exhaustive summary, it is important to focus on some of the most important nuts and bolts of planning and providing an event to reach neighborhood kids who are not regularly involved in church. There are enough details to help you lay a good foundation and put your own personality into what you do to reach neighborhood kids.

It is important to note that this article is based on the assumption that "kids who don't regularly go to church will come to a site in their own neighborhood to hear the Gospel." That is a safe assumption since we have seen success with the activities and approaches that are described in this section.

Incarnational Example

In our opinion, the first and most fundamental issue involved is the example of the Lord Jesus in the incarnation. In bringing the Good News to humankind, the Lord in his infinite wisdom did not simply send us an invitation to "come and see" what he had for us at his place. He sent his one and only Son to become one of us where we already were, in our world . . . our place . . . our neighborhood.

We strongly suggest that you consider planning events to reach neighborhood kids in a place where unchurched neighborhood kids already are, rather than at your church. Ask the Lord to guide you to a safe, non-threatening location near the neighborhood elementary school or place where neighborhood children regularly play. This could be a school yard, a park, an apartment complex, someone's yard, a recreation center, and so forth.

Having events at a location that neighborhood kids are familiar with will help you establish a positive influence and will help you connect with many kids who for various reasons may not come to a church right away. The non-threatening location helps you earn the right to be heard. You can use this initial event as a springboard for a healthy relationship and involvement in their lives, especially on a spiritual level.

There are liability issues that arise with doing an event at a location other than your church but those are easily dealt with. Almost all churches have allowances for off-site events such as home Bible studies, small groups, church picnics, and so forth. An event for neighborhood kids should fall under that same category. In addition to insurance policies that may already be in place, make sure that insurance for off-site locations are included or can be

> **W**hatever your event is, make it fun and make a memory. Neighborhood kids will come. Once they are there, you have a chance to establish relationships with them and that is where the real work begins. Fun and relationships earn us the right to be heard and provide opportunity to speak into their lives.

added. Check with the business office or senior pastor of your church regarding this detail.

Day and Time

It has often been noted that the most unsupervised hours of the day for kids are week days between the end of school and early evening. Consider planning an event during this time. This timeframe may not always be best for volunteers, but many neighborhood kids have time to spare during these hours.

Spiritual Element

It is important to incorporate a spiritual element from the start. This does not mean it has to be all spiritual, but it is an error to have an outreach event that is purely food, fun, and games.

Sometimes there is the tendency to think that we should not be overly religious or spiritual at first, in the hopes of not running the kids off or perhaps coming on too strong. Keep in mind that the methods we use in our first approach will have a strong implication for what the kids expect from that point on. It can often backfire if we start out with little or no spiritual element and then try to add it later on.

It is most important to have a balanced combination of spiritual and nonspiritual elements. You can increase the spiritual dimension as your relationship with the children grows, but it is hard to add a spiritual component if you started somewhere else. That is, after all, why we are doing the event, so it is better to just be honest from the start.

The spiritual element may be a prayer at the end, a simple Bible story, Christian music, or a combination of these. Remember that it is the teaching of God's Word that brings about change in a person's heart. Choosing the right curriculum is critical. Make sure that what is taught is not over the heads of those who have yet to understand the basics of the Gospel, while still keeping the interest of those who think they've heard it all. Lessons that are highly visual and interactive work best. Traditional classroom style resources simply do not work.

Something else that often works well is to ask kids, one-on-one, if you can pray for them about something. You will rarely be turned down, and it is amazing how many times the walls just come right down by offering to pray for their needs. The children will soon be begging you to come back.

Communication

After the initial contact, weekly or biweekly visitation can be set up with the children and the families of the children involved. In the beginning, parents are asked to sign a permission slip allowing their kids to attend. Beyond the simple courtesy of letting the parents know where their children are, the permission slip also provides contact information and a point of communication with the families. This permission slip serves as the beginnings of relationship building with the family.

Sample Schedule

A sample breakdown of an effective weekly outreach event for neighborhood kids might look something like this:

- The location is secured several weeks in advance. If possible, a sign should be placed at the location with the event name displayed. Remember, it is wise to select a location where neighborhood kids already hang out so they quickly become accustomed to the location.

- It is valuable to have a pre-event event called a Blitz. This is a short high energy presence the day before the actual event that includes volunteers canvassing the neighborhood with flyers announcing the details of the event. The Blitz may include music, games, and possible food such as hot dogs. Contact information is gathered from children and parents in the form of permission slips so that follow-up visits and invitations may be made.

- Every effort should be made to touch base with area VIP's such as city or school personnel, property managers, recreation center staff, and so forth. Nothing is asked of them, but informing them about the event in advance will be to your advantage. Give them your contact information.

- Having toys, sport balls, and other game equipment available for the first twenty to thirty minutes of each event is a great way to facilitate group games and play interaction between kids and staff/volunteers.

- After play time, a whistle is blown and the kids all gather together. If weather and venue permits, they can be seated on the ground or plastic tarps. Next, there is a "spectator" game where the group watches two kids (often boy vs. girl) play something that illustrates a key point from the teaching. Players are selected by asking for volunteers who are seated with their hands raised. There is still a high level of energy but the energy is focused.

- Next is an opening prayer and explanation of special prizes for good listeners. We follow this with an object lesson and Bible story. Again, highly visual illustrations are best.

> As is the case with all kids, there is a great need for consistency in the lives of neighborhood kids.

- One important aspect of the teaching time is the transition between segments. With all the supplies at hand, a team teaching format is a positive technique. This approach involves one teacher in the forefront speaking while the next teacher is prepping. A smooth transition is made between speakers so the attention of the kids is not lost. Keep the pace moving and flowing at all times, with one speaker immediately following the next. Anything that can be given as a take-home item, a Scripture verse card or coloring page for example, is always helpful.

The format of this sample schedule is not that different than what might take place in a regular church program. Keep in mind though, that when the event is held regularly in a place other than the church, it will be attended. You may not have everyone attend every week, but you will see a large percentage of unreached kids when the right approaches are used.

Fun & Relationships

Someone once said, "High tech is good, but high touch trumps high tech every time. Every kid wants to have fun. The Lord made them that way, so go with it." Whatever your event is, make it fun and make a memory. Neighborhood kids will come. Once they are there, you have a chance to establish relationships with them and that is where the real work begins. Fun and relationships earn us the right to be heard and provide opportunity to speak into their lives.

We need to work hard to keep our perspective from becoming one of an event mentality. The event is just a means to an end of developing relationship where we are regularly a part of their lives just as we are with the kids in our own church. We already know that it's not really any one time with them that makes all the difference in the lives of our own kids, but rather the cumulative effect of a whole lot of times over a period of time. It is the same with neighborhood kids.

Transition

As is the case with all kids, there is a great need for consistency in the lives of neighborhood kids. With the continued breakdown of the family in all areas of our culture, a consistent presence in the neighborhood will bring us into contact with many kids who are lacking any consistent positive adult influence. Being there in their neighborhood on a regular basis deeply establishes the relationship, helps them to develop trust and confidence in us, and makes it much easier to transition this relationship to the context of the church. There can then be a natural gravitation towards the church that is represented at the weekly event.

Establishing a relationship with the kids will also communicate volumes to the kids' families, which makes it easier to "bridge" the gap between the kids and their parents. One effective follow-up approach after a consistent relationship is established is to hold a special event where the kids invite their parents.

Buy-in from Key Players

The only way to have sustainable successful ministry is to connect the unreached child who has started attending with kids who are already involved with existing church programs in the area. Get a buy-in from key players such as church leadership, staff and volunteers, and the parents of the kids in the church. This is important in order to avoid problems that can arise when neighborhood kids actually do become involved in our churches.

Sometimes there will be behavior issues that accompany the new kids, and it is important to communicate in advance with those (volunteers and leaders) who are actually going to have to deal with them. If not, when problems do arise, the church volunteers and leaders may feel they are required to deal with issues that they did not sign up for. Casting the vision for reaching neighborhood kids in advance is valuable, and even allow key players to be part of the decision to begin such efforts. Overcommunication in this area actually pays off.

May the Lord bless and keep you in him as you seek to take Jesus to neighborhood children!

Kevin Reynolds is Co-Founder/Co-Director of House of Faith, a ministry that works with over 3500 neighborhood children and youth in San Angelo, Texas. Kevin is also a speaker who travels throughout the United States and internationally, training others to reach neighborhood kids.

Kevin@hofministries.org
www.hofministries.org
www.handsandfeetbook.com
www.echoexperience.com

Communities Connecting for At-Risk Children

by Sandy Rakes

One-third of the 40 million children across the United States are at-risk academically, socially, economically and/or spiritually.

What can we do as a church? Plenty! *Great Kids Explorer Club* is a model program in Volusia County, Florida, that has bridged the gap between schools and churches in a respectful partnership. Our goal is not to bring religion into the schools but rather to bring the school children into our churches.

Our mission is to inspire other churches to develop their own outreach ministry to help at-risk children recognize their God-given unique talents and unique value through academic and Christian character building education and by surrounding the children with positive role models.

> "Children in low-income families often reach adulthood without the tools, experiences, and connections to help them thrive. These children are more likely to suffer from preventable illnesses, fail in school, and become teen parents than children from more affluent families — and they are more likely to be unemployed as adults." — Annie E. Casey Foundation

This "free" early intervention program helps young children ages five through twelve develop self-respect and a desire to do their best while earning better grades, becoming more confident, and becoming better equipped to make healthy decisions. This is being accomplished through positive reinforcement of good behavior, mentoring in a structured learning environment, tutoring, and Christian Character lessons.

Both Christian and secular educators agree that education is the number one way to make positive social change. Young children are like Jello®, you have to get the good stuff in before it sets. Great Kids is designed to raise children's confidence in order to elevate their expectations of success, thus pushing them to reach their highest academic and personal potential.

The *Great Kids Life Skill Enrichment Program* provides three hours of weekly interactive educational mentoring/tutoring conducted in a small group teaching environment, giving children the assistance in reading and math needed for them to catch up with their peers.

Study Buddies

Volunteer "Study Buddy" mentoring/tutoring groups of three to five students per adult gives the children the personal attention they need to be inspired to *want* to learn and then teaches them *how* to learn.

Academic Stations

Academic stations for the younger children work well. Station One is reading circle and Station Two is skill. Each group should be at least 45 minutes and very structured.

"Improving children's ability to read is the single most important way to help them gain the skills and confidence needed to break the cycle of poverty and make a better life for themselves." — Save the Children US Programs

1. **Reading Circle:** *The Scholastic Big Book* series is perfect for kindergarten through second grade. Words from each story can be made into vocabulary flash cards, and the teacher guide gives ideas for learning activities. Repetition activities are keys for young learners, so we suggest each book be used three weeks in a row.

2. **Skill:** This is a time to practice basic spelling, language arts, and math skills. Reproducible activity books are available at your local teacher store. We require our kids to complete three work sheets and then they may go on to homework.

We keep our third through fifth grade children together and give them three 30-minute activities: Skill, homework, and reading adventure.

1. **Skill:** Skill lessons are the same as it is for the younger children except grade appropriate. School issued spelling words can be developed into lessons that are designed to help them spell the word, use the word, and research the word. We also give math practice lessons based on our county's curriculum map.

2. **Homework assistance:** Children receive help on their challenging homework.

3. **Reading adventure:** Children listen to books on DVD as they follow along using tracking skills. This project should be designed to illustrate that reading is fun and not encumbered in a lot of tutor type activities.

Program Goals:

- **Improved attitudes and effort:** The use of mentoring (motivation and accountability) and tutoring helps children improve their grades while learning how to make healthy decisions.

- **Improved behavior and social skills:** Social skills and citizenship training should be woven into all activities by teaching children to follow direction and to respect rules and recognize and respect each other's differences. Children need structure and to be held accountable. It is most important for all tutors to "say what you mean *and* mean what you say." Anything less is confusing and counter-productive.

- **Improved reading skills:** Education is the number one way to make positive social change. *Great Kids* is helping to break the cycle of poverty and dysfunction through education starting at age five, when it is needed the most. Small group reading circles work very well.

- **Improved character:** Today children are being de-sensitized by what they see on TV, in movies, and by playing violent video games. Many children are growing up without knowing right from wrong. Christian Character Development is taught in a big group setting at the end of the academic time. We suggest matching values to Bible stories that show the children how God wants us to live and treat each other.

Stories to Bless Your Heart

Over the last fifteen years we have helped hundreds of children. Here are a few stories to bless your heart.

Last year Travon was a first grade student who started out the year below grade level in both reading and math. He was completely unmotivated to learn due to a lack of confidence. He would not even attempt to read a book or do simple math equations because of his fear of failure. Within a couple of months of attending *Great Kids* his grades improved and his mom reported, "He now enjoys going to school and learning new things because of the confidence he has gained from going to the *Great Kids* Program."

Anna joined *Great Kids*. She was below grade level and lacked the self-esteem to participate in activities and make friends. After three years with *Great Kids*, Anna's personality and grades improved drastically. She is now on grade level and looking forward to middle school. She has also joined a small group Bible study at the partnering church. Anna wrote in an article for the *Great Kids* newsletter, "I may have dyslexia and ADHD, it doesn't mean I'm helpless. You must push yourself if you want to succeed."

Jonathan's biggest challenge was himself. He lacked the motivation and willingness to work hard. He was in danger of failing the fourth grade, and his mother was at her wits' end. He was moved to fifth grade even though he was still below grade level in reading. Jonathan returned to *Great Kids* for his fifth grade year and there was little difference in his motivation. Midyear, something happened. His attitude started to change, and he began actually trying to do well. His behavior, attitude, and effort changed for the better. He ended his fifth grade year on grade-level and was promoted to middle school. When asked how did we help you? He replied, "You didn't give up on me."

There are children like these in every community. They need you to love, nurture, and teach them. I hope God touches your heart and inspires you to start an at-risk ministry in your church.

Best practices in establishing your at-risk ministry with your local elementary school:

- Approach your school with a servant heart.

- Develop a Memorandum of Understanding Agreement (MOU). This will outline each partner's responsibilities.

- Schools oversee the selection of the children; provide report cards, and other vital information.

- Churches provide the classroom space, volunteers, and learning materials.

- Provide a dual-enrollment, one for the academic program and the other for the Christian based program. Don't require religious participation as a requirement for assistance. Most parents sign up their child for both, so let parents decide, and respect their decisions.

- Research the school's reading program, and develop learning activities based on what the kids are learning in their classroom.

- Once the ministry is established and you have a relationship with the parents, invite them to participate in your "seeker" activities.

- Always remember it's all about the kids.

Jesus said, "Bring the children unto me." As a church it is necessary to go get them. They are waiting for you to reach and connect with them in a way that nurtures their mind, body, and soul.

Sandy Rakes is the founder and executive director of Great Kids Explorer Club, *a not-for-profit faith-based organization. She grew up in a dysfunctional family similar to many of the children she serves and she has made it her life mission to give at-risk children a brighter future through love, encouragement, education, and by teaching them that Jesus loves them and has a purpose for their lives. This has been possible through her faith and the love and support of her husband of thirty-five years, Terry.*

For more information about Great Kids Explorer Club *and how this organization can further help you in developing a similar ministry in your church, log on to greatkidsclub.org for a free "Tool Kit," or e-mail Sandy at greatkidsclub@bellsouth.net. Together, we can make a difference one child at a time.*

The Inside Scoop

A little boy was running in our church when he and mom were visiting. No one else was around when the mom said to her son, "Don't run in God's house." His answer, "It's OK Mom, God's not home."

Roger Theimer
Associate Pastor of Children's Ministry at King of Kings Church in Omaha, Nebraska.

I had been invited to join the fourth, fifth, and sixth graders from Christ Fellowship on their mission trip to Mexico City. I was asked to teach workshops on Classroom Management and Attention Deficit Disorder. I also addressed the one hundred senior pastors who came to learn more about children's ministry. The kids from Christ Fellowship performed during the large group gathering time of the training portion of our mission trip. I thought their ministry would only involve singing as a choir but was impressed to see them also minister through the use of mime, a testimony, and a powerful solo in Spanish.

My heart was moved as we traveled to the mission outreach in the afternoon. It became apparent that the chaperones and children had not been told that we were going to one of the dumps in Mexico City. Thousands of families live at the base of the ever-growing dumpsite. They make their living by sorting through the refuse and selling glass, wood, metal, and plastic. One of the mothers on the bus commented about the deteriorating neighborhoods as we got closer and closer to our destination. About that time Rick Hubbard, the leader of the mission team, got everyone's attention on the bus and asked if anyone wanted to pray.

It was a fourth grade girl who raised her hand. She would love to pray. Special consideration had been given to selecting this girl for the mission trip. Since she has muscular sclerosis, the leaders knew that extra time and extra care would be necessary. I was glad to hear that they were willing to accommodate her needs so that she could come on the trip. Then I heard her pray. She stood and raised her hand as if to reach the hand of God. She sounded like an evangelistic preacher as she interceded for the needs of the children we would meet. She prayed for the members of our mission team and asked God to use us in powerful ways. We all knew that God had heard her prayer. There was no need for anyone else to pray.

What an amazing life-changing experience our time was at the dump. Several of the kids from the Florida church had brought a soccer ball. Language was not a barrier as they started playing with the boys and girls from Mexico who arrived at our gathering place on top of the dump. While some of the adults set up a portable platform, backdrop, generator, and sound system, the children were busy breaking down cultural and language barriers as they played and introduced themselves.

Christian clowns from one of the local churches performed and introduced our group. The singing and ministry time began. It was apparent that age was not a factor. These kids were ready and able to tell the story of Jesus and leave an encouraging message. A lot of lives were changed that day . . . primarily the lives of those of us on the bus!

Judy Comstock, writer and editor

Preteens

But the LORD said to me, "Do not say that you are too young, but go to the people I send you to, and tell them everything I command you to say."

(Jeremiah 1:7, GNT)

L7: Basic Training
A Four-Part, Three-Week Leadership Event!

by Jessica Johnson

L7 stands for, "Live the Seven" the seven words Jesus spoke at the age of twelve, found in Luke 2:49, and those words are . . . "I must be about my Father's business!" This fast-paced four-part, three-week event helps kids step out in areas of leadership by developing who they are in Christ, teaching them life principles essential to life as believers, and training them in the basic elements of ministry. This event requires time and commitment, but has proven for us to be well worth the effort. Tweens will come away with the confidence that comes from endurance and the satisfaction of having finished a good race. After completion of all the requirements, they will enjoy a graduation attended by pastors and parents and friends.

L7 meets for three hours, once a week for four weeks. The best time we have found is summer mornings when kids are out of school. This is also a time when they are not usually at church, making the class seem new and different and creating more expectation.

It has been said that, "I must give up that which is acceptable in order to achieve that which is otherwise unobtainable." These three weeks and four classes give kids an opportunity to really tune into the Lord and grow in their service for him. We believe that the life of Jesus is the greatest model for our kids! He had an awareness of his calling and purpose and was serious about his Father's business plan for his life, even at the age of twelve! We want nothing less for our kids. This program is designed to get kids out of their comfort zone, helping them build the confidence of God in their hearts and letting it show through their lives.

> A big part of the success of this program is that once kids graduate they have a meaningful place to serve in the ministry.

A big part of the success of this program is that once kids graduate, they have a meaningful place to serve in the ministry. In our church, once they graduate, we often call them into ministry through having them stand at the church entrance, welcoming the adults into service using the introduction and handshaking they learned in class. They also ask if they can pray for an adult entering the service that they would have a good service and receive everything the Lord has for them. Our kids have prayed for healing and many other things for people as they enter the building. You will be amazed at how well people respond to young people who step out in ministry and how it encourages them to step out as well. It begins to dawn on them . . . "if a ten, eleven, or twelve year-old can do that, so can I!"

After *L7* graduation, find places for them to serve younger kids, pray for their own peers, clean the facility for work projects, serve food, and so forth. But don't just ask them if they want to help, call them into ministry, call them to serve! Have them wear their *L7* shirts and prepare themselves spiritually and mentally. All of these opportunities to minister in your local church tie them to the larger vision. They no longer see church as a place where they "have to" go to but as a place to give their lives away. They realize they are valuable and needed by leaders and by Jesus to accomplish his great purpose. This solves the typical problem of kids leaving the church after their teenage years because they can't assimilate or integrate into the adult congregation.

Our kids have been serving alongside adults from the tween-age on up as they become adults themselves. They work in tech and lighting departments, go to outreaches, and help on workdays. . . . Say goodbye to the generation gap!

We love it when kids tell their parents they need to be somewhere to minister as opposed to parents being involved in ministry and kids just tagging along. Our *L7* graduates often travel with us to *J12 Encounters* at other churches. They come wearing their *L7* shirts and name badges, helping lead worship, excitedly greeting kids and parents, and praying with kids during ministry time.

Solid, Aware, United

These are the three core teachings platformed throughout the four weeks of the event with the following theme verse:

Hebrews 12:1-2, NKJV: "Therefore we also, since we are surrounded by so great a cloud of witnesses, let us lay aside every weight, and the sin which so easily ensnares us . . . looking unto Jesus, the author and finisher of our faith, who for the joy that was set before Him, endured the cross, despising the shame, and has sat down at the right hand the throne of God. "

> We love it when kids tell their parents they need to be somewhere to minister as opposed to parents being involved in ministry and kids just tagging along.

Solid: we look to "Jesus the author and finisher of our faith" (Hebrews 12: 2, NKJV). Everything that we need to know to live out our lives on earth was encompassed in Jesus. When he came to earth he showed us how to live fully human, filled with the Spirit of God. He showed us how to live connected to our Father and Creator. He showed us what to do.

When we look at him, we get a clear picture of who we are. This causes us to live with dignity and confidence. We often say, "The Jesus they see in me may be the only Jesus they ever see." We have the privilege and personal responsibility to share Jesus through our own eyes, hands, and feet.

Aware: When we become aware of who we are in Christ, we become aware of the vast needs around us. We know we have the answer that is needed, and with Christ living in us we have the ability to do something about it. However, being Christ to people often comes at a price but always gains an eternal reward. "Jesus . . . who for the joy that was set before Him, endured the cross, despising the shame, and has sat down at the right hand of throne of God." Jesus was aware of what being willing to die on the cross would do for humanity. He kept his eye on the goal, the redemption of humanity, He endured the cross (paid the price) and is now sat down at the right hand of God (an eternal reward).

United: When we become aware of the needs around us and are persevering in meeting those needs, we realize we can't do this job on our own. It is going to take all of us, side by side, working together and encouraging each other. ". . . since we are surrounded by so great a cloud of witnesses . . ." All of those that have gone before us, those parents and leaders that are surrounding us now, our brothers and sisters in Christ, are cheering us on to greatness for God.

The secondary teachings:

• **R&R "Read and Rewrite":** They learn how to read the Bible from a daily reading plan and journal about what they are reading. The homework assignments contain journaling, so they immediately get to put what they are learning into practice.

• **Give God 12:** This stands for giving God twelve minutes a day! Whether it's in prayer, memorizing and meditating on the Word, or confessing his Word. For at least twelve minutes a day, they are saying, "Lord I'm yours and I am giving you my time."

• **M&M "Memorize and Meditate":** We challenge tweens to find a Scripture that really speaks to them and memorize it so they can always have it with them. What is memorized can be meditated on anytime, anywhere!

• **P&C "Prayer and Confession":** We encourage them to find a Scripture that speaks to their situation, or someone else's, and use it in prayer and confession concerning that situation. This helps them pray accurately, praying what the Word says about a situation.

• **T&T "Tests and Testimonies":** We teach them to share their testimony of what the Lord has done in their life with others, using "story" as a means to share the good news!

• **Activity time:** All of the activities are designed to give them the opportunity to put what they are learning into practice. This involves role playing with greetings and introductions, praying with others, sharing their testimony in front of the class, and more.

• **Craft time:** These activities are centered around giving and serving. They do projects from creating handmade cards to give to first-time visitors or kids who are sick, making bracelets for orphans with notes letting them know they have been prayed for, to prayer walks around church campus.

• **Coaches:** This is a time when leaders really get to connect with the kids. They spend time going over their homework, answering questions and encouraging each of them in the class.

• **Snack time:** Eat snacks!

Before We Begin

Before we begin this event, we have a meeting with the parents. They are informed of all that will be happening and how important it is for them to be involved and encourage their kids through the program. We are very strict concerning rules such as arriving early for check-in and completing homework. All of this is training for our young leaders and gives them great confidence when they complete the program.

The parents sign an agreement form before their child begins the program. We have found that this really connects us to parents and lets them know how much we want to invest in their kids and how important they are to us. Our goal, in the end, is to raise up a generation of young people that say, "I must be about my Father's business" and equip them with the tools to do it.

Jessica Johnson, writer, speaker, and creative developer, is co-founder of the ministry of Jesus | at | 12. *She is married to Gregg Johnson and together in 2002 they founded the ministry of* Jesus | at | 12 *in response to Gregg's life-long call to reach a generation before they need to be rescued. J12 is based on the story of Jesus found in Luke 2:49-52 where he declares at the age of 12, "I must be about my Father's business." We believe his life, at the age of twelve, is a template for our young people today. Gregg and Jessica serve as J12 Pastors at their home church, The Rock, in Anaheim, California, as well as travel nationally and internationally sharing the vision of* Jesus | at | 12 *through conferences, camps, church services, and J12 Encounters. For more information, our website is: www.J12.com.*

L7: Basic Training

Coach's Binder

L7 Coaches Binders include:

1. Welcome Letter (below)
2. Coaching Guide Sheet (below)
3. Homework Check lists
4. Copy of homework for all weeks of level they are coaching
5. Weekly L7 class schedule (sample included on CD Rom)

L7 Coaches

As a coach, you will be the one that your tweens have the most personal contact with. Each week will have a breakout time that will be spent with your assigned tweens. This is a great time to develop relationship with the tweens, encouraging them to continue on with the class and their homework. To make the most of this time, you need to read through their homework they have been assigned so you understand what they have been learning and can ask relevant questions. The better prepared you are, the more effective you will be and the more impact you will have. Below is a list of items you will need to do each week with your group.

1. Pray for each tween. God will be working in them and there will be many things trying to keep them from finishing and distract them. There may be things they bring up during your breakout time that gives you insight for how and what to pray.

2. Call them once during each week to see how they are doing and encourage them. You have no idea how exciting it is for a tween to get a call from a leader!

3. Use the checklist in your binder to mark their progress. They must be on time and complete their homework each week. If they aren't able to do it, we don't tell them they are "kicked out" but let them know they weren't able to meet requirements so we want them to take it next time. We want them to get everything out of it that they can and allowing them to short circuit that through not doing assignments isn't helping them. Graduating must feel like an achievement, because it is. They must feel the confidence that goes along with having paid a price for something. They will value the Truth that they have answered the call to become ministers.

4. Go through the coaching sheet of questions for that week. Feel free to pull or use anything from that weeks homework into the discussion if it helps the tweens "get it". Have a full understanding of the goal of the homework and the class so that you aren't just asking questions from a list but are engaging the kids, and training them.

COACHING GUIDE SHEET

These are some helpful tips and questions to get your group headed in the right direction. Have fun! (BE SURE TO ALWAYS DO HOMEWORK CHECK FIRST AND THEN MOVE TO DISCUSSION.)

This is your first time with your new group. Consider these kids to be "your little flock" for the next 3 weeks. Really get to know them and allow your anticipation and excitement over this discipleship class come across in all you say and do. Let them know you will be praying for them and calling them during the week to check up on and encourage them. Encourage them to pray for each other during the next weeks as well.

WEEK 1

This weeks focus is on becoming SOLID. Encourage them to do ALL of their homework so they can graduate the program. Encourage them to have fun with asking the questions to people in the homework. (It's number 3 in the homework) Explain to them that the point is for them to get used to starting conversations with other tweens and adults. Take time to pray, and let them pray for each other about the class, the homework, etc. Let them know you will be praying for them during the week and giving them a call to see how they are doing.

WEEK 2

This weeks focus is on being AWARE because we care. If we don't know, we don't care. Some things you might ask or say: Ask them how the homework went. Talk about what they experienced. Ask them what their favorite TAG is and why. Ask them what the toughest thing was about being in discipleship. Pray over those things that the Lord would help them with it this next week.

WEEK 3

This weeks focus is on being UNITED, One mind, One goal, One way, "and the one way is "Jesus". Some things you might ask or say: Ask them how it went when they prayed for the 3 people. Discuss the 3 things they wrote down about how to be more aware of the needs around them. Talk about ways that they can be united with each other and stand together as Christian brothers and sisters and as disciples as well. Encourage them to keep up the homework. Pray that the Lord will help them as they prepare to give their testimonies next week.

WEEK 4

This is your last time with your "little flock". Talk about the highlights of the past weeks and what they are going to do differently or how they have changed since L7. Pray with them to continue on in strength and boldness. Also pray that the Lord would be with them as they give their testimonies.

L7: BASIC TRAINING

Sample Schedule

Name	Time	Assignment
	0:30	Check-in
	0:25	Lesson 1: SOLID
	0:35	Breakout groups (half kids stay for activity time –other half go to craft room
	0:20	Snack break
	0:35	Breakout groups switch (activity time – craft room)
	0:30	Journal groups
	0:25	Lesson 2: How to journal
	0:05	Pray & Dismiss

Notes

For the rest of the weeks, move the journal group/homework check time to the beginning of class. Everyone gathers together in the main room, we pray over the day and then break into journal groups. This schedule was created for larger numbers of kids. It may not take you as much time to move the groups to different rooms or projects. Adjust the time to what fits your needs.

Your class may only last 2 ½ hours as opposed to the full 3. The goal is to keep the time moving. This is a fast paced schedule, which holds the interest of the kids and keeps them engaged. Transition time is included in these times so be sure you end the sessions with enough time so you don't get behind schedule.

© 2010 Abingdon Press

L7: 8 Week Timeline

Reminders/Tips and Pointers

This timeline was designed to facilitate large numbers in a large church. Make any adjustments to fit your needs.

8 Weeks Out

- Gather a core team of volunteers for the following positions:
  - If you are a smaller church some of these roles can be combined.
  - L7 service Coordinator – go to person for everything
  - L7 coach's coordinator – in charge of coaches, child placement, and homework questions.
    - If any child has not completed their homework, they should be sent to you for review. If a child has not completed the homework – I usually give them until the next week to have all of it completed, letting them know that they have to retake the class if they don't have it by next week. I also talk to their parents after class and keep them posted on what is going on. In some cases, our kids can't read or write very well. In these cases, I ask the parent to help. If the parent reads through the homework, discusses it with them and writes the child's answers, that's fine. I still know they are getting the information they need and they are doing the work. If a child doesn't have an involved parent then I would ask the coach to meet with them a separate time and go through the homework with them. "Truth is intention". If a child has intended in his or her heart to do their best and do all that has been asked, then I'm happy. If they meet with their coach and are understanding and learning from the material, then they've accomplished the goal. If a child is trying to get out of doing the work and hoping to slide by, they are not ready for leadership and therefore I have less grace. This is what I do and these are my suggestions. Ultimately you will make the judgement call. I urge anyone to err on the side of what is best for the child for their life-growth.
  - L7 snack coordinator
    - Yummy!
  - L7 "Do Room" coordinator
    - This is the person in charge of crafts. Gathering supplies, working with volunteers, showing kids what to do and helping them do it.

© 2010 Abingdon Press

- L7 Tech – this is for mics, music and DVD (there may be a couple of other video clips you may want to use)
- L7 lesson teachers
  - Meet with core team of volunteers and let them know:
  - What individual assignments will entail, (2)that all of them (except lesson teachers) may need to get people to assist them (3)specify a date by which they need to let you know who is assisting them, (4) walk through general overview of L7 program
  - Request 3+ large rooms for L7 usage in your church
  - Coaches Coordinator should begin to recruit coaches

6 Weeks Out

- Have another meeting with core team to further detail L7 lesson schedule
- Get names and emails from core team of their assistant(s)
- Make L7 flyers to advertise the date, time and location of the program.
- Make L7 signups (student's name, student's mailing address, parent/guardian's name, parent's phone #, parent's email, student's t-shirt size)
- Begin announcing L7 and recruiting kids at all services or when kids are gathered.
- Begin passing out Flyers
- Begin showing L7 video in all services
- Recruit Check-in volunteers for each week of L7
- Recruit a person of high energy to play games, review L7 lessons, etc., during check-in time each week
- Have L7 sign-up sheet available before and after all services with one team member available to answer any and all questions
- Recruit 3-4 people to oversee check-out each week
- Snack Coordinator should begin planning weekly snacks whether they get them themselves or recruit volunteers to bring, etc.

4 Weeks Out

- Have a meeting with the "Do Room" coordinator to make sure all activities are prepared and discuss what items need to be purchased
- Meet with L7 coaches coordinator to discuss how to divide groups up for coaches
  - You know your kids best, try to place them in groups that will be most effective, place females with female coaches and males with male coaches and we usually try to separate good friends so they won't get distracted
- Meet with lesson teachers and communicate with them what they will be teaching on, length of teaching, and any activities to be performed during that teaching time
- Snack coordinator should have snack signup at all services (divide snacks down by items needed)

2 Weeks Out

- Continue promoting L7 in all services
- Continue signups
- Have Coaches Coordinator meet with coaches to explain what their responsibilities are throughout the duration of L7.
- Begin printing and forming L7 binders and Coaches binders
- Make any necessary purchases
- Check-in needs to make sure they have name tags for kids for each week (print first name largely with marker because they will need them for activities)

1 Week Out

- Meet with core team to make sure that everything is set up, everyone is clear on set-up, inform them of what time they are to arrive
- Set up all rooms for L7
- Check on tech and make sure all media/music is previewed
- Complete preparation of L7 binders
- Go over schedule sheet (run sheet) with Service Coordinator
- Make sure Coaches Coordinator has final list of L7 tweens so that he/she can divide them up by gender and by coach. - Make copies of Parent Letter and prep for 15 minute parent meeting that will take place during check-in time the first week of L7.
    - o What parents need to know: We want to see their kids gain everything from the event that they possibly can. We have set it up with certain guidelines for them to follow, fasting certain things and focusing time on certain things. It's really only 3 weeks so they can do it and it will change their life! Following the rules and guidelines are very important to the success of the class. If we are lenient, then attitudes often become lazy. We instill wrong teaching that says you can be lazy, or not follow the rules and it doesn't matter. We never want to enforce that teaching. But we do want to enforce that if they do their best, give this class everything they have, they have an opportunity to graduate. They will have completed something that was not easy to do, giving them confidence in themselves and a belief that they can accomplish other things if they work hard and follow the rules. This is a great lesson for life in general and that is why it is at the core of how we set up the program.
    - o Now go through the guidelines with the parents so that they know the commitment they are getting into as well. It becomes a family affair. Kids are dependant on parents for rides, etc. and they must be on time. They also must attend every class so if a parent isn't able to bring them, they need to find them a ride or take the class next time around. Missing one class is 25%. It isn't fair to the others that are giving up things in order to be there. (I am always positive with parents letting them know it will be best for Johnny or Susie if they wait and take it next time to they won't miss out on any part because it's all too good!) Trust us, this level of commitment will produce tenacity and confidence in your young people with a zeal for being like Jesus! After explaining everything and answering

    questions have the parents sign the agreement form committing to partner with their child.
- o Check in with teacher for week one lesson; make sure they have lesson ready to go and answer any possible questions (does not apply if you are using DVD)
- o Call Snack Coordinator and make sure all snacks are covered.

Day of First L7

- Finish setup of L7 rooms
- Setup Check-in station: need attendance sheets, kids receive their binders, name tags for each week (kids must wear them on their chest so we can see their name!)
- Coaches Coordinator will need to place last minute L7 tween signups in coaching groups and letting coaches know.
- Snack Coordinator – setup snacks
- "Do Room" Coordinator: set up craft area, communicate what the activity is for assistants so they are prepared to help throughout activity
- Service Coordinator: make sure all volunteers have each weeks schedule. Remind people of the times they are needed and expectations. Available to answer questions and work out any problems that might arise.
- Parent Meeting – We do this 30 minutes before first class starts (set a specific time or you will have parents trickle in and have to explain and re-explain)

*Repeat all of Day 1 of L7, minus the parent meeting for the remaining weeks of L7.

L7: Basic Training

Homework

Live the Seven At Home

Homework each week contains daily Bible readings for journaling, prayer (to self and/or out loud). Other assignments contain activities that help them interact with others such as introducing themselves to people, asking questions of interest, finding people with whom they can pray, etc. One of the weeks targets sharing their testimonies and helps them practice and get comfortable sharing about their relationship with the Lord.
*All Bible reading reinforces what they are learning from the class teachings. All activities help them step out and actively "be about their Father's business."

Suggestion: Create homework assignments that encompass what you want your kids to learn about leadership or target your ministries specific areas of need. You may have an area of service that your church is involved in for which kids could be specifically trained.

Gender Wars

The Ultimate Preteen Sleepover!

by Kurt Goble

The chaos is organized. The spontaneity is planned. The lesson is prepped. But your preteens won't notice. They'll be too busy having a blast during this experiential lesson in resolving conflict. Preteens love the spontaneity and excitement of this event.

This is one of my favorite preteen events. The sleepover is designed for a group of ten to eighty students, but you can make adjustments for larger or smaller groups. It is a fellowship and discipleship event, designed to build relationships between students, connect them to the church, and learn something about resolving conflict. It will work differently according to your facilities and volunteer staff, but I'll share how it plays out in my ministry setting.

The Premise

The sleepover is actually billed and promoted as two simultaneous events. We do not call it "Gender Wars." We plan a "Boy's Night" sleepover in one area of the church and a "Girl's Night" in another area. The boy's event is advertised as a night of pizza, soft drinks, games, and movies. For the girls, we advertise a low-key event with dinner, movies, and baking cookies. When our students arrive, they are greeted in separate places by separate volunteers who are running "separate programs." Little do they know that their paths will cross in fun and exciting ways throughout the evening.

The Preparation

Without the knowledge of our preteens, the volunteers who are working with the girls and boys have met for over an hour beforehand. We have reviewed the schedule and planned out every step of the way. We have discussed how we will stay in communication via text messages. We have coordinated our plans for who will go where, when they will go, and what routes they will take. Everything is carefully planned. But the kids will never know it.

The First Strike

When the boys check in, they are told to leave their sleeping bags and pillows in the lobby. Thirty minutes later, the boys are downstairs eating pizza.

Meanwhile, the girls are at the opposite end of the campus finishing their dinner, when one of the volunteers has an idea, "Hey girls. You know how the guys are sleeping over too? I just saw all their stuff in the church lobby. Let's go hide it in the kitchen! Then we can leave them a note saying that they have to do something for us if they want to find out where it is!"

Another volunteer suggests, "Let's make them sing us a song!"

At this point the girls are really excited. They make a "ransom" note, put it in the lobby, and move the boy's bags to the kitchen; running and giggling the whole time.

When the boys finish their pizza, they are told, "Okay guys, go grab your bags and bring them back here."

Of course, the boys come back two minutes later without their bags. One of them is holding the note. They are excited. Jumping up and down, they exclaim, "The girls took our stuff! We have to sing them a song to get it back!"

Boys Strike Back

We decide what to sing, and practice it a few times, and then head off to find the girls. There is lots of laughter as the boys sing to the girls.

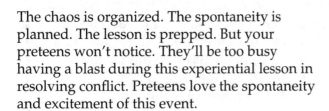

After the performance, they tell us that our stuff is hidden in the kitchen.

But on the way to retrieve the guy's things, I have an "idea." I share it with the boys, and they get ready for their revenge.

I show up by myself in the girl's area five minutes later. "Hey, Girls! Where did you really put our stuff?"

"It's in the kitchen."

"No, it isn't."

"Yes, it is. We left it there. We promise!"

"Okay. You'll have to show me, because I looked, and it's not there."

The girls lead the way to the kitchen, and when they step in, the boys ambush them with Nerf Guns. (Silly string or squirt guns will work as well. Just be prepared to clean up afterwards.)

The girls run out and, of course, begin to plan their lighthearted "revenge."

The evening continues with a series of harmless pranks. Leaders are planting ideas in the students' minds while squelching ideas that might not be so good. As the boys play their

games, and the girls make their cookies, they intermittently go back and fourth "getting" one another. We will send a couple of boys to sneak in and turn off the lights in the girl's room. The girls will put marbles in the boy's pillowcases. The boys will jump out and startle the girls as they make their way to another area of the campus. All of the pranks are harmless, fun, and coordinated by the volunteers and staff.

Finally, it is time for bed. At least, that's what the students think. Leaders announce to the students that it is time to get ready to go to sleep. When kids are quieted, and in their sleeping bags, it is a great time to have an "impromptu" discussion.

The discussion guide can be memorized by a leader, or hidden in his or her Bible. Both boys and girls groups follow the same guide.

Discussion Guide

"That was fun, wasn't it? It was like our own little war between us and the (boys/girls)!"

"What was your favorite part of our little feud?"

"What was the best trick we did to them?"

"What do you think was the best one they did on us?"

"Okay, so that was fun. But have any of you ever been involved in a real feud, where somebody kept doing mean things to you, and you just kept it going?"(*Encourage the kids to share their stories about people they struggle with.*)

"Real feuds aren't so much fun, are they? This makes me think of a couple of feuds in the Bible. One of them happened when Paul was upset with Peter. Peter was not treating some Christians as well as others, and this made Paul angry. We can see what happened in Galatians 2:11."

Galatians 2:11, NIV: When Peter came to Antioch, I opposed him to his face, because he was clearly in the wrong.

This is one of my favorite preteen events. The sleepover is designed for a group of ten to eighty students, but you can make adjustments for larger or smaller groups. It is a fellowship and discipleship event, designed to build relationships between students, connect them to the church, and learn something about resolving conflict.

"How did Paul handle the situation?" (*Point out how Paul confronted Peter directly, and stated his problem. He didn't complain to others, or gossip, or treat him badly. He had enough respect for Peter to state his problem so they could work through it together.*)

"How can we learn from Paul's example?"

"There is another story about how King David tried to resolve a feud with King Saul. Saul was jealous of David, and trying to kill him. We're going to read 1 Samuel 24:1-17 (NIV) to see what happened . . ." (*Read the passage.*)

"How did David resolve his conflict with Saul?"

"How can we repay people good for evil?"

After the discussion, a volunteer will have another "idea."

"You know what would be fun? Let's come up with a fun way to peacefully resolve our feud with the (boys/girls)."

A girl volunteer will say, "Hey, let's take the boys some of the cookies we made."

Another volunteer adds, "We could make them a treasure hunt, with clues to lead them to the cookies. They'll think we're trying to get them again, but they'll find cookies instead!"

The girls have a great time making clues and hiding them.

The boys decide to share their extra soft drinks with the girls. (We happen to have lots of extra cans of soda in an ice chest.) They make notes to attach to the ice chest that say things like, "You Girls Rock!" and "Let's Be Friends." They deliver the ice chest to the girl's area of the building.

After a good night's sleep, we gather all of the kids for a big breakfast before their parents arrive to pick them up.

For this event to be a success, the concepts and details must be highly adapted and customized to your own church setting. The schedule and pranks will have to work for you. This event requires a lot of preparation and planning. But the experience that your preteens receive will be well worth it!

Kurt Goble has made more mistakes than anyone in the history of Children's Ministry. But he loves sharing what he's learned from all those mistakes. For fourteen years Kurt has served as children's pastor at First Christian Church of Huntington Beach, where he shares God's Word with kids through innovative programs. He is a graduate of Bethel College and a curriculum writer. He and Heidi are happily married with two kids.

Service Project Camp

by Annie Waterman

Instead, whoever wants to become great among you must be your servant, and whoever wants to be first must be slave of all. For even the Son of Man did not come to be served, but to serve, and to give his life as a ransom for many.

(Mark 10:43-45, NIV)

"For I was hungry and you gave me something to eat, I was thirsty and you gave me something to drink, I was a stranger and you invited me in, I needed clothes and you clothed me, I was sick and you looked after me, I was in prison and you came to visit me." Then the righteous will answer him, "Lord, when did we see you hungry and feed you, or thirsty and give you drink? When did we see you a stranger and invite you in, or needing clothes and clothe you? When did we see you sick or in prison and go to visit you?" The King will reply, "I tell you the truth, whatever you did for one of the least of these brothers of mine, you did for me."

(Matthew 25:35-40, NIV)

Wow! I'm convinced — how about you? These familiar passages take on a deeper level of meaning when thinking about what it means eternally to provide opportunities for our kids to serve. We have a responsibility to model, teach, and involve our kids in service.

Youth service is also something that is gaining attention on a national level. According to Diane Hedin (1989), "[t]he situations in which young people learn most are ones in which they have the opportunity to determine what needs to be done at developmentally appropriate levels of responsibility." When students are given the opportunities and responsibilities of decision-making in a task that is interesting and important to them, they tend to think more deeply about the issues at hand and "use their most complex thinking skills" (Hedin 1989) to solve the problem. I say, what better place than in our families and church to teach about service! Providing an opportunity for our kids to serve in their church, community, nationally and internationally makes sense.

A camp for sixth graders (those entering or exiting their sixth grade year . . . or fifth grade if that is the last year in children's ministry at your church) was born from participating in organized camps of this nature. While driving two hours to pick up and deliver campers to a work campsite, a few of us thought, "We can do this in our neighborhood. We don't have to send our kids away from home to teach them to serve." From that conversation the seeds were planted for a Service Project Camp that would teach and model service right in our own community. It is a privilege to come alongside preteens and show them how they can serve in ways that will make a difference. What the kids end up learning is that through serving they not only help others but receive blessings in return.

For two years now, we have been offering a week-long camp in conjunction with our evening Family Vacation Bible School. The coordination with Family VBS allowed for some built-in structure and family dinner each night at the church. Of course, this was just an added bonus for our church, but not necessary to doing a similar camp at another church.

We chose our projects for the kids with the idea of showing them ways they can serve in their church, in their community, and internationally without leaving home. Some of the projects require involvement from others in the church for the sake of relationship and numbers. Some of the projects are things the kids can feel equipped to do outside of the camp. By taking a holistic approach, the participants come away with a virtual "tool kit" of service projects. By having the kids stay overnight, they are able to develop relationships with peers. The kids end up not only serving together but debriefing, hanging out, doing Bible studies, and eating together.

> Our kids leave camp excited to continue serving and having had a bonding experience with other kids they will then be going on to youth group with.

Serving Internationally

Find a local organization that serves people internationally. In our area we have access to *World Vision* and *Project Cure*, to name just a few organizations. Take campers to the site, if possible, and let them see the work taking place and how people are contributing. Invite others in the church to partner with you and meet a

specific need, such as collecting items, joining in a specific volunteer effort. In our case, we had our VBS families contribute items that were then packed into boxes for our project. The kids were able to tour the facility, but due to the minimum age requirements to be working on site, we packed the boxes at the church and delivered the finished product to the warehouse.

Serving in the Church

What church doesn't have multiple projects that can be done by a group of eager, available kids? This, of course, takes some planning and oversight. It is wise to not assume that the help is wanted if not planned out ahead of time. Ideas might include: cleaning the parking lot, picking up items in the sanctuary, organizing materials in the classroom, copying printed items, setting up or tearing down for an event, writing or addressing cards, and so forth. Our campers helped prepare some craft items for VBS, set up and cleaned up a meal, and cleaned out supplies in the Children's Ministry classrooms.

Serving in the Community

Does your church have a ministry in the community that could use some help? Is there a place close by the church that would be blessed by some manual labor? Our church has a ministry to several apartment complexes on the north side of town. We connected with the manager of one of the apartments and went for a day of painting, weeding, cooking, and serving lunch to the residents. It was a hard day of manual labor, but the kids enjoyed it, especially talking and serving lunch to the residents. Now when this ministry is discussed in church, the kids have a sense of ownership and knowledge of not only the location but the people themselves.

Homelessness Project

The kids and their parents were made aware of the details of this project prior to the camp. It is important to have information upfront so the parents have the chance to discuss any of their concerns with the leaders and talk with their children.

A few days before the camp started we asked parents to supply a large box for their child. On the last night of camp the kids will be sleeping outside in their box "shelter." Our campers knew that they were leading up to this project on their last day (night) of their camp. There was plenty of discussion each day to prepare the kids.

The kids created a small city out of the boxes and were able to sleep in the clothing they brought with their sleeping bags and pillows. In the morning, we woke them up early and they were told to pack up their boxes and sleeping supplies. They had limited time to dress and were given the choice of a yogurt or cheese sticks for breakfast.

Back at the church, the kids watched a video on homelessness and the issue was discussed — the profile, how to interact with people who are homeless, and most of all how to be a servant and listener.

The kids and staff then traveled together to a designated part of town where they passed out donuts and coffee to people living on the streets. There was plenty of time for conversation with the people being served.

After leaving the area, the kids proceeded to a soup kitchen for senior citizens who are homeless. The kids served lunch to folks and then had an opportunity to sit and eat with people. Here's the exciting part. The kids were energized by their experiences. They weren't depressed or overwhelmed but rather interested and engaged. They did a lot of journaling when they returned to the church and excitedly discussed ways they could continue to be involved in similar outings.

The sixth grade service project camp is near and dear to our ministry. The cost is minimal and is used primarily to fund the projects that the kids are doing. Meals are kept simple, transportation and lodging is covered, but church resources are used as much as possible. Our kids leave camp excited to continue serving and having had a bonding experience with other kids they will then be going on to youth group with.

Annie Waterman is Children's Ministry Director at Colorado Community Church at the Aurora Campus. She has a Bachelor of Arts from the University of California in Psychology and a Master of Arts in Counseling Psychology from the College of Notre Dame. Annie is the mother of two sons. She is passionate about providing spiritual growth opportunities for kids.

Sixth Grade Outreach Camp Information

What to Pack:

• Bible / notebook / writing instruments

• Sleeping bag / pillow

• Toiletries: toothbrush/paste, deodorant, soap, shampoo

• Towel / washcloth

• Pajamas

• Clothes for Tuesday, Wednesday, and Thursday. *An old shirt for the apartment project would be good (painting, weeding, and so forth).*

• • • A VBS shirt will be provided for each kid — they will wear it each day and it will be washed on Monday, Tuesday, and Wednesday nights.

Special Packing Items:

• Please bring lunch, in disposable containers, on Monday when camper meets at church.

• Need a box large enough to sleep in on Wednesday night. Kids will be sleeping outside and the boxes are their shelters. Boxes can be dropped off at my house or to the church. I need boxes by Tuesday. If you need to break the box down to get it to me that is fine, I will duct tape them Wednesday evening (as needed).

• Cell phones are allowed. I want the kids to feel they have access to you whenever they need to (and vice versa). I request that texting be only done during free time (not after lights out or during activities). **Please talk to your child about this.**

• MP3 players and / or gaming systems — PLEASE NO. We may watch a movie and have time on the Wii / video games during down time, but any movie will be G or PG (not PG 13), and games for the Wii will be teen at most (Rock Band and Guitar Hero tend to be favorites and ones that many folks can play at once).

All items should be dropped off with your child on Sunday when they come to VBS. They will be taken to the house and set up for the next evening. Please bring all items (or as many as possible) on Sunday. If anything needs to come on Monday with your child, make sure it fits in a backpack that they can easily identify and take responsibility for.

Schedule

Sunday:

2:00 PM – Arrive at church with all belongings — go over details

2:45 PM – 5:00 PM — VBS preparations / dinner set up

5:00 PM – 6:00 PM — Dinner with Peter and Amey (in Upper Room)

6:00 PM – 6:20 PM — Opening VBS time in Sanctuary

6:20 PM – 6:50 PM — Help with dinner clean up (Peter and Amey with kids)

6:50 PM – 8:15 PM — Bible study, games, hang time with Peter and Amey

8:15 PM – 8:30 PM — Closing VBS time — everyone in Sanctuary

8:30 PM – 8:45 PM — VBS clean up / parents pick up your camper

Monday:

11:00 AM – Arrive at church — bring disposable sack lunch, wear T-shirt

11:00 AM – 3:00 PM — Project Cure kit packing, transport to warehouse, tour of Facility, lunch and return to church

3:00 PM – 4:15 PM — Dinner set up and any VBS prep

4:15 PM – 5:00 PM — Free time in Kid's Space

5:00 PM – 6:00 PM — Dinner with Peter and Amey (in Upper Room)

6:00 PM – 6:20 PM — Opening VBS time in Sanctuary

6:20 PM – 6:50 PM — Help with Dinner clean up (Peter and Amey with kids)

6:50 PM – 8:15 PM — Bible study, games, hang time with Peter and Amey

8:15 PM – 8:30 PM — Closing VBS time — everyone in Sanctuary

8:30 PM – 8:45 PM — VBS clean up — leave for accommodations

9:15 PM – 10:00 PM — Free time / settle in

10:30 PM – Lights out

Tuesday:

8:30 AM – Breakfast

9:30 AM – Depart for apartment project

10:00 AM – 2:00 PM — Work at apartment — serving lunch, weeding, & painting

2:30 PM – Return to church — help with dinner set up and any VBS prep

4:00 PM – Free time in Kid's Space

5:00 PM – 6:00 PM — Dinner with Peter and Amey (in Upper Room)

6:00 PM – 6:20 PM — Opening VBS time in Sanctuary

6:20 PM – 6:50 PM — Help with Dinner clean up (Peter and Amey with kids)

6:50 PM – 8:15 PM — Bible study, games, hang time with Peter and Amey

8:15 PM – 8:30 PM — Closing VBS time — everyone in Sanctuary

8:30 PM – 8:45 PM — VBS clean up — leave for accomodations

9:15 PM – 10:00 PM — Free time / settle in

10:30 PM – Lights out

© 2010 Abingdon Press

Wednesday:

> 8:30 AM – Breakfast
>
> 10:00 AM – Depart for Church project
>
> 10:30 AM – 4:00 PM — Work at church and in strip mall on various projects (lunch served)
>
> 4:00 PM – Free time in Kid's Space
>
> 6:00 PM – 6:20 PM — Opening VBS time in Sanctuary
>
> 6:20 PM – 6:50 PM — Help with Dinner clean up (Peter and Amey with kids)
>
> 6:50 PM – 8:15 PM — Bible study, games, hang time with Peter and Amey
>
> 8:15 PM – 8:30 PM — Closing VBS time – everyone in Sanctuary
>
> 8:30 PM – 8:45 PM — VBS clean up – leave for accommodations
>
> 9:15 PM – 10:00 PM — Free time / settle in / clean up all belongings possible
>
> 10:30 PM – Lights out (sleeping in backyard in box and sleeping bag)

Thursday:

> 7:00 AM – RISE AND SHINE — pack up, minimal breakfast
>
> 8:00 AM – Depart for Church
>
> 8:30 AM – Preparation with Pastor for Homeless project
>
> 9:00 AM – 2:30 PM — Homeless project, help serve lunch at the Summit
>
> 3:00 PM – Return to church — help with dinner set up and any VBS prep
>
> 4:00 PM – Free time in Kid's Space
>
> 6:00 PM – 6:20 PM — Opening VBS time in Sanctuary
>
> 6:20 PM – 6:50 PM — Help with Dinner clean up (Peter and Amey with kids)
>
> 6:50 PM – 8:15 PM — Bible study, games, hang time with Peter and Amey
>
> 8:15 PM – 8:30 PM — Closing VBS time – everyone in Sanctuary
>
> 8:30 PM – 8:45 PM — VBS clean up — Picked up by family

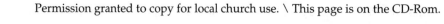

"Takin' it to the Streets"

More information on outreach projects

Date:	Activity:	Description:
Monday: June 14th	Project Cure	Packing medical supplies/visit facility
Tuesday: June 15th	Apartment Project	Painting laundry room/weeding
Wednesday: June 16th	Church	Cleaning church/businesses
Thursday: June 17th	Summit Senior	Center Coffee to homeless/lunch to seniors

Project Cure:
This outreach is one of our Strategic Ministry Partners. Its mission is providing medical supplies to dozens of improvised countries around the world. Contact Person: Fred Smith. Phone: 888-555-1212

Nome Apartments:
This ministry has been in operation for over ten years. Its mission is to be "The Church On the Block" providing caring adults the resources to minister to at-risk children and youth in the urban core of Aurora. Contact Person: Jane Smith. Phone: 888-555-1212

Church:
The mission is to serve the local church by cleaning and general maintenance of the property and the surrounding area including the local business. Contact Person: Annie Waterman. Phone: 888-555-1212

Urban Immersion Mission:
In co-operation with Pastor Jim, all participates will engage in transformational serving projects in two separate locations. 1.) Serve Denver's homeless on the square adjacent from the Denver Rescue Mission by offering coffee and donuts. 2.) Serve lunch at the Summit Senior Center for 40 plus homeless and low income adults.

Pastor Jim will be equipping and training all participants prior to this educating and heartfelt need to serve the "least among us." Contact Person: Pastor Jim G. Phone: 888-555-1212

Registration Form for Sixth Grade Service Project Camp

For kids entering Sixth or Seventh grade in Fall 2010

Dates: Sunday June 13 — Thursday June 17   Location: See Schedule

Cost: $75 per child

The Camp fee is attached to this form: **Yes** ❑ **No** ❑ Check Number_____

Parent / Guardian's Name:_____

DOB_____ **Family E-mail address:**_____

Address:_____

_____

Phone Number:_____**(home)** _____**(cell)**

Child Name:_____

DOB_____ **Age by Camp**_____ **Grade in Fall 2010**_____

Date Form Received:_____ Date Payment Received:_____

For more information on the particulars of this camp please contact Annie at awaterman@ccc.org or 888-555-1212.
Extensive information and Parent Consent forms will be sent home in May.
Limit of 13 kids.
Volunteers needed: parents who could volunteer one day on a service project would be greatly appreciated. Let Ms. Annie know your availability.

General Notes and Consent Form for Sixth Grade Service Camp

Must be attached to the 6th Grade Camp Registration Form

Special Note: ***Sixth Grade Camp Participants should be prepared to be outside and extremely active for 3 to 5 hours a day. Due to the nature of activities, minor injuries may occur.***

I have read the Special Note: _____

(parent signature required)

I give all Leaders permission to treat minor bumps and bruises. This may include the application of bandages or ice. Parents will be notified of all injuries, no matter how small. For injuries that may be of a more serious nature such as a head bump, bad bruise, or cut a parent will be notified immediately and treatment can continue on-site if the parent agrees. In case of a serious injury that would require transport to a hospital, I give all Church Leaders permission to make arrangements for ambulance transportation to a hospital if I or my emergency contact cannot be reached in a timely manner.

I consent to this Special Note: _____

(parent signature required)

I give _____ Church permission to photograph or video all children whose registration accompanies this form. Photographs or video may be used only for the promotion of the Programs at Colorado Community Church or produced as a movie or slideshow that would be shown to the members or parents of Colorado Community Church.

Photo Release Consent *

I consent to the Photo Release Consent: _____

(parent signature required)

Special Needs

If you have a child with Special Needs and would like to sign them up for 6th Grade service Camp, please contact our CCC Children's Ministry at 888-555-1212.

Does your child have Special Needs? (please circle below)

Yes   No

Permission granted to copy for local church use. \ This page is on the CD-Rom.

© 2010 Abingdon Press

EVENTS THAT WORKED FOR US 173

The Main Event: Special Events for your Preteens

by Katie Gerber

More life changing decisions are made during special events than any other time in your ministry calendar. So why do events with your preteens? Think about it, if your preteen only comes three times a month and you multiply that by twelve months. That is only thirty-six hours a year you see your preteen. That is almost the same amount of time an overnight event is. Events give you more of that one-on-one time with your student that you do not usually have on a Sunday morning. Here are a few tested ideas.

Incredible Love

It's important for the students to realize that the world doesn't revolve around them. Give them opportunities to serve others. Older adults are a great group to tap into with an event like Incredible Love. It is an overnighter event where we serve brunch to the seniors of our church.

Students arrive on a Friday night and spend the evening preparing for the brunch and doing fun team building games, sleep at the church, and then serve Saturday brunch. During the brunch we do our best to try and bring a little preteen world into the older adults' lives and a little of the older adults' lives into the preteen world. We have done a few preteens games with the seniors, and we always end with a hymn sing. It is very special seeing multigenerations singing songs that a lot of our preteens aren't used to singing.

It is very important to prepare and set expectations for your preteens before the seniors arrive. Brainstorm different conversation ideas and talk about how they should act. If you let them know what their expectations are, they will rise to it.

Schedule for Incredible Love

Friday
6:00 PM – 6:20 PM — Arrival and Activities
1. Making valentine cards for the Seniors
2. Four-Square taped on the floor
3. Circle Ball taped on the floor

6:20 PM – 6:45 PM — Rundown of Expectations and details
6:45 PM – 8:00 PM — Set up for Saturday
1. Make Favors
2. Decorate Tables
3. Sharpen Pencils/Put in Cup
4. Table Cloth, Silverware, Napkins
5. Valentine cards
6. Reserved for fifth & sixth grade cards
7. Set up morning program
8. Get two students to open/close prayer

8:00 PM – 8:40 PM — Game
8:40 PM – 10:00 PM — Movie/Snack (Facing the Giants)
10:00 PM – 10:30 PM — Prayer & Movie Wrap-up
11:00 PM – 11:30 PM — Get Ready for Bed
11:30 PM – Lights Out

Saturday
7:15 AM – 8:00 AM — Get up/dress/pack/ Light Breakfast
8:00 AM – 8:20 AM — Devotions
8:20 AM – 8:30 AM — Rundown of morning/final preparations
8:30 AM – 9:15 PM — Meet & Greet/Seat Guest (Coffee, Drinks)
9:15 AM – 9:40 AM — Prayer by Student: Serve breakfast & eat
9:40 AM – 10:00 AM — Get to know you games
1. Boggle (with Foam Letters)
2. Discussion Question (table)
3. Two Truths & a Lie (share two things that are true and one thing that is not true and try and guess the untruth)

10:00 AM – 10:20 AM — Sharing Talent (Dancers, Couple of Piano players)
10:20 AM – 10:45 AM — Hymn Sing (All students on stage)
10:45 AM – 10:55 AM — Students give their table the pictures to take home, & their addresses
10:55 AM – 11:00 AM — Prayer & Dismissal

Example Overview

When:

Where:

What Went Well:

What Went OK:

What Would We Change:

Administration & Other Details:

Mission Possible

Mission trips can be done with preteens if you have specific details all in order. First, make the project accomplishable. The students need to see their project completed. A few great mission projects would include painting (get an adult to do the trim), yard work, cleaning, and leading younger kids in a mini VBS. We take our city preteens to a church in the country, partner with them on a project, and have the preteens lead their children services on Sunday. We never go more than two hours away, and we do not stay in a hotel. We either tent it or sleep inside the visiting church. Really, you can make a "Mission Trip" right in your backyard. Find people in your church who really need some extra help around their house.

Preteens can and do serve well, however they need breaks, lots of breaks or else they get frustrated and a little unmotivated. We would break up the work with special activities during the day, whether it was going swimming or

planning their Sunday morning worship service for the kids. This really helped keep them stay motivated.

Mission Possible Schedule

Friday July 21:
12:01 PM – 2:30 PM — Prayer Circle with Parents

2:30 PM – 3:30 PM — Set up Camp

3:30 PM – 5:30 PM — Go to Site/Serve

5:30 PM – 6:30 PM — Dinner

6:30 PM – 8:30 PM — Go back to Site/Serve

8:30 PM – 9:30 PM — Head back to Camp, Get cleaned up

9:30 PM – 10:00 PM — Campfire, S'mores, Devotion

10:00 PM – 10:30 PM — Get Ready for Bed

10:30 PM – Good Night

Saturday July 22:
7:00 AM – 7:30 AM — Wake-Up/Breakfast

7:30 AM – 8:00 AM — Morning Devo's

8:00 AM – 12:00 PM — Go to Site/Serve

12:00 PM – 1:00 PM — Lunch at park

1:00 PM – 3:00 PM — Go back to Site/Serve

3:00 PM – 5:00 PM — Prepare for Sunday

5:00 PM – 5:30 PM — Supper

6:15 PM – 9:30 PM — Bowling

9:45 PM – 10:15 PM — Get Ready for Bed

10:15 PM – Good Night

Sunday July 23
7:00 AM – 7:30 AM — Wake-Up/Breakfast

7:30 AM – 8:00 AM — Morning D-Voes

8:00 AM – 9:00 AM —Tear Down Camp/
Pack Up

9:00 AM – 10:00 AM — Prepare for Children's
Worship

10:00 AM – 12:00 PM — Church

12:00 PM – 1:00 PM — Lunch

1:00 PM – 2:00 PM — Goodbye Celebration

2:00 PM – 4:00 PM — Drive back

Packing List
1. BIBLE
2. Sleeping Bag
3. Grubbing Clothes (Clothes that can get dirty & painted) Fri. & Sat.
4. Pillow
5. Tent if you have one *See how many we need
6. Toiletries
7. Swim suit-to be used for showering on Saturday night
8. Clothes for Church—nice jean shorts or jeans and a nice shirt plus one extra set of clothes for bowling on Saturday night.
9. Flip Flops
10. Sunscreen
11. Bug Spray
12. TENNIS SHOES
13. Sleeping Clothes
14. Flashlight
15. Towel for Shower on Saturday night
16. Medication if need be

Mystery Nights

A great way to jazz up any event is to call it a Mystery Night. Plan an event and only tell the parents where you are going. Give them a few clues, but try to leave them in the dark until they arrive at the designated place. Example of clues: Feet, Air, Flying . . . we took them to an inflatable bounce place.

Examples of where we have gone for our Mystery Nights:

Bowling	Roller Skating
Ice Skating	Cookout/Hayride
Polaroid Scavenger Hunt	Bounce Zone
Western Night	Movie Night
Amazing Race Night	Laser Tag
Indoor Rock Climbing Gym	

Sardine Night (Opposite hide and seek, two people hide and everyone goes and tries to find them, once they do they hide with them.)

Blast Week

A while back we noticed that we were loosing our preteen attendance at our VBS. We decided to try something special, an "Extreme VBS" just for preteens. We decided it would be great to run it at night and we only went from Sunday Night through Thursday Night. We came up with a simple formula that worked very well for us.

Dividing the night into three sections:
1. Special event
2. Food
3. Worship/Guest Speaker.

This event is a great time to invite different staff members, elders, or deacons to speak for you. Make sure you are not doing all the speaking; let the students hear from other people; they hear from you all the time.

Section 1 (6:30 PM – 7:40 PM) Special Event
Section 2 (7:40 PM – 8:00 PM) Food
Section 3 (8:00 PM – 9:00 PM) Worship time and
guest speaker

Here are examples of Special Events that we have done:
- Laser Tag
- Napolean Dynamite Night

- Survivor Night
- Fear Factor Night
- Rock Climbing
- Inflatables
- Amazing Race

Crossing

The final and most important event that we do is called "The Crossing." This is a yearly overnight event where we partner with our Junior High (Middle School) leader and say goodbye to our sixth graders. Once this weekend is over they are officially in Junior High (Middle School). You can do this event in many ways, but there are a couple of things that we do that make it very special for the students.

The weekend is divided equally amongst the preteen and Junior High (Middle School) leaders. The preteen leader is in charge of Friday Night, and the Junior High (Middle School) leader is in charge of Saturday. We usually give the students a chance to share their favorite preteen memory and show pictures/video of the past two years. We also have them each write encouragement notes to each other. We end Friday night with the "Crossing."

We try to find a bridge or a longer path that they have to cross over. I begin by reading a special letter and then tell them they are about to cross over into Junior High (Middle School). I leave them and go to the middle of the path where they are going to cross. One at a time they are sent to me, I say a personal goodbye, put a special cross necklace on them, and say "Welcome to Junior High" (Middle School).

Once they get to the end of the walkway, the Jr. High leaders and students are there to welcome them. If a current seventh grader had attended the crossing in sixth grade and showed great leadership they are invited back to participate in the crossing the following year.

After they have "crossed" they are officially in Junior High (Middle School). We normally allow them to stay up a little later. In the preteen ministry we are pretty strict about their bed time because they need their sleep. So right off the bat they are allowed to stay up later in their rooms

talking. At least the girls talk, I don't know what goes on in the boys room. I'm guessing they are talking too . . . ha, ha, ha!

The next day we try to get all the students on some team building/rope course with a zip line or a rock wall. This is a great way for the new Junior High (Middle School) students to form trust.

On a side note, if you have a church camp or any other camp nearby that has all these facilities this is a great place for the crossing to take place.

Crossing Schedule: Subject to Change

Friday:

5:30 PM – Check-in & Load Buses
5:45 PM – 6:45 PM — Travel to Camp Allendale
6:45 PM – 7:00 PM — Unload Bus/Get settled in dorms
7:00 PM – 7:45 PM — Preparing to Cross
  *Give encouragement card directions
  *Go down Memory Lane
  *Show slide show presentation of the past two years
8:00 PM – 8:30 PM — *Volunteers say goodbye & pray with them
  * Katie will say words of encouragement to all the kids and give them each a cross/letter
  *They walk to the Jr. Highers
8:30 PM – 9:30 PM — Jr. High get-to-know-you games
9:30 PM – 10:30 PM — Campfire
  *Smores
  *Testimonies
  *Worship time
10:30 PM – 11:00 PM — Get ready for bed
11:00 PM – 11:30 PM — Chat time with the Jr. High students (Down time in their dorm rooms)

Saturday:

7:15 AM – Wake up/ Pack up
8:00 AM – Breakfast

8:45 AM – 9:15 AM — Devo's
9:15 AM – 10:00 AM — talks about what Jr. High/ Middle School is going to be like and maybe a few Jr. High/Middle School stories
10:00 AM – 12:00 PM — Climbing Wall/Zipline/ split up into 2 groups
12:00 PM – 1:00 PM — Lunch
1:00 PM – 3:00 PM — Climbing Wall/Zipline/split up into 2 groups
3:00 PM – 3:45 PM — Encouragement Cards/Pass out Cards
3:45 PM – 5:00 PM — Final prayer circle/ load bus
Head back to church

12 Practical Tips to Help Make Your Preteen Event go Smoother

1. Designate someone else to do your registration.
   - This will free you up to answer the hundreds of questions you will be getting from parents and students.
2. Always have a plan B, C, and D planned.
   - What happens when the bus is 45 minutes late?
   - Student breaks a tailbone during a game?
   - It's raining for your outside event: NOW WHAT?
3. God's Word is the Last Word.
   - For all overnights make sure you have a plan for getting everyone to sleep. Instead of threatening to call their parent's or moving them, why don't you let them talk an extra 5 to 10 minutes and then do "God's Word is the Last Word." Once you pray, that's it, no more talking.
4. Absolutely no electronics allowed.
   - They can live one night without their cell phone/gaming system.
   - They are distractions and keep them from participating with the group.
5. Announce the departure time at least twenty to thirty minutes earlier than when you have to leave. Unless you plan on leaving students behind which is completely up to you.
6. Always have a Nurse or an Assigned Medical Person along on overnight trips.
   - Our goal is to have one with us at all times, this doesn't always happen.
   - Preteens are prone to accidents.
7. If at all possible visit the location you are going to ahead of time.
   - A side note: make sure that your map is correct. Please don't rely solely on computer directions because they can fail you.
8. Make friends with your Junior High/Middle School pastor or leader.
   - Your preteens are heading there next anyway and you want the best transition possible for them. Invite a few Jr. High leaders on your events beginning after Christmas.
9. Create a Medication Box for all student prescriptions/drugs.
   - Have it at the check-in table so parents can put it in write away. Include baggies, sharpies, pens & paper in the box for the parent to write instructions.
10. Parents like to feel secure when they are dropping their student off. Have Emergency Cards made up so that they are informed with all the up-to-date happenings of your event.
    - I put my name and my cell phone, where we will be heading, what time we will be returning, and any other important information they might need. (This has been a huge hit with the parents.)
11. Always evaluate your event when it is over.
    - Our children's minister makes all of us do this and it should be in her e-mail box no later then a week later. (For me, I try and do this as soon as I am finished so it is fresh in my mind.)
12. Send a thank-you note to all your volunteers who came on the event with you.

Memory Lane

There have been many moments along our Preteen events journey that I wish I could turn back and have a "re-do." Here are just a few; enjoy.

Buses Buses Buses: When traveling by bus make sure you ask them to arrive at least thirty minutes before your students are to arrive. I have had to wait and wait and wait, and sweat it out praying that the bus would show up on time.

Those Hockey Games: So, I thought taking our preteens to a minor league hockey game would be fun. I mean, surely they are family-friendly. Right? Little did I know that when the home team scores a goal they chant a nonfamily-friendly chant. I was mortified that I had taken a group of impressionable preteens and promoted an event that was saying really not nice things. If I would have gone to see a hockey game before, I wouldn't have chosen to take the students. From this moment on I visit every place/event ahead of time.

No Electronics Allowed: A few years back I had a student bring his brand-new Blackberry to our youth group. Yes, I had a fifth grader with a much better phone than myself. We were playing a game and he happened to fall right on his brand-new Blackberry (a few days old). Guess what happened. It broke. That was a fun conversation to have with the parents. "Yes, I know that you spent a lot of money for that phone and I am sorry that the phone was broken, and no the church will not be replacing it. Have a great day and remember Jesus loves you."

Games, Games, Games: I love to research and try out new games with the students. One game I saw showed taking an Alka Seltzer® tablet and making it into a necklace. Each person was given a necklace to wear along with a cup with water. Water buckets were placed around the playing area. On the word go, the students would run around trying to make everyone else's Alka Seltzer® fall off the string by throwing cups of water on each other. The last one with the Alka Seltzer® still attached to their string/necklace wins. Sounds like a VERY fun game right? Well, I didn't realize that Alka Seltzer® sizzles and tends to get into eyes when placed close to the face. It stings really bad and makes preteens cry. I will never, ever, play with Alka Seltzer® around students necks again.

Communion Meditations: I am famous for having a great thought right before I talk and saying that thought out loud without completely thinking through the whole idea. One Sunday as I was literally walking up to the stage an idea of a Communion meditation went through my head. So I throw the one I had practiced out the window and went with this fleeting thought. My subject went from a mouse found in my house, to the mice cutting through the rope of Aslan in the Chronicals of Narnia, to going to the movies, to Jesus dying on a cross. My subject went all over the place.

I am all about listening to the Spirit, but sometimes you need to slow down and really think through what you are going to say. We only have such a short time with these students, don't waste any moments with them. God put you with those students, give them the best that you have.

After graduating from Cincinnati Christian University in 2001, Katie Gerber served nine years at East 91st Street Christian Church in Indianapolis, Indiana. She started a new preteen program and with God's grace it grew from twenty students to over one hundred and fifty. For the last two years at East 91st, the focus of Katie's ministry changed to include all large group worship and teaching for kids four years old to fouth grade. In 2010 God called her family out East to Joppa, Maryland, where she and her husband both serve on staff at Mountain Christian Church. She is currently the Children's Elementary Director and launched a new preteen program called Mt. 54. *Katie and her husband Pat reside with their beautiful daughter, Hannah, in Edgewood, Maryland.*

Serving His Kid,

Katie Gerber
Elementary Director
Mountain Christian Church
1824 Mountain Rd.
Joppa, MD 21085
410-877-1824
katiegerber@mountainchristian.org

The Inside Scoop

When one of my quiet preteen students who was not known for sharing personal issues began talking about her mother, I listened closely with an understanding that she had a real concern. Sameer told me that her mom had "rocks in her side."

Now, there was a little language barrier, but I thought I understood what she said. Her family had come to the United States as refugees from a war-torn country. Women in this country were often abused. I began picturing her mother on the ground with rocks being thrown at her. I had obviously watched one too many television news shows.

As Sameer continued talking about her mother, I realized that she was talking about her mother's health. Her mother had not been a victim of abuse . . . she did not have rocks in her side . . . she had gall stones.

I learned a lesson that day about not jumping to conclusions. I told Sameer that I would pray for her mother to quickly recover.

Judy Comstock, writer and editor

As a consultant for a major Christian publishing company, I would annually participate in VBS curriculum review nights at Christian bookstores. On one such evening, the four other VBS representatives and I were chatting with early attendees at our respective display tables. Suddenly, a gentleman standing next to my table collapsed. It became clear that he was in physical distress and required help.

"Does anyone know CPR?" I cried out, and thankfully, a nurse and friend quickly came to his aid. An ambulance was soon called, and our event halted until he was carried out by attendants.

With sirens fading and a somber atmosphere, the eager bookstore manager quickly introduced me as the first presenter of the evening. My VBS presentation title? "God's Wonderful Surprises."

Cindy Ziemba, Director of Children's Ministry
Ward Evangelical Presbyterian Church
Northville, Michigan

Emily Tisdale was in kindergarten when I became her Children's Pastor. Her mother assisted with the children's choir and her dad, a custom furniture maker, helped construct a large set for children's church. Emily and her family were faithfully involved in the church. One of my memories of Emily took place a few months before her fourth grade year. I happened to be walking in front of Emily and her mother as they headed to the girls' cabin to gather her belongings. Lynn Tisdale asked her daughter what her favorite part of camp had been. As I eavesdropped, I expected Emily to say how much she enjoyed the crafts, swimming, and archery. Emily's response was an early indication of her desire for spiritual things. Her favorite part of summer camp had been learning about The Tabernacle each morning during the chapel Service.

It is not surprising to me that Emily Tisdale has responded to God's call on her life. She and her husband, Carlos Romero, work as missionaries with the Mayan Indians in the mountains of Guatemala. She describes herself as "sold out for Jesus." Emily is also a mother of three children and is involved in a program to provide milk, vitamins, and medicine to undernourished children. Her favorite scripture is Ephesians 2:10, NIV, "For you are God's workmanship, created in Christ Jesus to do good works, which He prepared in advance for you to do."

Judy Comstock
Writer and Editor

Special Needs

Let the little children come to me;
do not stop them; for it is to such as these
that the kingdom of God belongs.

(Mark 10:14b)

Hark! The Herald Angels Sing

An Angel Breakfast Celebrating Ministry to Children with Special Needs

by Patty Smith

When my son Patrick was diagnosed with autism, my approach to ministry changed dramatically. The children's ministry I was leading no longer was meeting the needs of all of the children. Providing ministry to children with special needs was now a necessity, not only for my son but also to the other children God would soon send our way. A team was assembled and we prayerfully and creatively shaped the new ministry — HALOS.

HALOS, Helping All Loved Ones Succeed, partnered each child with special needs, ages three to twelve, with a dedicated ministry partner or "Angel." These specially trained, passionate, and patient angels guided the child with special needs during typical ministry opportunities, modifying and adapting the curriculum, environment, and relational moments to meet the needs of their special friend.

The response was tremendous. We heard success stories from parents, the children, and Sunday school teachers. Angels told stories about how their special friend was ministering to them! Our God-inspired efforts were building the kingdom.

Children with special needs experienced Jesus' love, typical children demonstrated Jesus' love as new friendships were formed, and parents discovered firsthand the love and support of being part of a community of believers who valued all of God's children. We were living out the meaning of our acronym. HALOS ministry was helping all loved ones succeed!

As children's ministry staff members, we wanted to celebrate the success of the ministry, but more importantly honor the angels and special friends in the ministry.

We tossed around several ideas based on the why, how, and what of the HALOS ministry.

Why did the ministry exist? To bring the Good News of Jesus Christ to children with special needs.

How? Through creating ministry opportunities that were safe, friendly, and age-appropriate.

What? By pairing ministry Angels with children with special needs.

Finally, one of the planning team members shouted a familiar Bible verse that was echoed by other Angels, "Do not be afraid, I bring you Good News of great joy!" The planning team cheered as they affirmed that the Angels in our HALOS ministry bring the Good News of Jesus Christ to children with special needs joyfully and safely each week.

The HALOS Angel Breakfast, a special Christmas event to honor the Angels, special friends, and families in our HALOS ministry was born!

In addition to honoring the members of the ministry, this event also provided a special place for children with special needs and their families to experience the Christmas story. Often typical Christmas pageants, worship services, and programs are too long and noisy for children with special needs. Keep that in mind as you plan your special needs ministry Christmas celebration.

Here's how we planned, executed, and followed up the event.

Spread Your Wings

We invited everyone in our congregation to be a part of this special event. Our team prayed about who had the gifts we needed to make this event extra special. When a potential servant was mentioned, a team member called that person and invited him or her to serve on the team. The response was overwhelming. And, here's why. We invited people with passion to serve children using the gifts God had already given them. We didn't ask people to do something they'd never done before. We simply harnessed their passion for doing what they love!

The list of ministry partner roles we offered included:

Angel Breakfast Director

Responsibilities:
- Creates an event of fellowship, fun, and family time on the first Saturday in December where special needs ministry volunteers (angels), children with special needs, and their parents share in celebrating ministry together and the birth of Jesus Christ.
- Leads a team of ministry partners to execute the event. Works closely the children's ministry leader.

Heavenly Decorators

- Create a kid-friendly environment for the Angel breakfast. Make clouds out of foam core board and hang them from the ceiling. Use gold, silver, and white tablecloths. Create fluffy cloud centerpieces out of tufts of polyester fiber fill.
- Form small halos out of gold and silver chenille and stick them in the polyester fiber fill.
- Make or purchase angel frames and put a photo of each child with his or her angel in the frame. Place these frames in the center of the white clouds on the table.
- Top off your table decorations with fun angel-themed relationship builders. NOTE: It's important to avoid conversation starters here since some kids do not speak using words. Keep them simple and be sure to include options for kids who cannot speak or hear. We wrote our conversation starters on strips of gold ribbon and draped them around the clouds.

Heavenly Hellos

- Greets guests and guides them to their table. Helps carry breakfast plates to tables for families.

Heavenly Chef

- Plans menu for breakfast, taking into consideration the dietary needs of the children who will attend.
- Shops for food supplies and paper products.
- Recruits chef's helpers to prepare and serve food during the event.
- Directs and cheerleads cleanup after the breakfast.

Angel Worship Leader

- Recruits Angel Worship team members that may include children's choirs, men's choirs, or other people who love to make a joyful noise. Gathers worship team members to practice songs.
- Chooses songs for Angel Breakfast.
- Leads participants in music during breakfast.
- Prepares, in cooperation with Angel Tech Team, PowerPoint® presentations with song lyrics and images.

Angel Tech Team Leader

- Recruits people to take photographs and operate the tech equipment during the event.
- Works closely with the Angel Worship Leader and the Angel Breakfast Director to ensure PowerPoint® presentations are compiled and photographs are taken before (during ministry moments) and during the event.

Scarf Angels

- Have youth in your church create Christmas scarves to give the guests at your Angel Breakfast. The scarves are easy to create. Follow these directions:

1. Purchase a few yards of patterned, colorful fleece fabric.
2. Make a scarf pattern out of paper or cardboard.
3. Have youth trace the pattern on the fabric.
3. Cut out the scarf and fringe the ends.

Before the Event

- Shout It from the Mountain Tops (early and often).
- Survey the members of your special needs ministry and determine what time works best for them. Then pick your date and time.
- We held our breakfast on the first Saturday morning in December. It began promptly at 9:00 AM. and ended at 10:30 AM. These hours worked best for our kids.
- Place The Angel Breakfast on your church's calendar, as soon as possible. This will prevent conflicts with other ministry programs and encourage maximum participation by HALOS ministry members.
- Start publicizing the event in September. Let Angels, their special friends, and family members know about The Angel Breakfast in December. If possible, send out save-the-date postcards months in advance. You can do this via snail mail or use electronic invitations from services such as Evite (evite.com) or Smilebox® (smilebox.com).
- Six weeks before your event, send via e-mail and snail mail the official invitation for the Angel Breakfast to Angels, and parents. Be sure to include all pertinent information and communicate clearly the purpose of the celebration. Follow up the invitation with personal phone calls.
- Place reminders in the church bulletin, newsletter, and on posters around your church. Keep the upcoming Angel Breakfast front and center in the minds of your church members.

Plan Your Menu

Children with special needs usually have dietary restrictions or special food preferences. Your Angel Breakfast can easily accommodate their food needs by following these recommendations:

Breakfast Baskets

Create individual breakfast baskets for each special needs child, the child's Angel, and parents. Call parents and ascertain each child's favorite foods and place those items a colorful basket. We had many kids that followed gluten-free diets. Our breakfast baskets contained gluten-free muffins, breads, bagels, fruit salad, and a variety of jellies and jams. Coffee, juice, and heavenly hot chocolate were offered self-service.

Breakfast Buffet

Call parents and ascertain each child's favorite foods. Make a list of all the items. Create a breakfast buffet using the items most frequently mentioned by parents. Our buffet contained gluten-free pancakes/waffles, breakfast potatoes, sausage, bacon, fruit, eggs, and fruit salad. In addition to the standard breakfast condiments, we offered sugar-free syrup and a dairy-free butter alternative. Be sure to label the items on your buffet as gluten-free or casein-free, when appropriate.

Bring Your Own Breakfast (B.Y.O.B)

Give families the option to bring their own breakfast. Many families choose this option especially when their child requires liquid meal supplements and other hard to find specialty foods. When families choose this option, provide food for the ministry Angel and parents.

When families arrive, have greeters escort them to their table where they can unpack their breakfast.

Serve juice, coffee, tea, and other breakfast beverages with any of these options.

The Breakfast

Welcome families and Angels and direct them to their special table. Pray and enjoy breakfast first. Most children with special needs follow a strict routine that includes specific mealtimes. After breakfast, you can follow this schedule or rearrange it to meet your ministry needs.

Hark the Herald "Angels" Sing

Lead everyone in a few Christmas carols. Choose a few upbeat songs and one slower song. Monitor the volume of your songs. Loud noises can be painful for some children with special needs. If you have children who cannot sing, offer a few musical instruments such as bells or tambourines for them to shake during the songs.

Use worship software like PowerPoint® or EasyWorship and project the lyrics on the screen. Add images to the lyrics as well. This helps adults remember the words and shows children what the words mean.

We sang "Joy to the World," Hark! the Herald Angels Sing," and "Go, Tell It on the Mountain." Keep in mind, less is more.

Go Tell It on the Mountain

Have your pastor lead attendees through a succinct, interactive, sensory-filled presentation of the Christmas story. Provide objects the children can touch, hear, taste, see, and smell throughout the story. Direct your "Angels" and parents to guide their children to interact with these items as prompted by the storyteller.

Good News of Great Joy! (Share Your Ministry Moments)

Treat guests to a special slide show highlighting your "Angels" and children with special needs in action. You can use a Smilebox® template to create your ministry moments side show. It's as easy as 1, 2, 3! Go to smilebox.com and follow the steps.

Be sure to include photos of every child, his or her Angel, and the parents if possible. If you're missing a photo of someone at the last minute, take a quick photo at the beginning of the breakfast and add it to your presentation. Make your presentation about two to three minutes long. You'll keep everyone's attention and leave them begging for more! Be sure to take additional photos at the breakfast. You'll use them as part of your follow-up.

Away in a Manger— Wrapped in Jesus' Love

Have your youth ministry create winter scarves as a mission project for the Angel Breakfast. Give the scarves to the kids, parents, and Angels in the ministry.

Create a closing blessing using the scarves as a reminder of the gift of Jesus' warmth and love at

Christmastime and always. Keep the blessing simple and easy to follow. We used this one: "When Jesus was born, they wrapped him in a blanket and placed in him a manger. This cloth comforted him and kept him warm. (*Drape the scarf over the shoulders of the person you are blessing.*) As you wrap this scarf around you and feel its warmth and comfort, remember the gift of God's Son and his great love for you."

Go Tell It on the Mountain Part 2

After the breakfast, add the new photos to the Good News of Great Joy side show and e-mail the side show to the attendees. It's a great way to thank people for attending the Angel Breakfast and remind them of the fun they had while there. You can also show the slideshow during your church's worship service and post it on your church's website or Facebook page.

Write thank-you notes to all ministry partners who made the event a success. Make sure your note is specific and personal, highlighting something special that the ministry partner did that made the event heavenly. Send the thank-you notes via snail mail, or e-mail a fun template from Smilebox®.

Conduct an Angel Breakfast event evaluation with team members, a few parents, and Angels. Celebrate successes and seek opportunities for improvement.

Our Angel Breakfast changed the lives of everyone involved. Yours will, too. You'll celebrate the birth of Jesus and "Bring the Good News of great joy!" to children with special needs and their families in a wonderful, angelic way. And, you'll honor the dedication and love of many "Angels" in your church.

Patty Smith currently serves The Tennessee Conference of the United Methodist Church as Director of Children and Family Ministries where she equips children's ministry leaders in over 1,000 churches. Prior to this role, she was the Senior Product Developer for Children's Ministry at Group Publishing. While at Group, Patty also served as the Interim Minister to Children and Families at Broomfield United Methodist Church in Broomfield, Colorado. Before joining the Group family, she served as Minister to Children and Families at Christ Church United Methodist in Fort Lauderdale, Florida.

Integrating Special Needs Children

by Pat Dallaire and Cindy Ziemba

For those who have a passion for children with special needs, nothing is as exciting as watching every child become a functioning part of a regular church group.

Since our goal is to integrate children with special needs into their same-age peers, we have developed a plan that allows most of them to participate in the regular setting with other children by facilitating some support. However, we also offer some unique opportunities designed with these children in mind.

1. **Friday Night Out** is a much-anticipated monthly adventure. We provide games, sports, Bible story, craft, and snack for the child with special needs and his or her siblings while parents enjoy a worry-free evening away from their children. The purpose of this evening is multifold. Some of our families with special needs children have difficulty securing quality childcare. The volunteers for this event truly enjoy this evening with the children. Additionally, siblings sometimes feel overlooked at home due to their parents spending hours making and keeping counseling, therapy, and doctors' appointments for the child in the family that has special needs. This evening is designed to delight each of the children who attend by planning activities with each participant in mind.

2. **Self-contained Classrooms** on Sunday mornings is an option for some of our severely autistic students. While they cannot tolerate a full hour in their appropriate regular classroom, they can attend church or a class for the part of the time that they can manage. Then they return to the self-contained classroom where they receive a one-on-one lesson and snack.

3. **Full Circle Parent Support Group** is a newly created group in which parents share resources such as quality care givers and agencies. As parents describe a need, we secure individuals whose expertise can be helpful in addressing that need. We have had a lawyer who addressed estate planning for the person with special needs, a psychologist who addressed adjustment issues relating to siblings of a child with special needs, and a social worker who discussed the stages of grieving that the parents of a child with special needs experience.

Other activities are designed specifically for our Adult Special Needs population.

1. **An Easter Egg Hunt** is an annual service project and fun event for our Adult Developmentally Disabled class. These adults initially hide Easter eggs for preschoolers and then participate in their own Easter Egg Hunt. The enthusiasm with which they hunt for their own eggs marked with their own names is humbling.

2. **Adopt a Planter** is an event in which the adult class plants a church planter. Part of the joy for them is to be able to watch the specific flower that they have planted flourish throughout the summer.

3. **Summer Picnic** is an annual summer event held at the home of a volunteer. Students play water balloon toss, bean bag toss, clothespin drop, and enjoy hot dogs and hamburgers. Students particularly enjoy playing games and hearing music that they enjoyed in their youth. Most of the adult class resides in group homes, so offering a picnic in the backyard of the home of a volunteer from our class is important to us.

4. **A Detroit Tiger baseball game** is always popular with this group. The Tigers donate the tickets and the students enjoy a day at the ball park regardless of who wins. This is also a great opportunity to apply principles learned in the classroom to community experiences. We pray for safety and fun before we leave. Upon return, we thank God for his protection.

5. **An All Saints Party** is a church-wide event held in October in which our adult students take great joy in dressing up in costumes to help with games and hand out candy to the children. Following the children's party, we have our own Adult All Saints Pizza Party.

6. **A Christmas Pageant** is presented by the adult class to friends and relatives each December. Students receive their parts in September and spend five minutes each class session reviewing their lines. By the time they present the pageant at Christmastime, the students are bursting with excitement.

7. **A Christmas Party** is always anticipated. Students have dinner, grab the microphone to lead music karaoke-style, play Christmas bingo, and receive a small gift.

The adult students enjoy the traditions that have been established at each of these events. We can't have a picnic without a water balloon toss. We can't have a Christmas party without singing with great gusto, "We Wish You a Merry Christmas." That sense of sameness is very comforting to them.

The successful integration of a special needs child with their peers is dependent upon several factors. We welcome and encourage children with special needs to attend our Vacation Bible School. VBS is an exciting week with over one thousand children in attendance each day. We involve a group of trained volunteers who are eager to assist the children with special needs. Children from several denominations attend. Parents of the children have mentioned that VBS at our church is the very first time their child has been able to participate in this kind of summer program.

On our VBS registration forms, we include space for parents to describe any special needs their child may have. This year a mother indicated that her child had sensory integration issues along with Attention Deficit Hyperactivity Disorder (ADHD). The mother was contacted prior to the first day of VBS to clarify what we needed to do to address the sensory integration issue. We e-mailed back and forth several times, agreeing that Andrew would benefit from a helper. He didn't like loud noises and he knew how to inform his teacher when there was a problem. It appeared as if he would need minor support, so he was assigned to a kind woman who was a new volunteer in our program. The e-mails from Andrew's mother were shared with the helper who also contacted the family to introduce herself.

The first couple of hours at VBS were uneventful, and Andrew participated appropriately. However, during his Bible lesson time he ran out of the building toward the parking lot. When he would not respond to verbal commands, three volunteers were immediately available. They surrounded him and attempted to talk with him. He reacted by trying to bite, kick, and pinch.

When I arrived, I asked Andrew if he would calm down so we could talk and he agreed. The other adults left and Andrew stated that everyone hated him, especially the teacher, and that everyone was unfair.

He said, "Everyone gets candy except me." Andrew's teacher tossed individual hard candy to anyone that responded to a question. Andrew said he was holding his hand up, but he was not called upon. (He didn't mention that he was lying under a table when he put his hand up!)

Walking him back to class, I asked him if he wanted candy. "Yes!" was his immediate answer. "What should you do if you would like some candy?" "Raise my hand," was his answer. "Yes," I continued, "And where should you sit?"

He smiled a little and entered the room. He sat on the floor next to the table. The teacher quickly understood what to do. She called on him at her first opportunity. He responded and she tossed him a candy. He looked at the candy unhappily. "What's wrong?" I whispered. "I don't like red," he said. The only color he liked was blue. I quickly went to the teacher's bag and exchanged the red candy for a blue. Andrew smiled.

This particular teacher was able to quickly assess the situation and respond appropriately. The rest of the day and the rest of the week went well for Andrew. Armed with more insight, Andrew was assigned to a new volunteer who set firm limits and praised him for appropriate behavior.

This illustration about Andrew highlights a couple of issues regarding integrating special needs children into the general church setting. Sometimes, for a variety of reasons, parents are not entirely forthright in their description of their child. Andrew appears to have problems more severe than his mother indicated. Our volunteers are trained to provide only as much assistance as is necessary. But, they are an important safety net if the child is engaging in behavior dangerous to himself or others. The more information that can be obtained, the better our staff can provide appropriate interventions.

Another issue that sometimes arises is the classroom teacher's perception that a special needs child is getting unfair preferential treatment. Some teachers might not have appreciated Andrew's request for a different flavor of candy. That is when the teacher is gently reminded: Fair is not equal. Fair is every child getting what he or she needs in order to succeed.

Making accommodations so that a special needs child can be successful are simple. Common accommodations we use are:
1. Preferential seating — sometimes closer to the speaker and other times away from the noise.
2. Having directions repeated either by the teacher or by the child's volunteer. Or, the child can repeat the directions for the entire class.

3. Allowing the special needs child to be an assistant to the teacher. This is especially effective for children with attention difficulties.
4. Offer a walk in the hall to break up a long period of sitting.
5. Mark the location of a Bible verse and highlight it in advance with highlight tape. (Highlight tape can be removed with no damage to the Bible.)
6. Preparing difficult parts of a craft activity in advance.
7. Allowing the special needs child to repeat part of a Bible verse instead of the entire verse. The child receives the same reward as the children who said the entire verse from memory.
8. Giving advance notice before a transition occurs.

The key to successful interventions is to know what is planned and anticipate difficulties the child with special needs may experience. The special needs child doesn't want to feel different from his or her peers. Our volunteers act as assistants in the classroom and help all the children in the room until the child with special needs requires direct help.

> Each volunteer would say that they are far more blessed by those they serve than are those they serve are blessed by them.

Special Needs programming has existed at our church for about fifteen years. For the past four years, it has been my privilege to be the director of our program. We have twenty-five volunteers who routinely assist approximately forty special needs individuals ranging in age from birth through the senior citizen age. Those who volunteer become protective advocates for our special population. Each volunteer would say that they are far more blessed by those they serve than are those they serve are blessed by them.

Pat Dallaire is the Director of Special Needs and Cindy Ziemba is the Director of Children's Ministry at Ward Evangelical Presbyterian Church in Northville, Michigan.

Take A Break Respite

by Gwen Boyles

Take a Break is designed for elementary- and middle school-aged children with special needs and their siblings. While their parents enjoy a few hours alone, the children are paired with buddies for the evening and choose from a variety of fun activities.

Take a "Break" Respite Schedule

3:30 PM — Volunteers report
4:00 PM — Greet, sign-in, meet buddy, start rotation through stations and playground
4:45 PM — 5:10 PM — Playground is open pending weather and lighting
5:15 PM — Pizza/subs dinner
5:45 PM — Worship
6:10 PM — Continued rotation through stations
6:55 PM — Back to Creation Station to pick up craft/wait for parent or back to Chill Zone/wait for parent

Sunday school rooms are transformed into the activity stations. The materials for each station are kept in labeled storage bins to facilitate setup and take down. Setup generally takes two people about an hour and take down is completed quickly by the volunteer buddies at the end of the evening. Laminated signs at each door indicate the activity available inside. Some stations have volunteers to greet children and coordinate play while others are self-starting.

Family and Friends

This activity station focuses on home-living activities. There is an area with sink, stove, dolls, playhouse, and dress up items. Play dough and drawing materials are available in this room. Add a special new item each session such as baby bathing, a doll to fix hair, magnet paper dolls, beads to make jewelry, loom potholders, and so forth.

Adventure Zone

This station involves a variety of building materials, such as interlocking and wooden blocks. Set these items out for imaginative play. At times, a volunteer will offer lessons in learning to use tools or woodworking projects. Some children enjoy hammering nails into wood blocks or using the electric screwdriver. Woodworking projects have included trays, bird feeders, and wooden crosses. Add a special new item each session such as car tracks, trucks, fireman hats, train tracks, a tent, and so forth.

Game City

This room is for active games as well as board games that have been set up on tables. A junior volunteer is in the room to help children learn how to play the games.

Creation Station

Three themed crafts are available each month as well as coloring sheets or worksheets that go along with the theme. Samples are displayed and all materials are organized so that the children and buddies can create together. A volunteer is in the room to replenish supplies and give creative suggestions.

Movie Time

A TV and DVD player are set up along with a variety of movie choices. Lights are low and beanbag chairs and regular chairs are scattered in front of the television for viewing the movie.

Chill Out Room

This room provides a quiet area for any child that might become over stimulated during the evening. There are puzzles and books available.

A "peace basket" is provided with packing bubbles to pop, stress balls, paper to tear, and a stuffed animal to hug.

Snack Shack

This station has fun cooking options. A volunteer helps the children make simple snacks to enjoy after dinner. Care is taken to allow for allergies.

Following supper is a time for worship. It is a gathering for all children who can handle the larger group setting. The children worship through music, skits, puppets, and object lessons. A volunteer coordinates and leads the worship experience. If a child is not comfortable in the group setting, that child and their buddy may return to the rotation stations.

Children

We keep a data bank of all children with special needs and their families who have a connection with our church family. Our respite program is held on the first Saturday of each month, October through May, from 4:00 PM to 7:00 PM.

Each month, about ten days before the event, we send an "evite" using the website www.evite.com. This website allows parents to RSVP and will also send out a reminder several days before the event.

Registration is required each month (through Evite) but application forms need only be filled out one time and corrected as needed.

Volunteers

Volunteers are the heart of the respite program. We keep a data bank of volunteers and their contact information. We use the same website (www.evite.com) to remind our volunteers that respite is coming up.

As volunteers respond, we fill in the monthly volunteer form and match them as buddies with the children who register or assign them to rotation roles. Many of our volunteers are family units.

Volunteer teens may be paired with a sibling of a special needs child. Younger volunteers join their parents and interact with their special buddy together.

Volunteer buddies arrive a half hour early and are given specific information about their "buddy" to help facilitate a fun and safe time together.

Other volunteers are needed to lead worship, coordinate snack shack, and crafts/woodworking. A nurse on-site is essential. It is smart to check in volunteers who will prepare the pizza/sub dinner. We order in from a local restaurant, but some preparation for serving is always necessary.

Someone is needed to coordinate the Evites for attendees and volunteers, as well as set up on the day of the event.

Check-in

Volunteers wear nametags on lanyards. Children wear self-sticking security badges with a coordinating number label given to their parents. This number is recorded on the monthly volunteer form as well as a contact number for the parents for the evening.

We are entering our fourth year of *Take a Break Respite*. Here is a letter from one of our families whose three adopted children with special needs attend the program regularly.

*Dear Spring Hill Baptist Special Needs Ministry,
We are so thankful for your care for our children last night! We have so very few people who love and care for our children, and we do get weary of the twenty-four hour day in and day out care for them. Our marriage was strengthened last night by the time you gave us to be together alone while our children were safe and playing happily. Thank you for your ministry to us even though we don't attend your church. Thank you for loving our kids! We are really grateful.*

Gwen Bowles is a Christ-follower currently serving at Spring Hill Baptist Church. She is wife to her best friend, Russell and the proud mother of two daughters, Lynn and Jennifer. Gwen is the doting grandmother to seven! She is a retired teacher having worked for thirty years teaching children with special needs.

"Take a Break" Respite Care Volunteers

Date:

	Volunteer/Buddies		Children/#	Contact Info
1.	_____	_____	_____	_____
2.	_____	_____	_____	_____
3.	_____	_____	_____	_____
4.	_____	_____	_____	_____
5.	_____	_____	_____	_____
6.	_____	_____	_____	_____
7.	_____	_____	_____	_____
8.	_____	_____	_____	_____
9.	_____	_____	_____	_____
10.	_____	_____	_____	_____
11.	_____	_____	_____	_____
12.	_____	_____	_____	_____
13.	_____	_____	_____	_____
14.	_____	_____	_____	_____
15.	_____	_____	_____	_____

	Junior Volunteers/Respite Siblings		Children/#	Contact Info
16.	_____	_____	_____	_____
17.	_____	_____	_____	_____
18.	_____	_____	_____	_____
19.	_____	_____	_____	_____
20.	_____	_____	_____	_____

Nurse:

Front Desk/Kitchen:

Crafts:

Woodworking:

Snacks/GroupTime:

Volunteer Children:

© 2010 Abingdon Press

Children with Special Situations

Child:

Age:

Assigned buddy:

Diagnosis:

Educational level:

Favorite activities:

Signs that an intervention may be needed:

Intervention strategies that work best:

Possible triggers:

Allergies/Restrictions:

Other:

Children with Special Situations Sample

Child:

Age:

Assigned buddy:

Diagnosis: Autism spectrum — high functioning

Educational level: Grade level and above — mainstreamed with behavioral assistant

Favorite activities: Playground swings, Candyland®, Legos® interlocking blocks

Signs that an intervention may be needed: Using inappropriate language
Eating shirt
Picking bug bites
Continual questioning during group
Invading personal space

Intervention strategies that work best: Offer fidget
Offer notebook to write down question to answer later
Redirect outside to playground to run
Distraction

Possible triggers: Clapping — Prepare him when it is coming
Some music — he doesn't like slow music but also sometimes says the upbeat music that he likes hurts his ears
Perceived competitive situations

Allergies/Restrictions: None

Other: May spit when upset

SPRING HILL
BAPTIST CHURCH

TAKE A BREAK

A Respite Care Program for Parents and Caregivers of Special Needs Children

When	Meets 1st Saturday of every month (NOT July, August, September)
Where	Spring Hill Baptist Church 2620 Frays Mill Road Ruckersville, VA
Who	Elementary school children (Kindergarten –5th grade) with special needs <u>and</u> their siblings
Activities	Children rotate through stations at their own pace with a buddy 1. Creation Station (crafts) 2. Snack Shack (children help prepare) 3. Family and Friends Room 4. Adventure Zone 5. Movie Time (TV/video/DVD) 6. Game City (video and board games) 7. Chill Zone (quiet book room)
Dinner	Pizza, sandwiches, finger foods, snacks—other food available upon request—indicate needs on registration materials
How to Find Us	From Charlottesville, take Rt. 29 north 6 miles past airport to left on 641 toward Advance Mills. Church is 1/3 mile on right. From Ruckersville and points north, take Rt. 29 south 4 miles to right on 611 toward Advance Mills. Church is 1/3 mile on right.

There is no cost, but registration is required two weeks in advance of session. For information or to register call Mary at the church office: 434-973-7473, or email her at: mary@springhillbaptist.org.

Permission granted to copy for local church use. \ This page is on the CD-Rom.

Parent/Guardian Respite Care Consent Form for Spring Hill Baptist Church

I,_____, on behalf of myself and my child,_____, apply to Spring Hill Baptist Church to participate in its Respite Care Program being held at the main church campus at 2620 Frays Mill Road (the "Facility"). I acknowledge, represent, and consent to the following:

1. I am the parent or legal guardian for the child for whom this document is signed. I have discussed my child's participation in the Respite Care Program with my child's physician, and have received my physician's approval for my child's participation. I believe that my child is able to participate in the Respite Care Program without undue risk of harm to my child's health or well-being. I acknowledge that Spring Hill Baptist Church will not assess or approve my child's fitness for participation. I voluntarily execute this Consent and have voluntarily chosen to allow my child to participate in the program.

2. I understand that Spring Hill Baptist Church is not a medical services provider and has not undertaken to provide medical care to my child. I acknowledge that participation in the Respite Care Program involves risks of injury, illness, and/or harm to persons and property, and I assume those risks on behalf of my child.

3. I give my permission for my child to be treated for illness or injury sustained while participating in the Respite Care Program, including, if necessary, the administration of emergency anesthesia or surgery, and authorize Spring Hill Baptist Church personnel to act on my behalf in ordering such treatment if I am unable to be reached.

4. I have received a full explanation of Respite Care Program from Spring Hill Baptist Church personnel and have had opportunity to ask questions of Spring Hill Baptist Church personnel and clarify any concerns I may have with the Program.

5. I understand that I may withdraw my child from participation in the Respite Care program at any time, and that Spring Hill Baptist Church may refuse to allow my child to participate or to continue to participate in the Respite Care program at any time if, at the discretion of Spring Hill Baptist Church personnel, my child's participation might endanger his or her health or safety, the health or safety of another participant or worker in the Program, or might adversely affect the goals and ministry of Spring Hill Baptist Church.

6. THIS DOCUMENT IS INTENDED TO ABSOLVE SPRING HILL BAPTIST CHURCH AND THE FACILITY OF ANY LIABILITY TO ME OR MY CHILD THAT IS RELATED TO MY CHILD'S PARTICIPATION IN THE ACTIVITY. Accordingly, I hereby release Spring Hill Baptist Church, its personnel, its volunteers, and the Facility (the "Providers") from, waive, and will never sue the Providers for any damage (whether damage to or loss of property, finances, life, body, mind, or emotions), cost, suit demand, claim, or other liability, that arises or is alleged to arise from or in connection with my child's participation in the Program. Such liability includes any liability that arises from a Provider's negligence (but not its willful and wanton misconduct). Such liability also includes any liability that arises or is alleged to arise from claims for contribution by another that my child or I have sued or from whom my child or I have received compensation.

7. I have provided full medical information regarding my child's special needs to Spring Hill Baptist Church personnel. I understand that I am responsible to arrange for all administration of medicine, provision of medical supplies, and delivery of medical care that my child may need during the course of his or her participation in the Program. I am not relying on Spring Hill Baptist Church personnel to provide my child with medical care.

8. References in this release to Spring Hill Baptist Church include its officers, directors, employees, personnel, volunteers, ministry partners, and other related organizations.

9. I acknowledge that acceptance into the Program is contingent upon the consensus of Spring Hill Baptist Church personnel that my child's special needs are consistent with the Program criteria and that my child's needs can be adequately addressed by Spring Hill Baptist Church personnel.

10. I have provided Spring Hill Baptist Church with contact information for me and an emergency contact in the event I am unable to be reached. I understand that it is imperative that I be timely in dropping off and picking up my child from the Program and understand that consistent failure to do so may result in my child's inability to continue participating in the Program.

11. I give permission for my child's picture and any interview provided by me or my spouse to be used in marketing and media presentations for the purpose of promoting the Spring Hill Baptist Church ministry.

_____

Signature of Parent or Guardian

_____

Date

Special Needs, Dietary Restrictions, Medical Conditions of my Child

_____

_____

_____

_____

_____

_____

Permission granted to copy for local church use. \ This page is on the CD-Rom.

© 2010 Abingdon Press

EVENTS THAT WORKED FOR US **199**

Parent/Guardian Interview Form

Child's Name _____ Birthday _____

Address _____

Telephone _____ E-Mail _____

Parent's Names _____

Education
Specific diagnosis
Is child in school? If yes, where?
Type of placement

Behavior
Is the child on medication? If so, what is it and how often does it have to be administered?
Describe the child's behavior (is he aggressive? Does he hit, bite, throw,. run away, yell, pull hair, self abusive?)
What do you do to control his behavior? **OVER**

How does he deal with people he doesn't know?

Food

What are the child's eating habits?

Is he allergic to any foods? If so, please describe the food and reaction.

Are there food restrictions?

What do you give him for snacks?

Independence and Prosthetic Devices

Does the child take care of his or her toileting needs?

Does the child feed him or herself?

Does the child dress him or herself?
Does the child use a hearing aid? Cane? Wheelchair? Walker? Have artificial limbs? Or any other prosthetic device?

Communication

Is the child's speech understandable to people who don't know him or her?
How does the child communicate basic needs? (such as asking for a drink or using the toilet?)
Does he or she use any sign language or a language board?
What special care needs should we be aware of?

Hobbies/Special Interests/Pets

OVER

PLEASE COMPLETE THIS INFORMATION FOR SIBLINGS WHO ARE ATTENDING

Child's Name _____ Birthday _____

Is he allergic to any foods? If so, please describe the food and reaction. Are there food restrictions?

_____
_____
_____
_____
_____
_____
_____
_____
_____

Is the child on medication? If so, what is it and how often does it have to be administered?

_____
_____
_____
_____
_____
_____
_____
_____
_____

Hobbies/Special Interests/Pets

_____
_____
_____
_____
_____
_____
_____
_____
_____

The Inside Scoop

One day I had a parent come up to me with a serious look on his face. Apparently the man's son had come up to him and quite seriously said, "Dad, I think Pastor Joel thinks he is God." Bewildered, the father asked, "What makes you think that?" His son quickly replied, "Well, every week as we get ready to go into worship he sings 'Be Still and Know that I Am God.'"

Joel Bullock

On a recent Sunday we had an amazing event happened in our Sunday School class. Matthew is a four-year-old child with autism. Each Sunday various items like shakers or musical instruments are used to keep him and the other children engaged in the Bible lesson.

As a change of pace, I let the children select a rhythm instrument from the music box. Matthew eagerly searched through the container to select the instrument he wanted to play. He first found the triangle and stayed on task looking through the entire box until he found the correct matching stricker to accompany his triangle. He came to group time and stayed for several minutes while playing his instrument.

One of the other teachers stopped to take a picture of this amazing development in this learning.

Besty Parham
Associate Editor, The United Methodist Publishing House

Summer Events

As long as the earth endures,
seedtime and harvest,
cold and heat,
summer and winter,
day and night,
shall not cease.

(Genesis 8:22)

Sizzling Summer Programs

by Keith McManus

Your children's ministry can experience growth during the summer while impacting your kid's lives through creative, fun, and entertaining programs that turn the ordinary "dog days of summer" into extraordinary "sizzling super days of fun"! It can be as simple as changing what you ordinarily do and tweaking your Sunday morning and mid-week programs.

We all have "regular" programs and schedules that we do throughout the school year, but why not change those during the summer months to allow your "regular" volunteers some much needed time off, allow others in your church to get involved for shorter periods of time, and introduce your students to something fresh and different that will keep their interests and involvement high. This is not as difficult as some may think.

Some terrific resources are available that offer effective programs for both Sundays and mid-week services that require fewer volunteers but keep the focus on high impact of ministry and teaching God's Word. Remember, variety is the spice of life and these changes can breathe new life into your summer ministry when you might have experienced a downward turn in the past.

One suggestion is to consider allowing your Sunday morning small group / Sunday School teachers to take a few weeks off during the summer and expand your large group time to include more praise and worship, interactive games, and creative programming. This not only reduces the number of volunteers needed during the summer, but it also changes the routine schedule and pumps new excitement into your summer months.

For example, we have adapted five summer-long programs that we rotate through, allowing our first through fifth graders to experience each

program once during their time in our children's department. We have themed each summer program as follows: Super Book Olympics, Bible Boot Camp, P.A.R.T.Y. Time, Eternity 500, and C.I.R.C.U.S. R.I.N.G.

Some of these programs are designed for team competition that involves dividing our children into teams with about the same number of students from each grade on each team. Some of the programs are designed to include competition between the boys and girls. Other programs combine team competition with individual challenges and rewards. We rotate the themes so that the style of programs and competitions are different each summer. All of the programs are packed full of fun, learning opportunities, and challenges that make summer sizzle.

Here is a look behind the five themed summer programs that we have used at Sonshine Avenue on Sunday mornings:

Super Book Olympics is a program that is available from *One Way Street*. It is themed around the Olympics and challenges the students to study and memorize the Scriptures using worksheets that go home each week. You may want to post the Scriptures on the children's ministry pages of your church's website. The Olympic style games and activities are used to review what the children have learned over the past week. This program uses team competition. The teams have the opportunity to win gold, silver, or bronze medals. There is always a Grand Opening Ceremony and a highly publicized Closing Event. This is a fast paced, yet simple program that all the children love.

P.A.R.T.Y. Time is themed around a huge party with gifts, balloons, and colorful decorations. It is an older curriculum that was published by

Charisma Life. P.A.R.T.Y. stands for "Personal Attitudes Related To You" and teaches on gifts given, gifts we can give, and gifts we can receive. We divided our party teams into boys and girls with competition being "party games" and reviewing the teaching lessons. We also do a weekly drawing of all the children in attendance that week for an advertized gift give-away. We had a huge party at the end of the summer program for the winning team as another incentive for this program.

Bible Boot Camp was themed around the military with camo, tents, and artillery. We divided our children into "troops" and they competed by bringing visitors, their Bibles, Scripture memorization, and offering. Points were awarded for winning the games that we played that reviewed each week's lesson. Along with the prize for the winning troop, the boys and girls were able to earn "medals" for attendance, Scripture memory, and guests that they brought. *Charisma Life* offered the first Bible Boot Camp curriculum that we used, and in recent years we have adapted the *Truth Quest* Bible Boot Camp material.

Eternity 500 is themed around NASCAR and "The Race" to get to heaven. The curriculum is offered from the *Train Depot* and works great with dividing your students into race teams. Like the other programs, points or "miles" are added up for a variety of activities or responses. The winning "Race Team" can celebrate in the winner's circle with a special party or trip.

Another themed program centers on the **C.I.R.C.U.S. R.I.N.G.** We used *Charisma Life's* curriculum from several years ago with each letter standing for a different lesson. As with all

of our summer programs, we awarded points or "circus stars" for a variety of things that the children could do, such as bringing their Bibles, bringing guests, Scripture memorization, bringing offerings, and winning one of the circus games we play. We had the boys vs. girls throughout this program with each of the teams working toward "Circus Tickets" that could be cashed in at the end of the summer during the Circus Festival.

The Circus Festival is similar to a fall festival with the advantage of being close to the beginning of new school year. We are able to attract new students and their families with this event. Each week we gave away special "treats" such as hot dogs, popcorn, cotton candy, and elephant food (peanuts . . . unless there are allergies) that one might experience at the circus.

There are many other ideas that can be captured and themed to make for a creative and fun learning experience on Sunday mornings for boys and girls during the summer. With this rotation approach, over the five-year cycle our investment in curriculums, sets and decorations, and the development of the themed programs allowed us to keep them and use them over and over again. Repeating the five programs only once every five years allows us to reach and teach the children with a new program each summer. This keeps your summers fresh and exciting for the leaders as well as your students. This approach gives your regular teachers and volunteers a break and allows you to be a good steward of your ministry finances. We actually have more funds to invest in other resources throughout the year with the recycling of curriculum.

In addition to changing your Sunday mornings, you may want to consider suspending your

> Everybody loves something new, and making your summer sizzle with a fresh approach to your worship service and discipleship program can have lasting impact for the kingdom of God as well as for your local church.

regular mid-week discipleship program to allow the opportunity to run shorter programs that provide a refreshing approach for studying God's Word. Again, this allows you to introduce new volunteers who may be willing to assist for shorter periods of time while allowing your "regular" volunteers to enjoy a little time off.

There are some wonderful programs such as *KidMo, TeamKid, High Voltage Kids, Truth Quest, High Point, Super Heroes,* and so forth that work great for just that kind of change up. We have provided a variety of approaches: TV Dinners where we studied the Word of God through the eyes of TV characters and series, wild and wacky Wednesday nights where no one ever knows what to expect. This program can provide intensive ministry training for your children or offer electives for students to choose from. The summer months give you the opportunity to try different curriculum, new programs, schedules, and promotional ideas without being "locked in" for an extended period of time.

Many churches will do a Vacation Bible School for one week during the summer months. Instead of taking the VBS materials and packing everything into a single week, stretch the program over your mid-week night for five weeks or longer. There are some imaginative programs out there that would be easily adaptable for a "summer program" and provide opportunities for some fun decorating and theme ideas.

By using learning centers or a rotation system that your boys and girls could go through each night, you can reduce the amount of volunteers needed to a minimum number. Each volunteer would only be responsible for one "element" of the lesson each night. For example, you could have one Bible Lesson Instructor, Craft Instructor, Game Instructor, Snack and Refreshment Instructor, and Real Life Story Instructor. This type of structure and setup divides students in the first through fifth grades into groups. Each group participants in each "station" or learning center and rotates through each station once during the entire program.

This also allows for your volunteers to prepare for one specific area and teach that same topic several times to different groups instead of being responsible for teaching everything for the entire lesson. Add an additional volunteer or two for an opening and / or closing rally and you have a full fledged two-hour mid-week summer program that rocks!

Be sure to start planning early and recruit continually. Advanced planning allows for more creative time to decorate, recruit, structure, and "plus" the entire program. It is extremely vital that the folks in your community know what you have to offer their children well in advance. Therefore, the sooner you have your summer planned, the sooner you can begin to advertise and promote your program.

Everybody loves something new, and making your summer sizzle with a fresh approach to your worship service and discipleship program can have lasting impact for the kingdom of God as well as for your local church. With some prayer, imagination, a creative team, and a fresh approach to your summers, you can avoid the summer drop-off and experience an awesome program that will help you maintain your momentum and lead your students into a fun, challenging, and life changing event.

Keith McManus is the director of Sonshine Avenue Ministry, Inc. and has invested over twenty-five years of his life in ministry to people of all ages across the United States and around the world. Keith seeks to fulfill the mission of the ministry by conducting rallies, crusades, youth camps, seminars, and conferences. His combined experiences, professional training, and passion for people are offered in an atmosphere that has an eternal impact on all who attend.

Sizzling Summer Program Ideas

Bible Boot Camp (*Charisma Life / Gospel Light*)
A game competition. Teaches children about the armor of God and training good soldiers for God's army. Includes basic training, what we wear, and the training of weapons.

C.I.R.C.U.S. R.I.N.G. (*Charisma Life / Gospel Light*)
Victorious Christian life is dependent upon success in our relationships: Relating to Others, Relating to God, and Thanksgiving. The lessons focus on these topics to create the acronym.

> **C**aring is Sharing
> **I**ncluding is Improving
> **R**eacting is not Attracting
> **C**hanging is Rearranging
> **U**sing is Losing
> **S**eeing is Believing
>
> **R**eceiving is Giving
> **I**nfinite Love
> **N**o Room for sin
> **G**rowing is Knowing Jesus

IT'S P.A.R.T.Y. TIME (*Charisma Life / Gospel Light*)
13 weeks dealing with **P**ersonal **A**ttitudes **R**elating **T**o **Y**ou.
Boys and girls will learn about
- Gifts given to them: healing, God's son, everlasting life,
- Gifts they can give to others: love, compassion, talents and edification
- Gifts to receive: faith, miraculous powers, prophecy, and power

It's H.O.T. (*Charisma Life / Gospel Light*)
13 weeks focusing on **H**oly **O**bedient **T**eaching. Themed on holy living that helps build spiritual foundations in the lives of kids. Teaches holiness in all we do.
- Obedience to God
- Parents and authorities
- Teaching others by your life

TV Dinners
TV Series Bible Studies.

The Entertainment Ministry
www.entmin.com
1-800-999-0101

Superbook Olympics (*One way Street*)
A game competition that helps in Old and New Testament Bible knowledge.

One Way Street, Inc.
11999 E. Caley Ave.
Centennial, CO 80111-6835 USA
www.onewaystreet.com

Eternity 500 (*Train Depot*)
Following Christ and not giving up, avoiding temptation, and perseverance. (4 – 8 weeks)
- Race to Win the Prize
- Worst Wreck of all
- Don't Quit on God

Train Depot
1802 Timber Haven Trace
Louisville, KY 40214
Phone: 502-367-0630
www.traindepot.org

KID MO
Four to five week video driven curriculum.

KIDMO LLC
1113 Murfreesboro Road
Suite #106-145
Franklin, TN 37064
www.kidmo.com

Teamkid
A fun, high-energy program that encourages Discipleship.

LifeWay Christian Bookstore
One Life Way Plaza
Nashville, TN 37234
(800) 458-2772
www.lifeway.com

Right from Wrong (*Josh McDowell Ministry*)
Teaches the concepts of truth and morality.

Josh McDowell Ministry
660 International Pkwy, Ste. 100
Richardson, TX 75081-6616
866-252-5424
www.josh.org

J.O.Y. University (*One way Street*)
Jesus, Others, and You

One Way Street, Inc.
11999 E. Caley Ave.
Centennial, CO 80111-6835 USA
www.onewaystreet.com

High Voltage Kids
Various Topics

High Voltage Kids Ministry
4501 Burrow Drive
North Little Rock, AR 72116
(888) 826-4883
www.highvoltage-kids.com

Veggie Connections
Veggie Tales VBS and Yearly Curriculum

Nelson Ministry Services
PO Box 140300
Nashville, TN 37214-0300
(800)441-0511
www.nelsonministryservices.com

L.I.F.E
Life Is For Everyone
Binder of illustrated sermons.
- Knowing the will of God
- Salvation
- Seasonal Sermons
- Set up like a Care Group (Life Guards)

Train Depot
1802 Timber Haven Trace
Louisville, KY 40214
Phone: 502-367-0630
www.traindepot.org

Truthquest
Various Topics

TruthQuest Children's Ministries
1500 Sheridan Boulevard
Westminster, CO 80020
Phone: 303-920-1463
www.truthquest.net

Highpoint
Various Topics

Gospel Publishing House
1445 North Boonville Avenue
Springfield, Missouri 65802-1894
www.gph.org/highpoint
1-800-641-4310

K.I.D.S. Church (*Gospel Light*)
Various Topics

Gospel Light
1957 Eastman Ave.
Ventura, California 93003
1.800.446.7735
www.gospellight.com

Super Heroes
Teaches confidence, forgiveness, courage, and so forth.

North Point Community Church
4350 North Point Parkway
Alpharetta, GA 30022
866-866-5621
http://resources.northpoint.org/store

Student Discipleship Ministry
Various Topics

P.O. Box 6747
Fort Worth, TX 76115
1.800.880.8736
www.studentdiscipleship.org

Don't forget Vacation Bible School materials from past and current years from all the different publishers.

Ready, Set, Go!

by Patty Smith

Have you ever been whacked in the head by God? It happens when we least expect it, particularly when we think that we are fulfilling his assignment for us. And believe me, when God whacks you on the side of the head, it hurts!

I was whacked one summer while I was in the water aisle at Target®. I was looking for my weekly purchase of Propel® when he whacked me. God said, "Patty, what are you doing to connect the fourth through sixth graders to Christ that I am sending you?" And I responded, aloud, "Nothing—yet." (Yes, strangers heard me, and giggled.)

KAGOY!

It's true. **K**ids **A**re **G**etting **O**lder **Y**ounger today and the research by trend analysts has proven it over and over again. Our precious ten- to twelve-year-olds are inordinately different. These kids are hardly kids anymore. These preteens or "tweenagers" as some people call them have been exposed earlier to more of life's realities — violence, racial tension, increased sexual awareness, technical sophistication, and so forth, than children their same age ten years ago. They're conscientious, encouraging, relational, profound, and altruistic. What a blessing!

What does a children's minister do to effectively minister to these radically different children? The challenge we face is to create ministries that concentrate on collaboration, service, and leadership. Ministry to preteens provides opportunities for children to partner together to bring peers to Christ, creates service programs and projects to allow youth to bring about positive change in their world, and values kids as leaders by providing places for them to discover and use their time and talents.

According to Alan Root, a "kid musicianary" to the preteen set, these kids "need to lead." They're "ready to be seriously challenged . . . challenged to memorize Scripture, challenged to worship in spirit and truth, challenged to make a difference at church, at home, at school, and in their community." By fifth grade, Root adds, kids are ready to switch "from being under the ministry of a children's pastor to being ready to assist the ministry of the children's pastor."

Start With VBS

A big part of any VBS program is creating an environment that will "wow" kids and set the visual landscape for your themed event. Decorations help kids explore a place they've never been before. They spark the imagination. Decorations say to kids, "We've created all of this just for you! You matter!"

Let's be honest. Decorating for VBS requires a lot of help. It's a task that can take weeks if done by a group of dedicated, creative, driven people. It's even a bigger undertaking if done by just a few equally passionate people. Wouldn't it be great if you had ten or twenty or even fifty extra people to help transform your church for VBS? You can!

Here's a fun VBS-related event you can do to engage preteens in ways that they learn and serve best! "Ready, Set, Go!" is a four-hour event that engages preteens to help build and create your VBS sets and decorations and provides a fun way for them to spread the word about your VBS.

Get Ready!

Plan your event with that group of preteens. If they are involved in planning the event, they will attend it and they will bring their friends. Cast the main idea for "Ready, Set, Go!" and seek ideas for how to accomplish each part of "Ready, Set Go!" Be sure to ask what time is best for your event. Our preteens preferred a late afternoon event. Your group may prefer early morning.

We created a target group of preteens and took them out for pizza. As we ate, we asked about their last VBS experience. What did they like about it? What did they remember? Why? Then we used their answers to shape how we shared the idea of involving them in "Ready, Set, Go!"

Recruit ministry partners to join the fun. Ready, Set, Go! is a great service opportunity for people who are creative, handy with tools, have a flair for design, love preteens, and don't mind getting messy. Involve your VBS decorating team, too.

> "Ready, Set, Go!" is a four-hour event that engages preteens to help build and create your VBS sets and decorations and provides a fun way for them to spread the word about your VBS.

We offered three ways people could serve: a team for Set, a team for Go! and an all-event team. Most people chose to serve the entire time.

Publicize your event in fun ways. Find a colorful, preteen-friendly image, and brand your event with it. Make flyers that shout, "This event is fun!" Use Facebook. Twitter about it. Post the information on your church's website. Mobilize preteens to spread the word via text messages.

Work with your VBS Decorating Team to finalize the plans for your VBS decorations. Determine areas where preteens can help. Ask your team: What decorations can preteens create independently? What decorations can they help create? What decorations can they assemble?

Our theme was "The Rainforest . . . Where God's Goodness Reigns." Our decorating team needed help outlining backdrops, painting backdrops and VBS characters, making paper vines, making large bamboo poles, stuffing bags to make boulders, and cutting large leaves. You'll use these specific needs as the basis for your stations during the "Set" portion of the event.

We brainstormed fun names for our stations. We had The Sharpies (they used Sharpies® to outline), The Color Crew, Vinemakers, The Bamboo Crew, Super Stuffers, and Crazy Scissorheads.

Collect all the supplies you need for the decorating part of your event. We set up a staging area for supplies and designated a section of the room for each decorating station. We placed a sign in each area with the name of the station and all the supplies needed for it. As people brought supplies, we placed them underneath that sign and crossed off that item on the list. This made it easy to determine what supplies we still needed, and it made it easy to move the supplies from the staging area to the room where we held "Ready, Set, Go!"

Preparing For Go

Create and print flyers or door hangers publicizing your VBS. Use the clip art from the VBS Starter Kit to make your flyers. You can also purchase door hangers from the publisher of your VBS curriculum.

Use Google® maps to identify neighborhoods adjacent to your church as your target area. Choose one or two neighborhoods to visit during Go!

Hire a company that offers hayrides, rents double-decker buses, or other creative modes of transportation to take your kids VBS caroling.

Recruit one of your worship leaders to lead kids in songs as they travel through the neighborhoods. If you plan on singing VBS songs, give a copy of the music to the worship leader at least two weeks before your event so they can learn the songs.

Get Set

Before preteens arrive, set up the decorating stations. Check and recheck your supplies. Make sure you have everything ready to go when your preteens arrive. Remember to use drop cloths in areas where you'll be painting.

Assign your volunteers to a station. Show the volunteers what they'll do when the preteens arrive. Since preteens are highly relational, encourage your volunteers to chat with the kids while they're working. The members of our VBS decorating team lead our stations and used fun conversation starters from the VBS Starter Kit. You can also find fun conversation starters on the web.

Create a Snack Shack that's filled with fun treats related to your theme. Use some of the snacks from your VBS or create fun ones of your own. Be sure to include a mixture of healthy and not-so-healthy items. Offer beverages, too. Restock your Snack Shack periodically.

Crank up the tunes. Music enhances *any* environment. Play songs that your preteens love. Include some of the songs from your upcoming VBS, too. Throughout the day, take requests from the kids. You can also invite one of the preteens to be a guest D.J. and let them play their favorite songs. If your room has a screen and projector, play music videos.

Set!

Welcome your preteens. Begin with a fun mixer that will help kids get to know one another better. Encourage your volunteers to participate in the mixers, too.
Lead preteens through a devotion that focuses on working together or the theme of your VBS. Try to modify one of the experiences in your

VBS curriculum . . . connecting with the decoration theme for the day. Make your devotion interactive, including time for kids to talk to one another and the leader. Close the devotion with prayer.

> Lead preteens through a devotion that focuses on working together or the theme of your VBS.

Start decorating! Let the kids choose where they want to go. They'll gravitate to what they like to do most. Let the kids know that they can participate in multiple stations. After about twenty minutes, invite the kids to switch decorating stations and try a new one.

Encourage! Encourage! Encourage! Walk around the room and offer words of encouragement to the preteens and volunteers. Be specific and authentic as you share. Remind them that they are contributing to the success of this year's VBS. They're creating a space that says, "Wow!"

Celebrate success. As preteens finish a backdrop, character, or complete the task at a station, lead the group in a huge cheer. Preteens need to see they're making a difference. Take pictures. Lots of them!

Sound the whistle! Lower the volume on your music and let everyone know they have ten minutes to complete their work. After ten minutes, challenge the preteens to clean up quickly. We used a video countdown and challenged kids to have the room cleaned up before the video ended. It worked!

After clean up, we moved everyone into another room for Go!

Here's what you'll do next:

Place preteens in pods of six and assign two leaders to each pod. Gather everyone and explain the goal of Go! is to invite families to attend your VBS.

Tell the kids that they'll be going on a hayride (or other mode of transportation) through a local neighborhood to VBS Carol . . . singing worship songs and inviting kids and families to VBS. (They'll be shocked! But, it's summer . . . surprise!)

Go!

Make a joyful noise. Board the hayride and hit the neighborhood streets praising God! Have your worship leader bring his or her guitar and a few tambourines or drums. Invite kids to sing and play along. Your music will draw people outside. Challenge kids and leaders to sing in rounds, clap while they sing, and dance. Make this experience fun.

Stop along the way. Ask your driver to stop periodically and allow kids to place flyers on doorsteps or hang door hangers on doors of the homes. Only allow kids to exit the "vehicle" on the house side of the vehicle. Discourage kids from running back and forth across the street. You'll cover both sides of the street by having the driver go up and down the street twice.

Take pictures and video on your trip. Use the footage the following week at church to celebrate your amazing preteens. You can also use the footage to make your own music video!

For the day, and especially the off-site caroling, provide permission slips for the parents to sign prior to your event day.

They've Gone, Now They're Back

And, they're probably hungry. End your "Ready, Set, Go!" with a fun, preteen-friendly feast. We had a Rainforest Fondue Feast. Kids dunked different types of rainforest fruits and nuts (we prescreened for allergies) in yummy white, milk, and dark chocolate. They loved it.

"Ready, Set, Go!" is an event rising preteens will anticipate each year. They can't wait to be old enough to join the creative, collaborative fun. Current preteens will start planning the event as soon as our VBS theme was announced. Similarly, the VBS Decorating team will look forward to partnering with the preteens to ensure that the VBS decorations are awesome. Together, these two groups will transform your church with the components that make the environment you desire for your theme to be evident. More importantly, "Ready, Set, Go!" will provide a place where service-filled preteens can use their gifts to serve God and others.

Get your church on board for "Ready, Set, Go!" Instead of a whack on the side of the head, you'll get a God-sized pat on the back.

As Director of Children's Ministry for the Tennessee Conference of the United Methodist Church, Patty Smith equips children's ministry leaders in over 1,000 churches. Prior to this role, she was the Senior Product Developer for Children's Ministry at Group Publishing.

psmith@tnumc.org
www.tnumc.org

More importantly, "Ready, Set, Go!" will provide a place where service-filled preteens can use their gifts to serve God and others.

An Intergenerational VBS

by Linda Tozier

An intergenerational VBS involves all ages of the congregation taking part in the activities together. Individuals discover God's Word through Bible stories, crafts, music, drama, and discovery activities in an age-diverse setting. Activity centers are adapted to meet the needs of each participant. At each center, young people learn together with older members of the congregation. Each activity center is led by a leader who provides the instruction for the lesson.

VBS groups travel together to each activity center as "families." Individuals discover how to achieve a more intimate relationship with God and have the opportunity to praise God within their families.

Benefits of an Intergenerational VBS

As various ages travel through activity centers, interactive leaning occurs together. Children and youth will benefit from older members' wisdom and knowledge of the Scriptures. Adults will benefit from the energy and excitement of the youth and children as they discover new Bible truths for their lives.

Your entire congregation will acquire an appreciation and perspective from each other. Children and youth learn from adults how God's truth changes lives. Adults experience renewed excitement for God by watching young people explore these truths.

Through sharing, all participants are inspired to grow in their relationship with God.

Grouping Your Families

Each congregation can decide the best format for grouping families. Families traveling together can consist of traditional family units of a mother, father, brothers, and sisters. Or families traveling together may consist of adults, youth, and children who are unrelated. Members will have the opportunity to bond as they travel together. Choose the best option based on your congregation.

Activity Centers

Bible Stories

Children, youth, and adults become a part of the Bible stories when they travel to the Bible center. These times can involve all of the senses as they bring the Bible stories to life. As they learn Bible Scriptures together they can spend time talking about the meaning of the verses and stories and how it applies to each person differently. With everyone in the family at different points in their faith journey, the verses may mean different things helping to teach everyone how God's word is ageless and timeless and has something for everyone.

Crafts

Craft time should be a relaxed and positive learning experience for each participant. Young people can appreciate the help and expertise from the adults, and vice versa. During this time, the youth will feel valuable if allowed an opportunity for leadership. This is a great time for all ages to share in creating a mural for display in the church. Long after VBS is over, all ages will be proud of their lasting accomplishment for their church.

Music

During music time all ages will interact by sharing talents together. Children and youth can share their musical talents with adults, who are able to accept and affirm their abilities. Adults will share their experiences of how music has played a part in their spiritual journey.

Families can rehearse music or drama to be used during assembly time. As they are encouraged to perform in these positive settings, individuals will feel accepted, gain a healthy self-esteem, and make a contribution to others and to their church.

Discovery Time

Families make discoveries of their own through science activities. Through this center, families work together to explore how science demonstrations relate to their faith.

Recreation

During this time, true intergenerational relationships can be formed as groups play and laugh together. Adults need to enjoy themselves and be careful not to compete with the children and youth. Children and youth need an opportunity for play and a change of pace from the other center experiences.

Snack

Snack time is a great way for group members to spend quality time together. Families can use this break time to make snacks for themselves, or you might choose several families to make the snacks for all VBS participants. This arrangement teaches children how groups can work together to share their talents.

If you begin your VBS with a dinner, ask the families to sit together so they can share experiences during that time.

Mission time

Hearing and discussing mission stories gives an opportunity for adults, youth, and children to talk about ways they can make a difference in their community. Adults will be able to help the young people realize how they too can be missionaries and bring the word of God to others. Perhaps family groups can combine craft and mission time to work on needed church or community projects, help a family in need, or make crafts for a local nursing home.

Another part of mission time can be telling your faith story with the others in the family. This can be difficult for some people. Sometimes if adults are able to tell children how they grew and came to know God, it will help the adult practice telling his or her story as well as open up the child to hearing someone else's story.

> The combination of concrete thinking of children and abstract understanding of adults can bring new meaning to each activity.

Reflection Time

Reflection time comes at the end of each VBS day as a way to review the Bible stories and apply the teachings to everyday life. Reflection time involves sharing ideas and life stories as well as playing games and having fun.

Worship time is a wonderful opportunity to share experiences about how God has touched the lives of people in each family. Sharing faith stories can influence other people's lives in ways we may never know.

This time also gives the family groups a chance to share prayer concerns. Praying for each other in a family setting can be very meaningful and help members of the family develop good prayer habits.

Throughout the intergenerational experience, everyone has a chance to learn and share. Adults in the family group need to be ready to be participants and let the activity center leaders in charge of each center be the leaders. The combination of concrete thinking of children and abstract understanding of adults can bring new meaning to each activity.

Linda Tozier is the director and senior editor for vacation Bible school at The United Methodist Publishing House.

Weekday Summer Event — Wet and Wacky Water Day!

by Susan Cutshall

Looking for a fun, exciting event to hold during the summer? Wet and Wacky Water Day is full of fun and surprises!

Summer is a great time to strengthen your relationships with the children you serve and it can also give them an opportunity to just be kids!

The stories of "Jonah and the Big Fish" as well as "Moses and the Israelites Crossing the Red Sea" are featured during the day as the inspiration for a "slew" great relays, games, and all-out hilarity!

Anytime you have a "play situation," it's important that you establish your boundaries and rules up front. Always stress that being safe is more important than being first.

The children were asked to bring two beach towels for the day. As they arrive, we play "Pass the Fish." Two children hold the ends of a beach towel with a stuffed toy fish in the middle. They then pass the fish to the next two children holding a beach towel by working together to launch the fish in the air. As more children arrive, they are challenged to get the fish passed down the line of towels without hitting the ground. As they improve, spread the children out further so it's more difficult to keep the fish off the ground.

The chart below will help you plan the day to make it fun and memorable. One of the most important things to remember is don't just be an observer, but have fun *with* the kids!

Activity	Needed Items	How to Play	Tips
Soggy Jog	2 pair of large sweat pants, 2 buckets of water	Divide into two teams. First child dunks pants into bucket of water, puts them on and runs around a chair twenty feet away and back to the next player. Make sure everyone gets a turn.	After one child goes, it doesn't matter if pants are inside out or not. You could add a sweatshirt for the second round.
Story—Moses and the Israelites	Book—*Interactive Stories from the Old Testament*	Kids participate in the story with actions and motions.	Be familiar enough with the story to have fun! Do the motions with the kids—exaggerate!
Crossing the Sea	Sprinkler and hose	Mark out two "safe" areas with a sea in between. One child is "Moses"— he or she crimps the hose cutting off the water to the sprinkler. The kids cross the "sea" but never know when the sprinkler will get them!	Be sure to review how the Israelites crossed on dry land and the Egyptians got wet.

Activity	Needed Items	How to Play	Tips
Drip, Drip, Drench	A large sponge, bucket of water	Played just like "Duck, Duck, Goose" except the sponge drips water on several kids before drenching one person in the circle, leading to a chase around the circle.	Try to start in a dry area of grass. Once it gets wet, things get slippery and kids fall easily.
Story—Jonah & the Big Fish	Parachute & small rubber fish	Have some parachute fun. First make the fish fly off the parachute by creating ripples. Next read the Bible story while everyone sits under the parachute.	It may get hot under the parachute. Discuss what it may have felt like for Jonah inside the fish for three days.
You Can't Hide!	Plastic squirt bottle filled with water	The person who is "It" has a plastic squirt bottle. "It" closes his or her eyes and counts to 30. "It" tags other players with a squirt.	Talk about Jonah not being able to hide from God when God had a job for him to do. We can't hide from God either.
Water Baseball	Plastic baseball bat and ball, sprinkler, bucket of water, basket with shaving cream, small swimming pool	First base is the sprinkler, Second base is the bucket of water — players dunk their head here, Third base is the basket of shaving cream, and Home is the swimming pool.	Play just like baseball! Have plenty of shaving cream on hand because third base is very popular!
Ice Fishing	Small swimming pool filled with water, add ice cubes	The kids take turns trying to catch the ice cubes using only their toes!	Have plenty of ice on hand because it will melt quickly!
Flying Sponges	Sponges and plenty of water	Play like dodge ball. You can play in a circle or run the gauntlet between two lines.	Make older kids throw with their non-dominate hand.
Water limbo	Water hose with nozzle	Kids try to "limbo" under the running water — lower it until they can't get under.	Every now and then, just squirt a kid with the hose!
Lemonade Relay	Lemons cut into quarters, packets of sugar and cups of water	Form two teams. First player runs to specified place, sucks the juice from a lemon, swallows the sugar from the packet, and drinks a cup of water. Player then jumps up and down ten times to mix the lemonade!	Have a camera ready for this one! The faces they make when they suck out the lemon juice are hilarious!!

Activity	Needed Items	How to Play	Tips
Water Toss	Resealable baggie filled with water	Kids form pairs and play just like the egg toss game	You can vary the amount of water in the bags to make it easier or harder!
Bob for Marshmallows	Big bowl of flour and large marshmallows	Play just like bobbing for apples, but they have to stick their faces into the flour to find the marshmallows	Have a hose nearby to spray the flour off of faces.
The Shrinking Soap Relay	One bar of travel sized soap and one bucket of water per team	Form teams. First child unwraps the soap, runs to the bucket of water and "washes hands" for thirty seconds. Player runs back and next child goes. The goal is to shrink the soap away first without breaking it.	If you are really brave, you can have a bucket of dirt at the starting line for them to get on their hands before it's their turn to wash!
Seaweed Relay	One Large bucket of water and one empty bowl per team	Form teams. Each child takes a turn running to the bucket. Dip hair into bucket. Run back to starting line, squeeze water from hair into the bowl. First team to fill the bowl wins.	You don't want to play boys vs. girls on this one!
Jump Rope Splash	Long jump rope and cups of water	With two people turning the rope, a child tries to jump the rope ten times while holding a cup of water — trying *not* to spill any!	Start with same amount of water in each cup. The winner is the one who has the most water left! Everyone else then throws their water on the winner!
Water Balloon Bottom Bust	Water balloons	Divide into teams. First child runs to the chair-chooses a water balloon and then sits on it to pop it. They then return to the line and the next child goes!	Have plenty of balloons made up ahead of time!

At the close of the day we sit down together and reflect on the fun we've had and how being part of a community of faith is a wonderful experience.

We ask the children to name their favorite activity of the day and also ask for ways we can make improvements. The kids are so creative and always want to tell you how you can do something better. Be sure to listen so that the next summer's "Wet and Wacky Water Day" will be even more fun!

Susan Cutshall has been the Director of Childhood Ministries at St. Luke UMC in Lexington, Kentucky, since 1994. Her leadership team has been credited for creating a children's ministry that is effective and attractive to a variety of families. Susan has been an avid supporter of International Network of Children's Ministry (INCM), has led workshops at Children's Pastors' Conference (CPC), and has been a presenter for Children's Ministry Seminars for nine years. Susan and her husband Greg have two children, Lance and Lauren. Susan is an avid Indianapolis Colts fan and has seen them play three times, in three different stadiums.

The Inside Scoop

For the first time in many years, a little country church in Oregon decided to offer Vacation Bible School. The leaders prayed that God would bless their effort to reach lots of kids in their community.

A western theme was chosen. To get the word out, they planned a Saturday kick-off with an invitation to come on Monday for a week of VBS. On that Saturday over one hundred kids arrived at the little rural church. All was going well with the games, candy, activities. There was a long line at the horse ride . . . a highlight of the kick-off event.

A little concern arose at the horse station when some of the leaders decided to give the horse a break since he looked a little strange. All of a sudden, the horse reared up and collapsed on the ground. Parents and children rushed over to see what had happened. Soon everyone knew. The horse was dead!

The leaders took the kids inside the church sanctuary. They improvised activities for more than an hour while others decided what to do with the horse. A local veterinarian was called. The vet arrived but he told them that there was nothing he could do . . . since the horse was dead. The leaders tried to reach the owner of the horse, but soon learned that the owner was out of town and unreachable.

Now what? The pastor arrived. Even though he felt bad about the horse, he made sure that the leaders knew that the horse could not be left on the church parking lot. The next day was Sunday and the gravel parking lot would be needed during the church service.

So, what do you do with a horse . . . on a Saturday afternoon . . . lying dead . . . in the church parking lot?

Call for a backhoe. The backhoe operator arrived and buried the horse in the middle of the parking lot. The children were dismissed to go spread the word about the Vacation Bible School.

Would kids in this rural community show up! Monday morning arrived. The kids started streaming in.

But . . . they forgot Romans 8:28, NIV: "And we know that in all things God works for the good of those who love him, who have been called according to his purpose."

You see, it wasn't the decorations, the games, candy, or activities that caused a stir in the community surrounding this little county church. It was the dead horse that the kids could not stop talking about. This was Romans 8:28 in action. The little church was blessed and lives were changed.

John Tietsort

Volunteer Events

And whatever you do, in word or deed,
do everything in the name of the Lord Jesus,
giving thanks to God the Father through him.

(Colossians 3:17)

Staff Motivation and Appreciation

by Patsy Dennis

Simple Ideas to do With Your Staff

Food & Fellowship Meetings
Be consistent with meetings with your teachers and assistants. Food is always helpful. It somehow forms relationships one with another. Listed are several ideas to enhance and make your meetings fun as well as communicable.

Play Money Auction — Give play money to each one as they arrive, (or) let them earn play money each month in the children's ministry by making phone calls to children, visitation of children, and so forth. Purchase several inexpensive gifts and wrap them so no one will know what is inside. Start the bidding and let each one bid for the wrapped gift.

2,000 Nickels Give Away — $100 is 2,000 nickels. Place your nickels in a box to give away: fifteen nickels to the person who made the most phone calls this month; forty nickels to the person who visited the most children in your ministry this month; twenty-eight nickels to the person who arrived at this meeting first; a handful of nickels to the person whose class brought their Bibles the most in the class last Sunday; thirty-five nickels to the person who wrote the most cards to children this month; fifty-six nickels given to the person who read the most chapters in the Bible this week; and so forth. (It is wise if you already have your nickels placed in a baggie with amount on the outside and the name of what you are giving the nickels for.) Make up your own.

Surprise Box Give Away — Decorate three or four boxes (or more) of inexpensive gifts to take to your meeting. Everyone attending the meeting places their name in a hat four times (if that's how many gifts you are giving away). At different times during the meeting, have a drawing to give a decorated box away.

New Year's Meeting — Purchase party hats and blowers to give to all who attend the meeting. At certain times of the evening (set a timer) the first one putting on their hat and blowing their blower will receive something from a "goody" box you have previously prepared. Inside this goody box should be items your teachers can use personally or in the classroom. Makes them feel special.

Valentine's Meeting — Make special valentine bags tied with red and white ribbons filled with things that are red and can be used by the teacher (classroom or personal). Give small boxes of candy boxes away by placing them all on a pretty decorated table. Number the boxes. Then let each teacher pick a number from a hat and when you call out that number, they can either pick a box of candy from the table or take another person's box of candy. Of course number one has to start by taking from the table. At the end, number one can go back and pick someone else's candy box or keep the one they have. When all is finished, look on the bottom of the box of candy and there should be a special code for a special prize. They may have traded that box around all night to one another.

March Meeting — Fill a bag of "green items" (candy, shamrock stickers, pencil, plants, artificial grass/clover, and so forth) to give away to each teacher or staff person at your meeting. Or give "one dollar green bucks" away for things your staff has done during the month.

Easter Month Meeting — Have an Easter Egg Hunt for the adults at your meeting by hiding special treats. Whatever they find, they have to give you a one-minute talk on how to use it to teach a lesson to a child. (You can teach a lesson on "anything.") Also make a nice little Easter basket for each with small things each one likes.

Example: Patsy is a beautician (hair lifter), she collects (clowns), loves (bubble gum), eats chocolate (tootsie rolls), loves to write (ink pen) and so forth.

Maypole Meeting — Have different colors of pastel streamers taped to a table centerpiece. Then tape the opposite ends of the steamers all over the room. When teachers arrive, let each one choose a streamer and follow that streamer to find a gift. Make the gifts funny or serious.

Graduation Meeting — Your meeting is probably focused on all your children graduating to another class at this time of the year. Have pre-assigned lists written on certificate-like papers and rolled up with ribbons tied around the scroll. On the paper also put handwritten comments about positive things you could say about that particular teacher.

Stars & Stripes Meeting — Have a red, white and blue flag cake for dessert. Wrap a box in plain red paper. Fill the box with red, white, and dark blue tissue paper coming out the top. Inside the box place special small gifts that pertain to making your children in each classroom "explode with excitement." Or you could give a homemade firecracker. Cut empty paper towel rolls in half. Place candies inside each half and then wrap the roll in red tissue paper. Then place yellow tissue paper at the top and twist each end together to close.

Vacation Meeting — Fix your meeting room to look like a beach with umbrellas on the floor. Have everyone sit on the beach towels on the floor. Take pictures acting silly (like your kids would). It's really fun. Make vacation packets to pass out with small candles, certificates for special restaurants, and so forth to give away. Be creative!

Back to School Meeting — Fill brown paper sacks with crayons, pencils, glue, rulers, erasers, and so forth. Give a sack to each person attending the meeting. Fill a grocery sack with lots of supplies to give away to "a lucky staff teacher" whose name is drawn from a hat.

Fall Festival Meeting — Have each one make up a small table game and bring it to "show 'n tell" at the meeting. Give away baggies of carnival surprises for questions answered during the meeting. Give away a better gift to the one who has the best carnival game.

Thanksgiving Meeting — Have a "Mini" Thanksgiving Dinner at your meeting. Assign each person a food item, but have them place the food in doll pots and pans and serve everything "tiny." If you want more later, you can have more. Make a small photo album filled with one page for each person on your staff telling all the good deeds they have accomplished in their class with their children. Make one for each teacher or put all in the same album and pass around during the meeting.

Christmas Meeting — Make the meeting special by candlelight and Christmas tree lights. Let each person tell of a special Christmas they've had during their lifetime. You'll be surprised of all the input each one will tell. Have a time of Christmas carols together and praying.

Caricatures — Add pictures of your teacher's faces to funny looking bodies. Then copy them and make overheads to show on a projector. This will be fun for all if you do it right, but do not make fun of someone. Have the funny body look good for the person. You might even add a paragraph or two about their hobbies and so forth.

Certificates for all — Designate a month for one or two of your teachers to have lunch or dinner with you. Or give each teacher a dinner certificate for two for the teacher and guest to have dinner on you or your children's ministry.

> Mail packages or letters to your staff periodically. Everyone loves to get a "surprise" in the mail.

Film Containers — Collect film containers and place quarters inside one and washers inside the others. Have your staff trade around the containers. The one holding the real one at the end gets to keep all the quarters. Always do fun things together. It's great for team building.

Snow Cook Out — Invite all the team together for a cook-out dinner when it starts to snow. Put on your coats and hats and grill to your heart's content. There's nothing like sitting on a picnic table in the snow eating grilled hamburgers or steaks!

Awards, Awards, Awards — At a special dinner or banquet give crazy awards for whatever reason you wish to your teachers:

phone book	for making the most phone calls to children
toy car	for visiting the most children
toothbrush	for smiling the most
toy sewing machine	for sewing drama costumes
toy piano	for leading worship
notepad	for writing the most notes
album record	for keeping children's church records
toy camera	for taking pictures of your kids
play money	for counting the offering
toy microphone	for running the sound system
game	for playing games with the kids the most
light bulb	for coming up with ideas

Switcheroo — Have the kids switch places with the director and all the teachers one Sunday. This is so much fun. Make sure you choose one of the kids who can lead and talk. Don't pick someone who can only follow. All the teachers can be students for a day along with the other children.

Kids Write Songs — Have the kids write songs about the teachers and sing them. Make a word describing each letter of their name on paper and give to them. This looks good if you use a computer and do it in Old English style writing.

S—Sensational
H—Happy
E—Ernest
R—Ravishing
R—Real
I—Irresistible

Staff Newsletter — Make a one-page newsletter to give out monthly praising all your staff to one another. Or highlight one special teacher each month including everything you know about that staff person. This is really encouraging to each other.

Teacher Contests — Have different contests between teachers: phone calls, home visits, teacher encouragement calls, letters written, Bible chapters read, and so forth.

Something's in the Mail — Mail packages or letters to your staff periodically. Everyone loves to get a "surprise" in the mail.

Cake Bake — Bake a special cake for each one's birthday and take to their home.

Balloons, Balloons — Place a bouquet of balloons on the teachers' classroom doors for a birthday or a special occasion. Encourage the kids to write notes to them.

This is Your Life Night — Invite special people in their lives to attend a meeting, dinner, or special night. You can have one special guest for each teacher or plan a special night or morning for each teacher at a designated date.

I Love Pizza — Order and pay for pizza to be delivered to your staff's home. Surprise them.

Green Eggs & Ham — Order a fast food breakfast and take to your teacher's family one Saturday morning.

You're Special Tree — Secure a branch in a small pot. Have the children in each classroom write out thank-you notes for their teacher, roll the notes up with a ribbon, and tie them on the branches of the tree. Give the tree as a gift.

Special Birthday — Make their birthdays special. Give a gift, make a card. Photograph a picture of the teacher with the class. Put a special announcement in the children's bulletin. Give the teacher a balloon bouquet, flowers, cards and letters from parents of the kids in their class, and so forth.

Six-Foot Candy Bar — Put little favorite candy bars on a six-foot stick and wrap for them.

Coupon Booklets — Make and decorate coupons on the computer to give to your staff to show your appreciation for them. The coupons could be for free babysitting, a free movie, or an afternoon tea with you.

Take My Picture — Video your teachers and show at a special meeting.

V.I.P. Person — Have a special V.I.P. day once per month or quarter and recognize that staff person in front of the children's church.

Team Events — Plan quarterly places for all your children's team to go with their families and especially include their children. They will certainly know you care when you invite all the children. Go to places where the kids can play and all have lunch together.

Did the Phone Ring — Make frequent phone calls to your staff. Leave a nice message on their answering machines. Call and ask questions about your children's ministry. If they can answer the quiz question about children's ministry, they can have a fast food meal on you!

Funny Hat Wear — On days when you need a laugh, have all your teachers wear crazy looking hats they make and wear to class.

Candlelight Communion — Have communion with all your staff families once in a while, or make it a special time together each year at the same time. You as the director bless each family together.

No Reason Party — Have a party at your home and invite your team "for no reason." Do silly things and eat silly food.

Snafu Dinner — Invite everyone to a mysterious dinner at church or at your home. A snafu dinner consists of: Eating from new clean ash trays, buckets, or anything you find that food could be placed in sanitarily. Drink from bud vases, cans, or whatever is sanitary. Plan a menu which includes funny names for each item served. Then give each person a choice of the entree, two vegetables, salad, drink, bread, and dessert. But have your names already lined up in the kitchen. Have your waiters take orders. They can order seven items. Silverware is already on the table. For instance:

> Bulbs (Potatoes)
> Mud (Chocolate Pie)
> White Juice (Water)
> Round Dots (Peas)
> Heaven's Delight (Angel Food Cake)
> Snort Snort (Pork Chops)
> Dark Juice (Cola)
> Hot Beans (Coffee)
> Loafin' Around (Meat Loaf)
> Slurp Slurp (Spaghetti)

Get the picture? Be creative on your menu. They only know what the first item is, not what the real item in parenthesis is. It's great to see their faces when they see what they've picked to eat. Some may choose three meats, two desserts, and two drinks for their seven items. It's hilarious!

Christmas Card for Me? — Bring Christmas cards for each person at a meeting or get-together. No one's name is on the envelope. Pass out the cards and have everyone write a special note inside the card to give to someone (not knowing who will get it). Then draw names. Each person writes the name he or she drew on the envelope. The director will take the cards and give them to the rightful people. Read cards out loud. This is very funny.

Sharing Time — Each teacher brings a favorite toy. Share something about that special toy and what it means to you or your children. Then tell how you could use this in an object lesson for your class.

Hiding in a Matchbox — Give a wooden matchbox to each teacher. Ask them to fill it with anything that will fit in the box. The person with the most items wins a small gift or recognition within the group!

Name that Carol — Play Name that Tune with Christmas carols by playing CD's and each one jotting down the name of the carol. Only play three seconds worth of a carol.

Grow Mustard Seed Grow — Give all teachers a mustard seed. Remind them that they can plant each child so that he or she can grow spiritually to be what God wants them to be.

Puzzle Envelopes — Cut a note into a puzzle. Mail the puzzle to your teachers. They will have to put the puzzles togethers to read them.

For the Mirror — Write notes backwards. Send the notes to your teachers. They will need to hold the notes up to a mirror to read them.

Memory Scrapbook — Collect memorabilia of things and pictures of each teacher you work with and make a scrapbook. Be creative and make each page exciting! Use wrapping paper or stationery or wallpaper pages for the background. Use stickers where appropriate. Cut pictures and frames with cookie cutters for fancy designs.

Monthly Meeting Invitations — Make invitations from just about anything. To remind your assistants of something, send an invitation made of a giant ink pen with all the information written down the blade of the pen. If you are going on a retreat, make stationery which looks like a cabin. Find a picture of each event, then photocopy and wa-la! You have it! Anything beats the old "hum drum" of plain paper.

Spoil Your Helpers with Things — Purchase inexpensive things to give those who help you.

Unique Birthdays — Always send a birthday card. Cut confetti and place inside the card and when they open it confetti will fall out. This spills out love to them. Try giving a cupcake or a Hostess® Twinkies with a candle in it. Give

> Give all teachers a mustard seed. Remind them that they can plant each child so that he or she can grow spiritually to be what God wants them to be.

certificates for places to eat inside birthday cards. Make a giant posterboard birthday card and let fellow workers write on the card. Write special weekly articles about the birthday person in the children's newsletters.

Staff Folders — Keep a folder on each person in your ministry who helps you. Place anything of paper they give you. Ask your teachers to complete surveys and evaluations about your ministry. Make caricatures of them and place in the folder. From time to time show each teacher what's in the folder. Sometimes things you've kept means a lot to them. It also helps to keep up with their years of service in your ministry.

Progressive Dinner — Just like the progressive dinners where you go to different people's homes make each room in your children's ministry a different place to eat. Fix the room so it's decorated to meet the need of your desired meal. One room for appetizers, one room for the main course, and one room for dessert and drinks. Each room should be placed so each one can have a seat. Designate a certain amount of time in each place. This is a fun-filled evening and breaks up doing the same thing each time you eat. Have music playing in every room to set the mood. You might even have a salad buffet room where each one can make their own salad. Another twist: Make each room a different country. The main course could be China where you eat on the floor on pillows, another room could be Italy with Italian food, and so forth. Of course choose music to fit the theme.

Japanese Dinner — Send out invitations to all your staff telling them you are having a sit down dinner and that they need to bring a pillow. Or make it a secret and tell them to come to a certain place hungry and bring a pillow. Have candelit decor and Japanese music playing softly. Hand them chopsticks and steer them into the room to sit on the floor with their pillows.

Spray paint branches of a tree white and place white twinkle lights on it for decorations. Place candles inside brown paper sacks with decorations cut into the sacks. Have fun!

Secret Gift Room — Sort of like Secret Santa Shop, have a room set up with items to purchase for a gift. Assistants can purchase items for each other during the year to help boost morale in the ministry. If one is having a difficult time, an appropriate small gift could be just the boost they need. Draw names among the staff and have them purchase items for the person they drew.

Secret Pals or Secret Friends — Have four events per year. On Valentine's Day draw names among everyone and get a small token gift for "Secret Sweeties," at Easter for "Secret Bunnies,"at Thanksgiving for "Secret Pumpkins," and of course at Christmas for "Secret Elves." Five days beforehand pick your target date on which items will be delivered. Have a delivery person or just have each person deliver their own. On each day of the five, you do this: First day give something the color of the holiday, the second day, give something paper, the third day, give something sweet, the fourth day give something shaped like the holiday, and the fifth day give something that costs two dollars. Reveal your secret friend on the fifth day by giving them a handmade card.

My Valentine Date — Invite your staff to bring a date or their spouse to a party given in their honor. Nothing for them to do but attend and have fun! Secure other help within the church to help you pull this together, like moms and dads of children's ministry. Decorate with red and white. Add twinkle lights and romantic music. Have waiters serve the dinner. Have a kissing booth and give away candy kisses. Have everyone tell about a special time in your children's ministry when they loved a child in a special way. Let them tell all what they think love really is. Do a game with candy hearts.

Think-a-thon — Designate a time and place and have all your staff come with pen and pad in hand. (If you want to use this for a fundraiser, get sponsors to pay five cents per idea you come up with.) Serve snacks. Let everyone give ideas on a certain topic. Think about all the things you would like to have in your children's ministry during the year and let everyone give you "off the top of my head" ideas. Write them all down under each topic. When you get ready to have that certain "thing" you will have lots of new and fresh ideas to pull from. At the end of the evening, put all the ideas in a box and draw one or two for a winning idea and give a restaurant certificate for two to the winners.

St. Patrick's Day Gathering — Decorate everything in green. Serve all green food. Ask everyone to dress in green. Do a point system game of twenty points for each item of clothing you have on that's green. Set up card tables and place four to a table to play board games with one another. After an allotted time, call "Switch" and have the number ones and number twos go to the next table. Have a funny skit sometimes during the evening.

Hawaiian Luau — Plan this party at a swimming pool or outside on the grass. Choose soothing Hawaiian music. If you are at a pool, fill the pool with balloons of all colors or float candles. Lights are a must for this party. Let your staff invite two or three people of their choice to be their guest to this festivity. Give out leis and plenty of prizes. And of course put umbrellas in the glasses. Have the guys wear Hawaiian shirts and the girls grass skirts over their shorts or moo moo style dresses with ankle leis.

Singing Valentines — Have a group of people make up musical valentine verses for your staff. Then have a talented singer go to each staff member and sing the valentine.

Cookie Grams — Have a group of kids bake cookies and go with you to deliver the cookies to each staff person's home. Include notes telling them how much they are loved by your group.

Friendship Baskets — Fill a basket with stationery, pens, stamps, stickers, and so forth for each one on your staff. On Friend's Day you can give them the baskets and tell them how much of a friend they are to you.

Re-Creating Toys — At Christmastime let your staff help gather and repair toys to take to children in need. This is a wonderful ministry in itself. If you have lots of places to visit, enlist more help from the teenagers. They love helping out.

Keep a Watchful Eye — Always watch for the people who are "child oriented" when looking for a volunteer to help with children's ministries. People who tend to be bothered by a crying or screaming child usually are not your "children's ministry" type volunteers. The ones who get down on their knees or bend over to listen when a child speaks can have an A+ when it comes to handling children. Be on the lookout for these type people. Make all your events look and sound wonderful if you are recruiting. Talk one-on-one as much as possible. Ask everyone you contact to pray about a specific need you have. Never tell negatives about your ministry, this will drive them away from you. Don't tell them all the things you do in one meeting. This will tire them out and they may be overwhelmed. Make your office an "open door" to them for whatever reason they need you and you will probably keep them for a while. Make them feel very useful. If they come up with a neat idea and you already have thought of it, give them the credit and say it's wonderful (if it is).

Staff Appreciation Banquet

Schedule a certain date and place to have your banquet.

Invitations — Invite your senior pastor and spouse, church board members, your staff's friends, and of course their spouses.

Banquet Place — Can you decorate? Can you play music? Is there enough room to seat everyone? Is the food to everyone's liking?

Awards — Make silly awards. Trophy shops will make inexpensive name plates. Add something that represents the award to a wooden plaque and then place each name plate on the bottom of the plaque. The plaques can be small wooden blocks you buy or make. Some ideas on silly awards:
- The one who telephoned kids the most: telephone
- The one who smiled most at kids: toothpaste and a toothbrush

- The one who wrote most notes to kids: paper pads
- The one who collected the most money: play money or toy calculator
- The one who sewed drama clothes: toy sewing machine
- The musician for worship: toy piano
- The one in charge of parties: play food
- The sweetest staff person: two candy kisses

Other awards:
Glue pink feathers on paper. Write "I'm tickled Pink" that you are on my team.
Give a gas coupon for the one making the most visits to children.
Give a box of stationery to the one writing the most cards to the children.

Slide Show or Video — Take pictures of each person during the year to show at the banquet. Get lots of funny shots as well as serious ones. The song "Working Nine to Five" by Dolly Parton makes this funnier.

Sensational Idea Money — Run a contest between all of them and the one who had the best of the best of the best idea for the year wins fifty dollars at the banquet.

Style Show — Have your teenagers do a funny style show for your guests:

Balloon Dress (Dress with balloons all over it), Pillbox Hat (Pill bottles on a hat), Slipover Dress (Undergarment slip draped over dress), Tea Dress (Dress with tea bags), Brushed Denim Jeans (Jeans worn while brushing leg with hairbrush), Bell Bottom Pants (Bells sewn on bottom of pant legs), Spaghetti Strap Dress (Cooked spaghetti over shoulders) and so forth.

Patsy Dennis lives in Versailles, Kentucky, where she has served as the Children's Pastor at King's Way Assembly of God Church for the past thirty-three years. Patsy is writing a book about sensational ideas. She shares her skills and expertise on a state level as the Kentucky District Children's Ministry Director for her denomination.

Team Building Event — Take Me Out To The Ball Game!

by Kal Otis

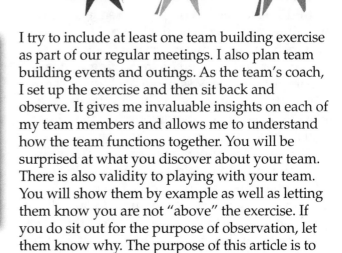

> O vercoming barriers to performance is how groups become teams.
> — Unknown Author

For years I have conducted workshops on team building. To make the principles of team building more palatable, I compare ministry to a team sport. It really doesn't matter what team sport you compare it to, the principles that make a team successful are the same in ministry. The primary goal is to win!

A team and their members have to undergo vigorous specialized training to perfect their own skills as well as learn to rely and play together to succeed. This requires practice! Since we are all on the same team, and yet not all the same, we've got to learn to play together. Team "bonding" is an important process that will help ensure a close-knit team. The team needs to become one in purpose and desire.

Team building events, exercises, and games are a fun way to develop cohesiveness. They tear down walls of communication, provide avenues that encourage discussion, and increase productivity. Successful organizations like IBM® use team building exercises as part of their creative meetings.

I try to include at least one team building exercise as part of our regular meetings. I also plan team building events and outings. As the team's coach, I set up the exercise and then sit back and observe. It gives me invaluable insights on each of my team members and allows me to understand how the team functions together. You will be surprised at what you discover about your team. There is also validity to playing with your team. You will show them by example as well as letting them know you are not "above" the exercise. If you do sit out for the purpose of observation, let them know why. The purpose of this article is to help you plan a team building event.

How to Plan a Team Building Event

When selecting a team building event for your team, it is important to know what you are expecting to get out of the activity. If you know your goals going into the event, you are more likely to make the right choice in selecting the venue and what type of activities you will plan for your team.

What is the main purpose for the event? Is this a recreational day, with a general goal of fun and camaraderie — or is this a purpose-driven venture into the dynamics of your group, with a goal of increased productivity, communication, and trust?

What is the time-frame for your event? Is this a one-to-six-hour event, a day, or multi-day?

Who are the key team members? Which team members are being included in this event — and is there anything significant you need to keep in front of you while planning this event?

Where will the event be held? Is this an on-site, meeting room — or off-site location, such as a conference center, park, or facility? Try different venues and see how they work. I've tried coffee shops, pizza places, a home of a team member, a camping lodge, a very large room with lots of space, a garden, a baseball field; you get the idea. See what inspires you and gives the team energy.

What is your budget? Here is one event that I have done that was a "grand slam" success. You can make this an annual event. Try not to get overwhelmed with the amount of information I am providing in this article. Personally, I tackle one concept only when I take my team out.

Event: Treating your volunteers to a baseball game is one way to show volunteer appreciation as well as build invaluable lessons and skills. To keep the cost low consider lawn tickets to a major league baseball game. This arrangement actually allows you to take time out to discuss the game and ministry strategy. I take my volunteers to a minor league outing. Travel together and arrive early. If you cannot afford to treat your team to a game, try visiting a local little league game for no cost, or watch a classic baseball movie together.

Uniform: I have fun designing baseball shirts for my team. You can personalize them by putting their last name on the back. Wear them to the game to enhance team spirit. They double up as Sunday morning attire.

> Everyone must know the "Big Picture."

Team Building: You can set the stage and peak their curiosity by arriving at the game and giving your team a list of questions that they can ponder as they watch the game. Midway through the game or during the seventh inning stretch, take time-out to discuss those questions. If you do not want to provide questions, you can ask your team to use their imaginations and simply draw parallels between what they do as a ministry team and the game of baseball.

Three Keys to Building a Winning Team

During the Championship Match, at any level, coaches, parents, and athletes gather around to see the two best teams fight tooth and nail for each run on the field. While the excitement, hard work, and talent are showcased and honored that day, the coaches are well aware that what they are watching is the result of months, if not years, of hard work and training.

There is a common thread behind all successful teams that is hard to see but is just as important as the physical traits of size, strength, speed, and natural strength.

Key #1: Everyone must know the "Big Picture." What are the goals for the team? At the end of the event/season, what ability level can the team expect?

For example in baseball: What is the "Big Picture" in baseball? Baseball players advance around bases by batting and running in an effort to score. Points, called "runs," are scored when a player on the batting team touches all the bases (including home plate) without being tagged or called "out." The team scoring the greater number of runs in the allotted number of innings wins the game.

Ministry Coach: Does every ministry team member know the ministry's mission statement, vision, goals, core values, and strategy? If your team does not know these important "Big Picture" items, your team is not playing on the same team or playing the same game. Do they know how to apply it every Sunday morning? Can they clearly articulate it to others?

Key #2: Everyone must know the specific skills needed to attain and work towards the goal.

As your team's coach, are you committed to a team approach? Do you know your team? Have you taken the time to evaluate your team member's skills and match them up with their position? What are the steps needed to reach the "Big Picture?"

For example in baseball: The objective for teams playing in the field is to get three players on the batting team out. A batter is out when 1) he hits a ball, fair or foul, that is caught by a fielder before it touches the ground; 2) he is tagged, or first base is touched by a fielder holding the ball before the batter gets there; or 3) he strikes out. A base runner is out when 1) he is between bases and is tagged by a fielder holding the ball or 2) he is forced out.

Skills — In the game of baseball you need runners, batters, catchers, fielders, pitchers, and umpires.

Equipment — A fielder's glove, baseball, baseball bat, cleats or sneakers, matching uniform, baseball cap, and batting helmet. For the catcher: face mask, chest protector, shin guards, and catcher's glove.

Knowledge — The rules of the game.

Ministry Coach: Does every member understand that team members score a "grand slam" when they lead a child to Christ? Do they understand that at the end of every lesson or story, it is vital to share the gospel message even though it might not be part of the written material? If not it's a "strike." Does every ministry team member have the skills, equipment and knowledge to accomplish the mission statement and goals? Do they understand how to use it? Do they know volunteer guidelines, standard of excellence, volunteer qualifications/requirements, safety and security procedures, and what your teaching guidelines are?

Key #3: Everyone must be willing to attend practice to work towards the identified goals and demonstrate consistent performance. Is everyone committed to working towards the goal? Do team members know how to examine errors without personal attacks? Does the group have the capacity to create new ideas? Is the team and the individuals prepared to take risks? Does each member know that he or she can influence the outcome? Are they willing to attend training meetings? Are they willing to commit to their own personal spiritual growth? Are they willing to invest time and energy into improving their own "game"?

This team building event has blessed me through the years. It is fun, energizing, and enlightening. Give it a try! The lists of team building skills that your team can glean from are endless when you take your team to a ball game.

Kal Otis has over 24 years of team building experience in both secular and ministry settings. In her current position as a Family pastor, she leads high performance teams that are both multigenerational and multifunctional. She has been instrumental in leading the charge of envisioning and implementing an integrated approach to Family Ministry at her church. She is passionate about equipping others to "think outside the box." A published author, she has been involved in evaluating church systems and assisting leadership to creatively align and synchronize all areas of ministry towards a common vision.

Creating Successful Children's Ministry Training Events

by Greg Baird

I can't wait to get to the children's ministry training meeting!

Our children's ministry training was so much fun this month!

I just used the ideas in my class that we learned in our children's ministry training session last week!

I'm always checking Facebook to see if our children's ministry director has posted something new that I can use to help when I'm serving the kids on Sundays.

I'm really looking forward to third grade team meeting with our children's pastor that we're having at the coffee shop on Tuesday!

Unfortunately, these are not things you hear very often from most children's ministry volunteers. Why is that? Because most children's ministry is not regular, relevant, or received very well!

One way to change that is to approach training with the "event" mentality. That doesn't mean that all training needs to be a "special event" as we might typically see that. It does mean that training — in whatever form — should be seen as something that is exciting, engaging and enjoyable, just like an event!

How do we do that?

Understanding General Principles For Training

- **Everyone** serving in children's ministry needs training! That means you, staff, core leaders, volunteers, substitute teachers, parent helpers, youth servants, and anyone else who serves.
- There are **different types** of training. Generally, training will fall into one of three categories:
  1. Introductory or orientation type training — this is primarily for new or returning volunteers.
  2. General skill development — learning how to interact with children, discipline methods, sharing the Gospel, or telling stories effectively are examples of this type of training.
  3. Leadership development — in order to effectively grow your ministry you must grow leaders, so investing intentionally with your core leadership is a must!

- Training events can accomplish **different purposes**, such as:
  1. Skill development — this is usually the central purpose of training in some form.
  2. Vision Casting — painting a picture of why we are doing what we're doing and what the future looks like is critical to keep your team engaged in the process.
  3. Communication — simple communication of things like calendar items or policy changes are a very important part of training.
  4. Team Building — connecting people in personal and relational ways only enhances what takes place in the classroom as they serve together.

- Providing a **framework** for the training you offer helps to facilitate its effectiveness. This is what moves your training from a requirement to an event that your team anticipates with enthusiasm. Your training must be:
  1. Practical and offer high value — your busy team members will disengage quickly if you waste their time.
  2. High quality — with today's easily accessible tools and resources, there is no excuse for poor quality. It's what is expected by today's leaders.
  3. Fun, engaging and experiential — long gone are the days when you can stand in front of your team and lecture for an hour. Active learning will make all the difference.
  4. Accommodating to everyone's ability level, personality and schedule — this is where many training programs break down, but don't do this and you won't keep an important segment of your team for very long (more on this later).
  5. Systematic and on-going — If you don't create an intentional plan for long-term team development, you will end up frustrated and ineffective, and so will they.

Offering Different Types of Training

No single type of training will effectively connect with all of your team all of the time. For example, if you only train through meetings, you will always miss the segment of your team that can't — or won't — attend meetings. Perhaps their work schedule won't allow it, or they're just the type that won't give up an evening to do this.

B e transparent and let them know that you face some of the same challenges they do, both in life and in ministry.

And just as not everyone will attend a meeting, there are others who will attend your training meeting but never read an email that you send. It's not their thing! Others won't check out the children's ministry page on Facebook, and still others don't really want to meet you for coffee.

As a young children's pastor, this really bothered me. I wanted (even made it mandatory!) all volunteers to attend our training meetings. But as I got older I realized that, in reality, I didn't respond to some forms of communication either — I was no different than my volunteers. I realized that, with my team, I needed a multi-faceted approach to training — something for everyone! So we started training through multiple avenues, and began reaching a larger percentage of our team on a regular basis. Some of the methods you might include in your training system include:

- Corporate — the large group, all-team event that often is held on an annual basis. There are many ways to hold this meeting — an off-site dinner, an on-site meeting, a casual "Beach Bash," or any number of other ways.

- Make it fun and engaging.

- Providing food is almost a "must."

- Do whatever you can do to make them want to attend — tickets for a "grand prize" drawing at the event; bring in a Christian comedian guest speaker; or let people know there will be a big announcement that they won't want to miss.

- Ask your senior pastor to attend and share with the team.

- Focus on "big picture" and save the more focused, departmental training for small group training.

- Offer a time of worship since many of your volunteers limit their involvement in the worship service in order to serve in children's ministry.

- An option to creating your own event is to taking your team to a conference or seminar planned by another church or organization. This will generally be more expensive, but is a great way of accomplishing the goal without as much effort.

- Small Group Events — skill development is rarely accomplished well with the whole team together. This is simply because of the diversity of the ministry areas represented — how can you train the nursery staff and your preteen team at the same time? So small group, or departmental, functions are necessary as well.

- Make them as informal and conversational as you can — meeting in a home or some other comfortable setting is always better than meeting at the church.

- Offer specific training on a specific topic, such as discipline in the classroom or telling stories effectively. You might also use the smaller group to do an initial orientation or basic training for new team members.

- Listen as much as you teach, addressing the questions and concerns with each team member.

- Use the opportunity to appreciate and affirm each member of the group both verbally and tangibly (a token gift, a meaningful resource, and so forth) if possible.

- Small group events are also great for core leader retreats and outings to help you focus on leadership development.

- Mentoring — mentoring one-on-one (or two) is a vital part of the children's ministry training system that is often overlooked. But mentoring can do things which large, and even small, group training cannot. It not only helps train the volunteer more quickly, it also allows the leader to develop a more personal relationship with the volunteer, helps to identify strengths and weaknesses, and allows the volunteer to be more candid with questions and concerns. It also communicates value to the volunteer when you or another key leader offers focused time and energy on their behalf.

- Build relationships and use this time to get to know and encourage your volunteers on a personal level.

- Be transparent and let them know that you face some of the same challenges they do, both in life and in ministry.

- Understand their strengths and weaknesses so that you can help them grow (personally, spiritually and as a volunteer leader) and get them in the perfect fit for ministry.

- Train core leaders to mentor their own team members so that the burden of time and energy is shared.

- Self-training — facilitating a regular course of self-training can be a very effective way to supplement other regular training methods. Ways to facilitate self-training might include:
  1. Providing written resources (books, booklets, magazines or articles, for example) for your team to read and perhaps discuss at the next small group event (you might create a single page discussion sheet with a handful of questions for them to answer in order to be more specific to your ministry).

2. Creating and sending a monthly newsletter (either a paper version or online email version).
3. Writing a blog (perhaps using your core leaders as co-authors) that includes training material.
4. Collecting articles on the children's ministry webpage that can be accessed at any time.
5. Creating short online video clips that can be accessed at any time.
6. Creating a Facebook page that occasionally offers training articles and ideas.
7. Doing a monthly podcast or finding podcasts done by others that can be used to train your team.
8. Connecting them to outside resources such as blogs or children's ministry member sites that offer training elements.

Building Step-by-step

Looking at all the options for training can be a little overwhelming. Understanding that no single method is going to work for everyone can be discouraging. Feeling like you don't have enough time or skill to do it all — much less everything else on your plate — can be frustrating. The good news is that you don't have to do it all, and you certainly don't have to do it all at once.

1. Understand your team — what are the dynamics of your team? What has been tried before that worked, or didn't work? What are your team members asking for? What areas do you feel are most pressing? Asking these and other similar questions will help you get a feel for what is needed for your team.

2. Prioritize and plan — once you have a general feel for what is needed, what type of training might be well-received and how to go about offering it, prioritize each method and create a plan to accomplish it. Begin looking for ways to enlist others in helping you create the training necessary for your team.

3. Build your training program one step at a time, refining and improving as you go. Through it all, your enthusiastic vision-casting is essential for helping your team understand the importance of investing in themselves in order to better reach the children they serve.

Not only is an effective training program essential for accomplishing the teaching goals you have for your kids, it is essential for equipping and retaining the leaders you have on your team. Making it a priority and building it step by step will go a long way toward helping you accomplish the overall purpose of your ministry.

Greg Baird is the creator of KidMin360 (www.KidMin360.com), a ministry committed to "Equipping & Connecting Children's Ministry Leaders." This is done through coaching, consulting, training, ministry checkups, and resources. Greg served as a children's pastor for twenty years in the San Diego area, including under the leadership of John Maxwell and David Jeremiah. He is married to Michele and has two sons, Taylor and Garret.

The Inside Scoop

In preparation for our new church school year I was telephoning people in the congregation who seemed like good possibilities for accepting a call to teach. Obviously, I had completely misinterpreted this particular person's interests when the response was, "Yuck! I would rather mop floors!"

Daphna Flegal
Lead Editor, The United Methodist Publishing House

I had been hired to coordinate the children's activities and their worship time for a denominational national convention in Washington, D.C. Since I had done this several times for the organization, I knew that adding a couple more faithful volunteers was a smart thing. I was happy when my husband Carl and our son Brian said they would help.

Every hour of the day and evening were carefully orchestrated for the convention. On the last day, the program plans in the children's area would include a clown skit, and Carl had prepared the "pull a needle through a balloon" illusion. Our conference puppet team and worship team with some great musicians were prepared. A couple of the leaders from the adult area saw me "in clown." They were going to announce that the convention the following year would be in Orlando. They asked me to help them in the ballroom where the adults were. I would fill in the answer, "We're going to Disney World!" in response to that well-known question, "Where are we going next year?"

Even though this was a cute idea, I had responsibilities in the children's area . . . that was where I was headed. After their persistent assurance that this announcement in the ballroom would take about five minutes, I told Carl that we would adjust the schedule. The kids' worship time would probably be long enough for me to help with the announcement and be back in the kids' area. However, if by chance I wasn't, then he could go ahead and do the illusion. I would certainly be back in the room at the end of his part.

Well, as often happens in the adult worship time, they were delayed in their schedule. I was standing at the side of the stage ready to go on and do my part, but the adult singing time went on and on. The worship had ended in the children's area. Carl had stepped before the kids to set up his presentation. I was told that his illusion went flawlessly. There was just one problem . . . I wasn't back in the room at the end to start the clown routine. Sooo . . . Carl did the illusion one more time. Perhaps there was a kid who missed the "punch line." There was a little more stalling before I made it from the other side of the hotel after the adults sang their last chorus and I helped with their announcement.

Carl is still willing to volunteer on these kinds of adventures . . . with the understanding that we will stay with the original plan . . . no matter what.

Judy Comstock
Writer and Editor

More Ideas

God deliberately chose things the world considers foolish in order to shame those who think they are wise.

(1 Corinthians 1:27, NLT)

The Move-In Event

by Judy Comstock

Everyone was excited about the new building. It was obvious that we needed more space. Even with multiple services, during transition times the halls in the children's education area were so crowded that movement from a classroom into the flow of hall traffic was tricky . . . almost dangerous.

After five services the weekend before Palm Sunday, we would relocate our department contents to the new building. The first weekend in our new building was scheduled for Palm Sunday. The celebration would include a traditional Palm Branch Parade with the children waving palm branches down the aisles in our new sanctuary as the congregation sang a meaningful Easter anthem.

Our new space included rooms for the children's ministry office, the director's office, the weekday preschool office, the children's ministry staff office, the director's office, the preschool office, nursery rooms, early childhood classrooms, elementary rooms, a large group gathering room, an indoor playroom in the nursery hall, and a resource room on each of the two floors . . . fifty-four rooms in all.

This new space required additional chairs and tables, new rocking chairs for each nursery room, and large-muscle indoor play equipment. All of these items would have to be unpacked and necessitated some construction. A new electronic check-in system would be implemented in our new building. We had to decide where the monitor for the security cameras would be located. The carpenters wanted to know where each bulletin board would be located. Who ordered that many bulletin boards?

The Facilities Staff did not have time to accomplish all of these tasks as they continued keeping the entire campus ready for various activities. Even though the new building was on the same campus as our current structure, this move would be a **Big Event**.

The strategic planning format described in the book *It Worked for Us…Best Practices for Ministry with Children and Families* (Abingdon Press, 2009) details what we used to create our plan. We formatted a spreadsheet with a column for action steps, responsible person, completion dates for each action step, a column for the cost or connection with the budget, and measurable results. It sometimes felt like I was living by this plan!

To create your Move-in Event Plan, I recommend that you involve an engineer or someone who thinks like an engineer and will utilize step-by-step processes. The engineer who helped us was already involved as a volunteer in children's ministry, so it was easy for him to understand the needs of our department.

Just to keep things exciting, it was decided that the walls in the hallways needed to be decorated with a design that involved more than taupe paint. Three artists were invited to present their

> T he strategic planning format described in the book *It Worked for Us…Best Practices for Ministry with Children and Families* (Abingdon Press, 2009) details what we used to create our plan.

proposals. The artist we selected had to work around the final interior construction steps, such as the installation of the carpet and tile and some challenges with the heating/air conditioning system. The artist and her team had only six weeks to paint the halls and large group gathering space of our 64,400 square foot building. Everyone knew that this decision would make a huge difference in creating a kid-friendly environment. We would do some painting inside some of the rooms later.

Our Move-in Plan was implemented three months before the big day. First, we inventoried everything . . . the items to be moved, thrown away or remain in place. We were blessed to have a volunteer in children's ministry with experience in the professional moving industry. He determined how we would identify items to be moved and how the destination would be clearly communicated. He used the box labels that are often used by professional movers. He got our moving boxes at a discounted cost. To get our supplies from one side of the campus to the other, we would stack boxes on flatbed carts and push them across the parking lots.

Establishing a method to easily locate items as they arrived in the new building was important. We didn't have time to hunt for specific supplies. A team of "unpackers" placed items in the appropriate new rooms. We recruited a team of volunteers who could follow directions. This kind of event requires teamwork. You may find that a professional mover should be involved to reduce your risk and liability when large items come into play.

It is important to know "who" was assigned to each task. Naming the coordinator for each division of labor eliminated confusion as our plans for the move-days were finalized. We

> It is important to know "who" was assigned to each task.

calculated milestones and constraints that would affect the plan.

Two months before the big move-in week we made certain that our consolidated written plan incorporated the "who, what, where, when, and how" of each step. We considered questions as simple as, "Will we ask our volunteers to bring their own box cutters?"

Here are some of the action steps that we listed in the room preparation objective of our plan:

- Stock the Resource Room.

- Stock the large group gathering room (Bible Theater backstage props and Front of the House audio supplies).

- Plan for these components: bulletin board team, room layout maps, cabinet content maps, plan to display photos of volunteers on hall walls outside each classroom, room safety procedures documents for each room, room number signs.

- Set up the Children's Library.

- Design and order vests to help parents identify greeters, staff members, and the Information Booth volunteers. Train the greeters and Info Booth volunteers.

- Print documents to assist members and visitors in locating specific classrooms.

- Recruit additional greeters, Info Booth volunteers, and classroom volunteers.

To implement our new Check-in System, these action steps were taken:

- Order the supplies and printers so that bar code cards and classroom nametags for each child could be made.

- Create a pilot program in three classrooms in the current building two months prior to the move.

- Establish Check-in training opportunities for staff members and volunteers.

Our weekday preschool classrooms and the weekday preschool office would not be moved until the end of the school year. Shared items were determined. How would the preschool teachers and the early childhood Sunday school teachers function without these items for almost two months? Did we need to order additional shared equipment, or not?

The new playground equipment was not installed until the summer months. This is a smart decision. Ordering the equipment and getting it shipped in a timely manner took longer than we anticipated. My advice is to allow an additional month. We had not considered that other preschools and churches across the country might also be ordering new playground equipment, which could delay our order.

Our scheduled indicators before our first Sunday were:

- Assign classes to specific rooms and create a directory.

- Establish a Shared-Space Policy for weekday and weekend children's programming. Our plan and other documents are included at the end of this section.

- Schedule tours and training for our volunteers and staff.

- Secure teams and set deadlines for setting up and decorating each room.

- Provide additional greeters and Information Booth volunteers. Give them the tools necessary to assist members and visitors so that their child's classroom could be easily located.

- Implement the new electronic check-in program.

- Define and communicate any necessary changes to the check-in and dismissal procedures for the fourth and fifth graders.

- See that the parent paging system in the sanctuary is installed and functioning properly.

- Determine staff assignments and hours for programming in the new building.

- Plan transition activities for the children for the final two Sundays in the current (old) building.

  - Plan activities for the children during the first month in the new facilities.

  - Secure plans for installation of the children's playground equipment.

  - Define the needs that will insure movement of the preschool classrooms and office by June 1.

  - Create teams and deadlines for planning summer programming.

- Establish a Spring Volunteer Appreciation and Fall Sunday School Kick-off.

> The children could tell that this new building would hold a lot of exciting possibilities as it would be used to help them on their Christian faith development.

Decorating classroom bulletin boards is not necessary, but we wanted the unveiling weekend to be impressive. Therefore, the theme that we had decided to use for our summer volunteer recruiting was reinforced on the bulletin board designs. A team of ten worked for three days and nights to decorate all forty-eight bulletin boards. This was quite an undertaking, but the fact that each classroom was not only stocked with supplies but decorated caught the eye of church leaders and parents. The children could tell that this new building would hold a lot of exciting possibilities as it would be used to help them on their Christian faith development.

Synergy with the IT Department, the Facilities Department, and the pastors who were planning the services for Palm Sunday was important. If your builder follows protocol, you will have limited access until the final inspection. To familiarize our volunteers with the new space, we worked with the Director of Facilities to schedule a tour as early as possible. This guided tour could not take place until after the final inspections.

It was vital that we calculated ways to help the children smoothly transition into their new classrooms and to know what to expect during the Palm Branch Parade. Most of them had not seen the new space. During the two weekends before the first Sunday, we created a "bare-bones" atmosphere in each current (old) classroom to capture the attention of our volunteers and the children. We followed these steps:

- Film a video tour of the entrance, check-in procedures, familiar faces, and the large group gathering room. We showed this video to the children during the last two weeks of programming in the current building.

- Incorporate transition discussions and celebration into the lesson plans. What spiritual decisions were made in the current building?

- Calculate the details, maps, adult leaders for the Palm Branch Parade. Order the palm branches.

- Plan the contents of the Children's Worship Packets that will be used in the sanctuary for Easter.

- Determine a method to assess the first two weeks of programming in the new building and to communicate necessary adjustments to our volunteers and to parents.

Church ministries often overlap with each other and this was certainly the case during our Move-in Event. Joint meetings with the IT Department, Facilities Department, Music Department, the pastor, and the leader responsible for the ushers were scheduled. To express our gratitude and build stronger bonds with the members of these teams, the children's ministry department planned a waffle breakfast and invited the members of these departments several weeks after the move. This positive decision helped us accomplish both of our goals.

If your church is building a new facility or remodeling, a smooth transition is possible. It is an arduous process, but a well-executed plan will be fulfilling. The process will help you get to the essence of how you do ministry. For example, we didn't realize that the building committee had ordered built-in classroom cabinets that didn't have drawers. At first this discovery was disappointing. In the end, it was one more example of how our old way of doing things was not the only way. We actually experienced less clutter by stocking items in labeled small plastic bins or containers and storing them on the shelves in the cabinets.

Rejoice at God's blessings and see your team and the volunteers rise to the occasion. Your success will rest on pre-planning and a positive attitude. Enjoy the process!

Judy Comstock has impacted children's ministry through her church staff experiences and 24 years with International Network of Children's Ministry as a board member and staff member. Judy wrote Children's Ministry *(Abingdon Press) and edited the book* It Worked For Us *(Abingdon Press). For 12 years, she had a dual career as a Director of Christian Education and Resource Teacher for gifted education in Dearborn, Michigan, where she worked with students from 20 elementary schools. It was her honor to also serve as a deacon in her church while living in Michigan. Judy is on the board of the Dare to Dream grant division of For Kids Only, Inc. She is a frequent writer for K! Magazine and has consulted on two Cokesbury curriculum projects. Judy is married to her best friend Carl and is the mother of one wonderful son.*

Shared Space Policy

Church of the Resurrection

KIDS COR Mission Statement:

*To mentor a child from birth to know, love, and follow Jesus Christ
and to help the family in becoming deeply committed Christians.*

Priorities:

Please remember that we are a church first. Secular decorations and wording will be secondary to Christian elements. All décor is subject to the Director's approval.

At Resurrection, we have a wonderful opportunity to share space with numerous groups seven days a week. Policies will be respected and reviewed by everyone on a weekly basis. This will insure a positive, Christ-centered experience for each program. Your compliance is appreciated. Thank you for helping with the sharing process.

It is very important that each classroom leader and program director read this policy. The Accountability Ledger in each room should be initialed on a weekly basis after classroom conditions are assessed. Since changes may be made to the policy, each classroom leader / director is asked to note attached addendums.

The following definitions are provided to benefit all users:

Accountability:

Program directors are ultimately responsible for making sure all policies are upheld and accountability ledgers are initialed on a weekly basis.

Bulletin Boards:

Boards are to reflect priorities for a church as stated in the earlier definition. Programs have equal opportunity to use boards in the classroom unless otherwise specifically stated or agreed.

Cabinets:

Cabinet space will be used as labels indicate. Please clear the counters and store all items in designated areas prior to use by another program. Program directors will take responsibility for issuing storage keys. Staff and volunteers using each space will assume responsibility for placing items in storage areas and locking storage cabinets. Keys will be returned to the appropriate director at a predetermined time and place.

Ceilings:

Children's artwork and appropriate décor may be hung from the ceiling in three areas. Specifically, items may be hung on the perimeter, not to exceed two ceiling tiles in from the walls. Nothing will be hung from the ceiling above the non-carpeted/sink area.

Community Items:

These items will be left in the open and will be acknowledged by all programs as items to be shared. Each program area that uses the items will share the cost for replacing or repairing items equally. The cost will be calculated at the end of each school year.

Storage of Non-shared Items:

Toys or equipment not included in the "community use category" should be removed from the room and placed in Room 2109. It is the classroom teacher's responsibility to remove and store non-shared items prior to another program's use of the room. It is the teacher's responsibility to return the item to the room.

Wall Applications:

Tape of any kind is not to be used on the painted wall surfaces. Staples, thumbtacks, and pushpins are not to be used on the painted wall surfaces. All displays must be contained on a bulletin, white magnetic board or on approved tack strips. Only approved labels should be affixed to the outside of cabinets. When, and if, labels are removed, the surfaced should be cleaned with approved solvent.

Marker Boards:

Only dry erase markers and erasers designed for marker boards should be used. Marker boards in the classroom and in the hall are also magnetic. The marker boards in the hall will be used as a communication center for parents who have a child in the classroom. Magnetic strips supplied for each room include: "Your Teaching Team, Parent Information, Today Your Child Will, Urgent, and Don't Forget." Signs not being displayed should be stored in the room cabinets.

Window Displays:

Outside wall windows should be decorated so compliance with the priorities is insured. The benefit of windows that allow natural light into the room should be optimized. Solid coverings over the windows are not allowed. There is to be no decorating of the hall windows beside the classroom door.

Shared Space Accountability Ledger

The Shared Space Policy has been read, items checked, room is ready for use by next users.

	Thurs	Mon	Thurs	Mon	Thurs	Mon	Thurs
Counters Cleared							
Bulletin Boards Reflect Church Priorities							
Storage of Non-shared Items							
Hallway Marker Boards Cleared							

Bring a Crowd To Your Church

Birthday Parties And How To Effectively Incorporate Into Your Children's Ministry

by Reagan Hillier

"The best birthdays of all are those that haven't arrived yet." — Robert Orben

Birthdays are events that call for celebration. Today, churches around the country are searching for programs to integrate visitors and new members, and innovative ways to increase membership. Hosting birthday parties is proving to be one of the most effective ministry outreach tools.

Getting Started

Churches are not in the birthday business, but rather in the business of life transformation. By incorporating a birthday party program into children's ministry, the church becomes **the** place to be in the community and provides an experience with memories that last a lifetime.

There is much to consider when adopting a new, effective program. Good guidance is imperative. Partnering with a trusted advisor that has experience both in creating play environments and children's ministry can help make the decisions for your program less complicated. Here is a guide that will lay the groundwork for an effective birthday party program:

1. **Understand your audience.** Each time a party is hosted at your church, the host will invite friends, neighbors, soccer/baseball/cheer team members, and relatives to the party. Based on a typical party of twelve to fifteen kids, this would result in approximately eighteen to twenty new visitors to your facility. If you host five parties in a week, that would be close to one hundred new visitors. It is important to understand and have a positive impact on this audience.

2. **Create a destination play space.** By incorporating areas for multiple use and versatility, families have the opportunity to incorporate the church into their daily routine. You may also want to consider incorporating a signature attraction or themed play environment that attracts a wide age range. Younger children have different needs than older children, who need more challenging elements. Custom play environments that engage all of the senses give children an exciting experience while providing invaluable learning opportunities. Turn to a trusted advisor to help with the planning process.

3. **Appoint ambassadors for your church.** Before, during, and after the birthday party experience, ambassadors for your church will be communicating with party hosts, attendees, and interested parties. The ambassador will also need to be available to conduct tours of the facility to interested parties. These are excellent opportunities to share your message with others centered on birthday parties. Take the time to consider the right person for this position. Depending on the amount of time required, a part-time position may need to be created.

4. **Staffing and scheduling.**
   a. Appoint a person to handle the number of parties per slot. The number will vary depending on facility. This person should conduct pre-party phone calls to parents to discuss the event. Be certain your venue can service the event and guests invited.
   b. Appoint a personal birthday party host/hostess for each group. Ensure the host genuinely cares about the birthday

child, as well as family and friends attending, by offering undivided attention and taking care of problems immediately.
c. Appoint a party coordinator or manager for setup, takedown, cleaning, and problem solving during the event.
d. Make sure the event is staffed properly. Hire congregation members to run the events. Members personally represent the mission of the church to guests. You must have dynamic people in these positions.

5. **Create the atmosphere and be in control of the event.** These think-ahead steps will help your guests have a good time, tell friends about it and want to return.
   a. Draft a well-designed event checklist.
   b. Offer party packages with a time limit, ninety minutes per party.
   c. Offer a private, fun atmosphere with personal attention and minimal frustration.
   d. Set the scene with balloons, music, party hats, and smiling faces.
   e. What is your draw? Play attractions, open space, interactive lessons such as cooking, crafts, or performers like a magician, or animals are some draws to consider.
   f. Consider group games that feature the birthday child and introduce everyone in the party to each other.
   g. Coordinate whether or not there will be food and beverages for each event and who is handling this. You may want to partner with a local catering company.
   h. Provide goody bags for kids to take home.
   i. Offer a safe and secure environment. Controlled access, organized check-in/check-out procedures, and background checks on all volunteers are processes being implemented for facilities with congregations both large and small.

6. **Consider how to market these events and money allocated towards marketing.** The church has the ability to provide free parties for the community, but you will need to market the birthday party program to members and the community.
   a. Word-of-mouth advertising is essential and the most credible form of advertising. Each happy guest can steer dozens of new ones your way.

b. Flyers or mailers. A flyer has one aim, to promote your program. Tell people what you can do by highlighting your offerings. Make sure to include the contact details.
c. Informational packet. Each guest attending a birthday party should receive an information packet about your church to take home. This should include details about your children's ministry, upcoming sermon series, and a coupon for redemption when they come back.
d. Advertise to local apartment complexes, low-income areas, or single moms.

7. **Tax and Legal.** There is much legality involved with instituting a birthday party program. Items such as insurance requirements and liability coverage. If the church is using this as intentional ministry, then the program qualifies as part of the church's goals and mission (this could include giving church information, devotion or prayer as part of the package). Unrelated Business Income (UBI) is acceptable for any church and not a huge issue. We highly recommend every church consult with counsel on these and other items.

8. **Next Steps.** Now that you've decided this ministry is right for you and your church, it's time to get started.
   a. Do additional research about startup requirements and ideas to incorporate.
   b. Cast the vision to the congregation.
   c. Be innovative!
   d. Decide on the space for the facility, what the big draw/attraction will be, and get the right people on board.
   e. When the facility is ready, launch the new program with a trial run party for the senior pastor. Everyone involved gets to practice and the pastor gets to experience the potential of your new outreach.
   f. Spend time in prayer that God will open huge doors and bring the right kids and parents to your events.
   g. Get ready to see God work!

Reagan Hillier is the president of Worlds of Wow, Argyle, Texas, www.worldsofwow.com. E-mail: Reagan@worldsofwow.com

Planning Events that Don't Suck The Life out of You

by Tim Scheiler

Three words: Best idea ever. That's exactly what I was thinking about an event I was planning for our families on a cool February evening a few years ago. Nothing could deter my passion for this idea . . . it was going to be great. No . . . not great . . .

It was going to be **amazing!**

After the idea was firmly implanted in my brain, I set out to begin making to-do lists, drawing diagrams, and filling in the details: The food would need to come from 'x', the t-shirts would come from 'y,' the craft would be located here, the game area would be located there . . . Oh! And the video . . . can't forget the video . . . all we need to do is write it, film it, edit it, burn a DVD and we're done!

This is going to be **amazing!**

How much time do we have? ten days? Easy . . . ish. Oh . . . we still have to make sure ministry is covered for this weekend . . . and the weekend immediately after. Why can't **amazing** ideas come earlier? Ok . . . no matter . . . Not as easy as I first thought but . . .

Amazing ideas are worth a little extra hard work, right?

Ministry on the first weekend came and went without a hitch, everything was covered and everything went smoothly. Time, however, was beginning to run out. As time ran out the idea began to fall apart, and I decided to sacrifice more and more to make sure . . . what was **amazing** in my head would be **amazing** in the real world.

First on the chopping block: the day off. Who needs it? Not me! So I worked all through my day off. Yes, that's normally the day that's devoted to my family and resting, but they were clearly less important than lining up craft materials and working on the all-important video. Besides, I'm sure they would understand, after all . . . they know just how **amazing** my ideas are.

Next, I would need to cut a few corners on prep for the weekend immediately after the event. It would be ok, right? I could come in extra early Sunday morning to get everything together and all would be fine. Besides . . . the kids are going to be so blown away by my **amazing** idea I'm sure that's all they'll want to talk about.

The day of the event came and the **amazing-ness** of my idea had started to become a little tarnished. The t-shirts still had to be picked up, the food still needed to be picked up, the craft supplies needed to be arranged, the games needed to be setup, and the video wasn't quite done. Even after all the extra hours I had put in, unforeseen complications had kept things from happening in a timely manner.

Things were looking less **amazing** and more stressful.

The event finally came, the crafts were good, the games were not bad, and the food (when it showed up) was cold but a hit. The video, the centerpiece to the whole evening, the thing I had spent most of my time on that week, the thing that I had lost sleep worrying about, the thing that had caused me to be short with friends, family and co-workers was . . . forgettable. No one seemed anywhere near as interested or excited for it as I was certain they were going to be. After the video played and we still had an hour to fill up I realized that I was out of gas.

My **amazing** bubble had just burst.

I had used up all my energy in the frantic preparation for the event and had nothing left for the event itself. I was tired, I was frustrated that my **amazing** idea didn't look anything like what was going on in the room, and in my stressed out state of mind I had forgotten to eat.

My colleagues could see that I was crashing and came to my rescue. We gathered, sorted out the rest of the evening, ate a slice of cold pizza, came up with a plan, and set to work. The rest of the night was tiring but good, the families had a great time, they loved the second half better than the first, and by the end of the night we were all smiling, ready for bed, and grateful we had survived another one of my **amazing** ideas.

I wish I could tell you this was a one-time event after which I learned my lesson. You've probably already sorted out in your own mind where I went wrong and how I could've avoided the stress, the frustration, the pain to my family, and the injury to my co-workers. The truth is we did too. We knew exactly what went wrong . . . but we couldn't stop. It was a way of life for us in ministry. Anything that happened outside of the weekend required every ounce of our time and energy, and everything must be sacrificed in order to see the idea come to life. The truth is we didn't know how to do it any other way. It was literally all or nothing.

There is a better way. If you are like I was, then hopefully you've already identified the destructive pattern of planning events that suck you dry, and hopefully you're on the road to recovery. If you know you need help but can't seem to figure out how to do things differently, here are some steps to getting back on the right path:

Step 1: Ask the tough questions.

I love to dream, to imagine, to think big about all the wonderful things the church could do for our families. It's fun, it's inspiring, and it's motivating. Sometimes the dreaming conversations are what got me out of bed in the morning.

Don't keep yourself from dreaming.

However, after you've dreamed up yet another **amazing** idea and you're convinced that it's too good not to do, ask yourself these questions:

1. Why are we doing this event?
2. Is this event life-giving for both my families *and* me?
3. If doing this event means we're adding something, what are going to stop doing?

If the answers to these questions are: "I'm not sure." "Maybe," and "I can't stop doing anything right now," then, you need to stop. Put that idea on hold until you know exactly why you're doing it, you're certain it will be a life-giving experience, and you're not just adding one more thing to an already over-crowded calendar.

If you're not sure what a life-giving event might be, ask yourself this: Is this a "non-event" event or an "event" event? That is to say: is the act of putting on this event an event in itself? If the answer is "Yes," you may want to reconsider. This has become our go-to idea assessor: "That sounds like it's an event-event. Is there any way to make that into a non-event event?" Try it. It works wonders.

Step 2: Plan within your means.

I am one hundred percent certain there is no end to the needs that you see in your ministry context, your passion for meeting those needs, or your creativity in figuring out new ways to meet those needs.

Remember: Needs ≠ Ministry.

In order to effectively minister to your families and meet the needs you see around, you must also have resources. Resources include: time, energy, passion, people, material, funding, venues, and so forth. Do not jump into doing something simply because you see a need. This will only lead to a severe drain on you as well as the other programs you're involved with.

Remember: Needs + Resources = Ministry.

These aren't resources that you wish you had, or you think you have. These are resources currently at your disposal. If you don't have the time, energy, passion, and so forth to meet a particular need or put on a particular event, then you must stop and wait until you have resources in place or rethink your approach in order to utilize what you have.

Step 3: Don't do it alone.

Have you looked at the stats on pastors lately? They paint a pretty sobering picture :

- 1,500 pastors leave the ministry each month due to moral failure, spiritual burnout, or contention in their churches.
- 70% of pastors constantly fight depression.
- 50% of pastors' marriages will end in divorce.

Your spiritual, emotional, and physical health is more important than any one event. The best way to ensure that you're not putting yourself, your ministry, or your marriage/family at risk is to be sure you have a team around you that is willing to speak the truth in love. Sometimes you will have no idea that you are doing too much. You need to bring people around you who can help you determine what events to do, why you're doing them, and how you're going to make them happen. Yes, this may mean that some **amazing** ideas remain ideas instead of becoming **amazing** events. It is far better to miss out on an opportunity to implement an **amazing** idea than to burn yourself out.

Step 4: Remember it's a marathon not a sprint.

A couple of years ago I decided to start exercising more. Actually what I should say is: a couple of years ago my wife begged me to exercise with her. I gave in and we began attending an outdoor boot camp program she had discovered a couple months previous. One of the ways our instructor determined our general level of fitness was the one-mile time trial. Basically, you run a mile, time how long it takes you and then, after a couple of weeks of the program, do it again. The idea is that over time your overall fitness will improve and you will get faster.

And so I did.

After the first six weeks, I was much faster than I had been at the beginning. I kept up with the program and met with a lot of success. I was faster than I had ever been and I was still improving! Then came the day when I wasn't getting any faster. After a few failed attempts at improving, the instructor pulled me aside and showed me something. My time for the first lap was hugely fast, but my time for the other three laps was much, much slower. In fact, with each passing lap I got slower and slower. That's when he told me something that didn't make a whole lot of sense: "You need to go slower so that you can go faster." The idea is that if you slow down on your first lap, than you will have more energy for the subsequent laps. Yes, you may lose a few seconds off that first lap, but you will gain much more with each pass.

I've thought how this same idea applies in the context of ministry. If we charge out of the gate into ministry at a dead sprint, we will end up moving slower and slower with each passing event, each passing Sunday, until we are too exhausted to keep going.

Ministering to the families at your church isn't a problem that can be solved. We do not fix people, we care for them, and this is a process not a product. It is not realized by moving faster and doing more but rather by understanding what family needs really are, keeping your spiritual, physical and emotional health a priority, and by planning events that don't suck the life out of you.

Tim Scheiler has been involved in youth ministry for the last thirteen years, having spent the last seven years as the Pastor of Elementary Ministries at Lake Avenue Church. As Pastor, Tim oversees a ministry for two hundred kids and leads a volunteer staff of sixty plus. Tim resides with his wife and two sons in Pasadena, California.
Contact Information:
Phone: 626.817.4560
Fax: 626.817.4660
email: tims@lakeave.org

Don't Shoot!

by Kurt Goble

Put down the camera and consider a few things before shutter-bugging your next event . . .

Today it is easy to capture images of your kids having a blast at your church event and then post those images online. Parents love same-day access to pictures of their kids at camp or enjoying VBS. But these innovations come with some pitfalls. Posting pictures and videos online can get you into a lot of trouble if certain precautions are not taken.

Problems!

The most threatening danger you face in posting pictures online is legal action by a child's parent or guardian. It is not okay to publish anyone's image without his or her permission, especially a minor. When you post something online, you are publishing it. If a parent sees their child's image on your website and has not granted you permission to use it, they could easily claim that you used their child's picture to promote your church. This is a form of advertising. Your church could be ordered to cease and desist, and sued for compensation and legal fees.

There is also an issue of undesired access. In most cases, pictures posted online are out there for anyone to view. This means that someone with ill intentions or someone with no connection to your church can access your website and see images of your kids. Legal issues aside, this is not what is best for the safety and well-being of our students.

This kind of exposure also leaves your images open to theft. In other words, someone could download a picture of one of your kids and manipulate it, sell it, or use it for their own advertising piece. Could you imagine going online and seeing a picture of your child on an ad banner? What makes matters even worse is the fact that once someone steals a digital image, it is impossible to get it back.

Finally, there is our own integrity. Do we really want to have pictures of our kids floating around on Facebook, our church website, or easily accessible photo sharing sites without their parent's knowledge? This is the kind of thing that can alienate families and dissolve trust.

Solutions!

Fortunately, there are ways to safely and legally capture images of all the fun and make them available to parents, staff, and volunteers.

Following are five key precautions that every church should take when dealing with images of the children who participate in their programs and events.

A Photo Release

It's best if you never take a picture of a child without getting their parent or guardian's permission. There are two types of photo release that are commonly used. One is a posted release. This is accomplished by posting signs at or near check-in and entrance areas. These signs must inform parents that pictures will be taken that day, and by leaving their child within our care, they release to us the right to use those images.

For obvious reasons, this kind of release is inferior to a signed release. Legally speaking, a parent's signature next to a release is the best protection you can have. There is no plausible deniability with a signed release. If a parent says, "I never saw a sign," that could be construed as your fault. But if a parent says, "I didn't read that statement before I signed it," then the negligence is clearly theirs.

A photo release does not have to be a separate form. Add your photo and video release statement to the language of your medical release form. Be sure to offer an "I agree" box for the parent to sign, or an additional line for their initial. A photo and video release should read something like this:

I hereby agree that _____ Church may use any type of audio and/or visual records of this event/trip for it's promotional and/or commercial purposes without further permission and/or compensation to me.

This short statement is your greatest protection against legal action when it comes to your use of photographs and video obtained at your event.

Designated Photographers
Designate one or two trustworthy volunteers to take pictures at your event. These should be some of your more experienced volunteers who have cleared background checks. You want to be able to tell a parent exactly who was taking pictures. You also want the assurance that you will be in control of all of the pictures generated from the event. This avoids the image that anybody with a camera is allowed to show up and start taking pictures. If you get people who know what they are doing, this can also help with quality control.

A Password Protected Photo Sharing Site
Post your pictures on a website that requires a password to access. You can give that password to parents via e-mail or flyers that are handed out at your event. In my experience SmugMug.com is the fastest and easiest to use. This service is provided at a very modest annual fee. We have used password protected albums for five years now, and parents are grateful that we see the value in protecting the images of their children.

Get Your Volunteers Onboard
These days most people carry a camera with them just about everywhere they go. And it is in their cell phone. I can pull my phone out, take a picture, and have it on Facebook in seconds. We take very clear and intentional measures to communicate to our volunteers

that they are not to post pictures of students online. We have even had to call volunteers and ask them to remove pictures they have posted. When so many people are armed with cameras that have immediate web access, it is important that we minimize their picture taking and web-posting activities. We also remind them that they are not our designated photographers, so our photo release was not designed or intended to cover them. (Although technically it does.)

Further permission
Finally, if we choose to use an image of a student in a prominent place such as our church website or printed promotional materials, we obtain special permission from the parent or guardian. Even though we could legally use these images under the umbrella of our original release, we extend a further courtesy to the family by requesting their permission through personal contact.

Now go for it!

Posting photos online is a great way to connect what you do to parents and families. It makes people feel that they are in touch with what is happening in your ministry. So if you haven't done so, I'd encourage you to try it out. Just make sure you do so in a way that protects your integrity, your church, and especially your kids!

_____

Kurt Goble has made more mistakes than anyone in the history of Children's Ministry. But he loves sharing what he's learned from all those mistakes. For fourteen years Kurt has served as children's pastor at First Christian Church of Huntington Beach, where he shares God's Word with kids through innovative programs. He is a graduate of Bethel College and a curriculum writer. He and Heidi are happily married with two kids.

The Inside Scoop

There is no doubt that Jason was a precocious first grader, but the incident started as a mix-up. Jason's parents, Jeannette and David, usually came in the same car to church with their two sons. However, this particular Sunday David had an early meeting with the Finance committee and getting Jason and his brother to church on time was all Jeannette could manage. Jason's brother had multiple special needs, and Jeannette felt like their schedule for this Sunday required two cars. So, David headed for the church an hour earlier in his own vehicle.

Somehow, when church was over, David thought that Jeannette had both of the boys and Jeannette thought that David had Jason with him. It wasn't until they got home that it was discovered that Jason had done the "Jesus thing" and was still at the church.

I had already discovered their error since Jason was with me . . . the last child in the children's church room. I called Jeannette and she told me that David was leaving their house to drive back to the church. They lived quite a distance from the church. Jason was hungry. He told me that he hadn't eaten any breakfast. I knew this family well and told his mother that we were going to buzz over to McDonald's, if that was okay. My son wanted a Happy Meal too. The three of us immediately went back to the church with the food. As Jason finished his French fries, David pulled into the parking lot. Of course, he apologized and Jason waved good-bye and got in his dad's car.

Apparently, Jason thought this after-church excursion was a good idea and tried to convince his mom that forgetting him at church would be a good plan every Sunday. After all, Miss Judy liked to take him to McDonald's.

Judy Comstock, writer and editor